PRAISE FOR *ASYLUM DENIED*

"This is a powerful story, human and legal. It is as tense as a fictional thriller, but it really happened. The hero battles official torturers in Kenya, then American bureaucrats out of the pages of Kafka."

ANTHONY LEWIS, author of *Gideon's Trumpet*

"*Asylum Denied* takes the reader from the dungeons of the Kenyan torture chambers to the labyrinth of the U.S. immigration system. It is both a thriller and an educational journey. It leaves you wanting to meet David Ngaruri Kenney, an extraordinary person who ran the immigration gauntlet, learned its secrets, and survived his ordeal."

RICHARD BOSWELL, University of California, Hastings College of the Law

"This is not only a poignant story about the heroism of an extraordinary Kenyan dissident, but also an exposé of the apathy, incompetence, and occasional outright cruelty that slither about in the darker corners of the immigration bureaucracy. As you read this chilling true tale, you will share the authors' anger, stress, sadness, and unbearable frustration—but be prepared for some surprises."

STEPHEN H. LEGOMSKY, Washington University School of Law

"*Asylum Denied* is several things in one enthralling whole: a vivid and moving story of persecution and resilience in East Africa, an infuriating and inspiring story of administrative malfeasance and lawyerly devotion in the U.S., as well as a love story and a reasoned proposal for reform. If there is any justice, the asylum system will be reformed and this wonderful book will be read by everyone who cares about what America is becoming."

TODD GITLIN, Columbia University

*The publisher gratefully acknowledges
the generous support of Adele M. Hayutin
as a member of the Literati Circle of the
University of California Press Foundation.*

Asylum Denied

*A Refugee's Struggle for Safety
in America*

David Ngaruri Kenney and Philip G. Schrag

UNIVERSITY OF CALIFORNIA PRESS

Berkeley   Los Angeles   London

University of California Press, one of the most distinguished
university presses in the United States, enriches lives around
the world by advancing scholarship in the humanities, social
sciences, and natural sciences. Its activities are supported by
the UC Press Foundation and by philanthropic contributions from individuals and institutions. For more information, visit www.ucpress.edu.

University of California Press
Berkeley and Los Angeles, California

University of California Press, Ltd.
London, England

Library of Congress Cataloging-in-Publication Data

Kenney, David Ngaruri, 1973–
    Asylum denied : a refugee's struggle for safety in America /
David Ngaruri Kenney and Philip G. Schrag.
        p.   cm.
    Includes bibliographical references and index.
    ISBN 978-0-520-25510-4 (cloth : alk. paper)
    1. Kenney, David Ngaruri, 1973–   2. Immigrants—
Government policy—United States.   3. Political
refugees—Government policy—United States.   4. Civil
rights—United States.   5. Human rights—United States.
I. Schrag, Philip G., 1943–   II. Title.
    JV6456.K46   2008
    323.6'31—dc22
    [B]   2007048703

Manufactured in the United States of America

17   16   15   14   13   12   11   10   09   08
10   9   8   7   6   5   4   3   2

The paper used in this publication meets the minimum
requirements of ANSI/NISO Z39.48-1992 (R 1997)
(Permanence of Paper).

*For Mackenzie Kenney and for
Leonard and Nora Schrag*

CONTENTS

Introduction

PHILIP G. SCHRAG

In 1939, on the eve of the Holocaust in Europe, Adolf Hitler allowed 929
Jews to flee Germany on the cruise ship *St. Louis*, bound for Cuba. He
was certain that Cuba would turn them away and that the world's democ-
racies would also refuse to admit them, proving that Germany was not
alone in its disregard for Jews.

So far as the United States was concerned, Hitler was correct. The
president of Cuba refused to let the ship land, in part because the minister of immigration had not shared the bribes he'd received for issuing
visas to the refugees and in part because Germany had fomented anti-
Jewish sentiment in Cuba. After being rebuffed in Havana, the ship's captain headed north. Sailing just a few miles off the Florida coast, so close
that the passengers could see the lights of Miami, the captain urgently
telegraphed President Franklin D. Roosevelt, requesting permission to
disembark. But in the United States, wracked by the Depression, sentiment against immigration in general and Jewish immigration in particular remained high. Despite national publicity about the plight of the
refugees and support for them from Eleanor Roosevelt, the U.S. government did not allow the ship to dock. It returned to Europe. About half
of the passengers from the *St. Louis*—most of those who were resettled
in countries that Germany soon invaded—died in the Holocaust.[1]

THE REFUGEE ACT OF 1980

Many twenty-first-century Americans believe that their government would never repeat such a mistake, that the United States would never again send people away to face likely persecution and death. In 1980, the U.S. Congress passed the Refugee Act. Under this law, the State Department annually selects tens of thousands of refugees, many of them living in camps run by the United Nations, and resettles them in the United States. The act also provides a system through which people who flee to our shores can apply for asylum. Any foreign national who comes to the United States, with or without a visa, may seek protection here. To win asylum, the individual must prove that the reason for fleeing his or her country is a well-founded fear of persecution on account of race, religion, nationality, political opinion, or membership in a particular social group.[2]

From 1980 until 1996, administration of this act improved steadily. In the early 1980s, many observers had charged the Reagan administration with political bias in its enforcement of the law—for example, favoring refugees from cold war adversaries while denying asylum to those fleeing human rights abuses in nations, such as El Salvador, whose regimes the United States supported. But these charges had faded by the early 1990s. The government established a professional corps of asylum officers and trained its members to interview asylum applicants carefully and respectfully and to decide claims based on the law rather than by reference to the foreign policy preferences du jour. In 1995, with at least tacit support from human rights advocates, the government resolved an administrative crisis presented by a growing backlog of possibly spurious asylum claims. It repealed rules that allowed applicants to work while their claims were being processed and substituted a new system under which most applicants had to win asylum before they could be employed. Almost overnight, the annual number of applications fell from about 140,000 to about 35,000; most observers attributed the decrease to the disappearance from the queue of claimants who only wanted temporary jobs and were not in fact fleeing persecution.[3]

After 1995, partly in response to a 1993 incident in which a Pakistani asylum applicant murdered two CIA employees in the agency's parking lot, Congress began to make asylum much more difficult to obtain. In 1996, Congress barred asylum for most persons who did not apply for it within a year of entering the United States. It also created a new system of "expedited removal," under which airport immigration inspectors (and, later, land border officials) could summarily deport, without hearings, many foreign nationals who arrived in the United States without valid passports and visas.[4]

In the aftermath of the terrorist attacks on the Pentagon and the World Trade Center in 2001, many members of Congress demanded even more restrictions. They believed that it had become very easy for fraudulent applicants, and even terrorists, to exploit the asylum laws and gain admission to the United States. Some members of Congress claimed that "the 9/11 terrorists manipulated our asylum laws to stay in our country,"[5] although none of those terrorists had been granted asylum. Others asserted that the asylum system had been "ripe for corruption for years" or had been "abused and gamed by terrorists."[6] The chairman of the House Judiciary Committee stated that "irresponsible judges have made asylum laws vulnerable to fraud and abuse" with the result that the United States grants "a safe haven to some of the worst people on earth."[7] Accordingly, the 2005 "REAL ID" Act imposed higher corroboration requirements on asylum applications and gave adjudicators greater leeway to deny asylum based on minor inconsistencies in testimony. Congress also tightened the standards for grants of asylum, requiring that asylum be denied to persons who had come to the United States both to flee persecution and for better economic prospects, unless fear of persecution was a "central" reason for their attempt to immigrate.[8]

Even after the Democratic Party won majorities in the House and Senate in the 2006 elections, members of Congress continued to view asylum applicants with great suspicion. Governments that abuse human rights often prevent their dissidents from leaving the country; they do not want eyewitness criticism from abroad. They do this simply by denying passports to their political opponents. Therefore, many victims of persecution, like the protagonist of this book, are unable to leave their countries unless they obtain passports in an irregular manner—that is, by "borrowing" passports from other people or by bribing or persuading officials of their countries to give them passports outside the normal processes. Yet in 2007, a leading liberal Democrat introduced a bill to make it a felony to use an irregularly issued passport to enter the United States, even if that use was necessary to flee from threatened torture or persecution. Being convicted of this felony would be grounds for revoking any asylum that had been granted. Under the bill, the Department of Homeland Security could waive prosecution but would not be required to do so.[9]

Statutes and proposals such as these are based on the ludicrous idea that asylum is easy to obtain and that terrorists can therefore evade immigration restrictions by masquerading as refugees. Actually, asylum applicants must go through an exacting examination, based on documentary evidence, to prove their identity and the truth and validity of their claims. Even if government officials believe an applicant's story, they may deny asylum because the story lacks sufficient corroboration, or because the application was not filed quickly enough after entering the country, or because the applicant was once convicted of a crime. A terrorist would be poorly advised to apply for asylum, because an applicant comes to the attention of officials who question every aspect of the individual's life. If the officials do not grant the application, they place the person in deportation proceedings.[10]

DAVID NGARURI KENNEY: A REFUGEE FROM PERSECUTION

The harrowing story of David ("Jeff") Ngaruri Kenney reveals the ordeals to which the U.S. government subjects those who seek refuge in America. Kenney was born in the early 1970s in a small village in central Kenya. The country, located on the East African coast, won its independence from Britain in 1963 after a prolonged armed struggle. Its first president, Jomo Kenyatta, was an independence leader, much loved both for his role in creating the nation and for the prosperity that he helped to bring to Kenya during his presidency. His rule, while authoritarian, was "relatively benign."[11] When he died in 1978, his vice president, Daniel arap Moi, took over.

Moi declared Kenya a one-party state. With the support of his armed security forces, he ruthlessly destroyed all opposition to his rule to ensure that he would remain in power. In the 1990s, he relied heavily on a domestic intelligence network, imprisonment, and torture to control virtually every aspect of the nation's political and economic life.[12] He also "turned Kenya into his personal fief, a kleptocracy under which [his party's] leaders looted with impunity. Corruption became the principal mechanism for regime maintenance."[13] The U.S. State Department reported that Moi's security forces committed "extrajudicial killings," noting that, according to the nongovernmental Kenyan Human Rights Commission, Moi's police tortured forty-nine people to death in the year 2000 alone.[14] Moi's human rights record was so bad that in 1991 the U.S. Congress barred economic and military aid to Kenya unless Moi began to restore human rights.[15]

In 1992, Kenney (at the time named David Wachira Ngaruri and nicknamed "Jeff") led a peaceful farmers' boycott to protest certain exploitive agricultural policies that Moi's government had imposed on him and his fellow tea farmers. In response, the security police nearly executed him, tortured him, and put him in solitary confinement for months. When he was finally released, he was subjected to police surveillance and controls. He had no future in Kenya, and he was told that if he engaged in political acts, he would be rearrested. With the help of several amazingly inventive U.S. Peace Corps volunteers, he was able to flee to the United States, where eventually he sought asylum.

Having put his troubles with the Kenyan government behind him, Kenney faced a new set of conflicts, this time with officials of the American government. This book chronicles his long struggle with many of the bureaucracies that regulate immigration: the Department of Homeland

Security (formerly the Immigration and Naturalization Service), the federal immigration court, the Board of Immigration Appeals, the U.S. court of appeals, and the Department of State. It reveals how the asylum system often works in practice and how difficult it is for individuals to obtain refuge through that system. The problems are particularly severe for individuals such as Kenney who do not have legal advice or assistance when they first apply.

Although asylum was at the heart of Kenney's struggle for safety in America, he also encountered many other aspects of America's immigration law—student visas, the diversity lottery system, the law of "voluntary departure," the Convention Against Torture, consular processing, waivers of nonadmissibility, and other arcane features of a statute that rivals the Internal Revenue Code in its complexity.

FROM LAWYER AND CLIENT TO CO-AUTHORS

I first met Kenney when he walked into the law school clinic that I direct at Georgetown University, seeking legal help with his asylum case. I assisted him at a brief court appearance to schedule his case, but I did not see him again for several months. I deliberately kept him at a distance, as I do with all clinic clients, because one objective of a law school is to train second- and third-year students by having them handle nearly all the contact with clients. Two students became Kenney's representatives for all practical purposes; I worked behind the scenes, meeting with the students every few days to discuss progress on the case and to review the documents they produced. I did not speak to Kenney again until a few days before his immigration court hearing, which I observed from the audience section of the courtroom.

Our relationship changed dramatically while his case was on appeal. Furious with how the immigration judge had resolved his case, I became his lawyer. Gradually over the years that followed, we became friends. As the book relates, our personal lives began to intertwine. When he was accepted into law school, my wife, Lisa Lerman, became his faculty advisor; and my children got to know him through our family celebrations, to which he was often invited. It was not always easy to cultivate this growing friendship and at the same time maintain the degree of professional objectivity and detachment that lawyers must have in order to render sound advice. It was therefore a great relief, after many years, to end our lawyer-client relationship and begin a new phase of friendship and collaboration, this time as co-authors.

We decided to write this book almost entirely from Kenney's perspective. We began with a series of meetings in which I interviewed him for a total of twelve hours. Drawing on my prior acquaintance with the case, our interviews, and the documentary record, I wrote a first draft of the book, which Kenney edited and supplemented. Then I took another crack at the manuscript, and in this way we passed it back and forth many times until each of us was satisfied.

The telling of Kenney's story was a joint effort in every respect, but we felt that each of us needed to write our own epilogue. While Kenney closes the book on a personal note, my epilogue relates his case to systemic problems in how the United States treats those who seek safety from persecution. Kenney's misfortune, as American officials slammed door after door in his face, stemmed largely from a single moment of bad luck: when a court clerk assigned his case to a judge who granted asylum far less often than the other judges who served with her on her court. Drawing in part on a statistical study that I undertook with two other authors,[16] I show that Kenney's case is far from unique. Far too many asylum applicants become players of "refugee roulette," their fortunes determined in large part by which particular government officials decide their cases. Every year, tens of thousands of individuals must attempt to persuade federal officials to grant them safety in America. All of them, winners and losers, participate in a system of adjudication that is not only exacting in its demands for proof of an applicant's bona fides but also disquietingly random.

Both Kenney's case and the larger statistical picture lead me to make several recommendations for reforming how America treats those who seek its protection. I do not share the perspective of members of Congress who think that asylum laws and procedures should be made more restrictive. My suggestions point in the direction of making them less random, more evenhanded, more compassionate, and more just.

America's immigration system, including its handling of asylum applications, is technical and complicated. We hope that by shedding light on this system, including some of its warts, through the story of a single asylum applicant, we can move at least some of our readers to insist that the United States improve its laws and institutions that are intended to protect the men and women who are victims of human rights violations throughout the world.

ONE

The Farmers' Boycott

After the security officers decided not to shoot me during the night in the forest, they blindfolded me again and forced me back into the van. Terrified, I lost track of time. Finally, the van stopped, and they told me to get out. The officers took me to a building and led me through it. They removed the handcuffs from my wrists and the blindfold from my face. As my eyes adjusted slowly to the light from the only bulb, I could see that I was in some kind of prison. Heavy wire links covered the window.

They ordered me to remove all my clothing. When I was naked, they pushed me through a doorway, and I fell into what seemed to be a dark room. Soon I realized that it was a small cement cell below the level of the prison floor: in essence, a pit. This was the beginning of the worst ordeal of my life.

I landed in cold water that rose up to my ankles. The lights went out immediately. There were no windows in the pit. I was very cold and in total darkness. I was completely disoriented and more frightened than I had ever been.

I ran my hands along the walls and felt the corners where they met. I stretched both my arms and touched the walls on each side simultaneously. I was in some kind of small tank or box. I heard the officers' footsteps receding as they walked away, somewhere above me, until I could no longer hear any sounds at all.

Then the water level started to rise. It came up to my knees, my waist, and then my chest. I thought that my jailers were going to drown me, because the walls reached above my head. I had no way to climb higher to escape the rising water.

After a while, the water receded, back to ankle level. This became the pattern for days: at apparently random intervals, the cold water would rise and fall. When it was high, I had to stand to avoid drowning. When it was low, I tried to curl up and rest on the wet floor. The cell was not wide enough for me to lie down without twisting myself around. I could not sleep for more than minutes at a time, because I was afraid that the water would rise and drown me while I was asleep.

The cell was entirely without light. I never had any food. There were no toilet facilities. To stay alive, I had to drink the water on the floor into which I had urinated and defecated. I could estimate how long I had been in that cell by feeling the length of my growing whiskers and by comparing how hungry I became with how hungry I had been a few years earlier when my brothers had forced me to live as a homeless person on the streets of my village. By those measures, I remained in the water cell for about a week.

Eventually, I had the experience of leaving my body. My mind seemed to separate from my physical being. I could see my body lying naked on the floor, as if I were floating above it. In my mind, I had long conversations with my dead father. Once, I walked over to my body on the floor and kicked it. I saw my own death, and I attended my funeral. I was only about twenty years old, but my life seemed to have ended.

· · ·

The government of Kenya consigned me to the water torture cell because I had led a protest on behalf of the tea farmers in my region. A few years before the protest, I had become a tea farmer in the hope of eking out a meager living on a small parcel of land that the British government of

Kenya had given to my father, Ngaruri (pronounced "ga-roo'-ree") Muchiri.[1]

My father was a Kikuyu, a member of one of the largest tribes in Kenya. He was born during the period of British occupation (Kenya had been occupied since 1895, first as a British protectorate and then as a crown colony). The colonizers imposed a system of government very similar to one against which Kikuyus had revolted centuries earlier. The British forcefully removed people from their ancestral lands, appointed village chiefs from different tribes, and granted them unlimited powers over villages. Village chiefs answered only to senior district commissioners, who reported to the provincial commissioner, who reported to the colonial governor. As a result, many village chiefs became petty dictators in their respective villages because their word was law. In what became known as the Mau Mau rebellion, Kikuyus resisted this despotism. This rebellion in the 1950s contributed significantly to the success of the independence movement in 1963. Ironically, the new African government, dominated by Kikuyus, adopted the autocratic system that the British had imposed. It used the regional administrators to suppress all forms of dissent in many rural communities.

In one attempt to stop the Mau Mau rebellion, the British had passed a land reform act in 1956. They took farmland from some Kikuyus and redistributed it to other Kikuyus who did not support the rebellion. The British also allocated five acres of mountainous land, suitable for growing tea, to each loyal farmer who would agree to grow tea for British companies. They hoped to bring enough prosperity to these farmers that future rebellions would be less tempting. Undoubtedly, the colonial government also saw in this arrangement some advantages for the British companies that would process and ship the tea as well as for British consumers.

My father spent his early years working for the British settlers. From that experience, he understood British thinking and found covert ways to use the colonial administrative system to protect the interests of his Kikuyu friends and relatives. The British later appointed him a civil administrator. He remained loyal to them, was elected as a young regional tribal chief, and never joined the Mau Maus. When the land reform act was passed, he encouraged other landless Kikuyu farmers to migrate to his region; and he helped them get land grants, including the additional five acres of tea-farming land. When enough farmers had congregated in the area, he founded the village of Kangaita. Later, my father ceased being a regional civil administrator, but because of his work in building Kangaita and helping other homeless Kikuyu families to regain farmland, the village people elected him the *munene*, the head of the council of elders of Kangaita.

Kangaita lies in the southern foothills of Mount Kenya. Snow-capped twin mountain peaks rise behind the forest where the village ends. By the time I was born, about 120 people lived in the village. As a little child, I imagined that the mountain was a fixed cloud that never cleared from the sky. Later on, my father told me it was the mountain of God, and I grew up believing that God lived there. On the southern side of the village, fields of tea plantations sprawled across the hills in a beautiful landscape as far as the eye could see. When I was a child, I loved to stand in the village square at the beginning of the long rainy season and watch amazing storms approach and dissipate over the hills before reaching our village. I used to think that we were the most blessed people in the world because we lived closer to God and could watch the rain fall from the sky.

My father had been married once before but was separated from his first wife before he married my mother, Maria. When my mother was a child, her father had beaten her mother to death. He remarried, and there was ceaseless friction between my mother and her new stepmother. When my mother was fifteen years old, my father appeared on the scene, and my maternal grandfather gave my mother to him as a ward, assigning her to cook and clean for my father. Though they later married, I think that they never loved each other.

Before I was born, my mother had four children who survived infancy. According to my uncle, she also gave birth to three children who died in infancy or at very young ages, at least two of whom may have perished through her neglect. All of my surviving older siblings were products of

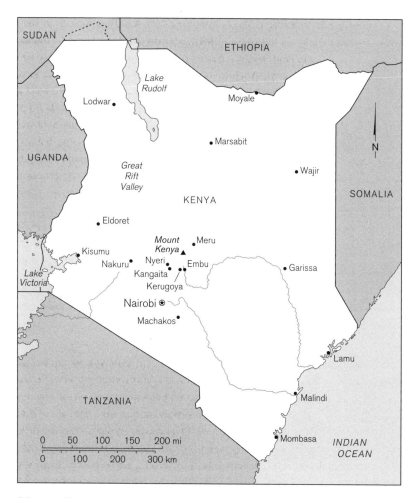

Map 1. Kenya

affairs that she had with men other than my father. I was the first of three children that she had with my father.

Today, I am seven feet tall, unlike typical Kikuyus, who are shorter than five feet, ten inches. But I was so small at my premature birth that everybody, including my mother, expected that I would soon die. I believe that I was born in the early 1970s, but I don't know exactly how old I am. While

Aunt Keru

my father was away, my mother went into labor and gave birth to me while she was collecting wood alone in the forest. Later, my father inscribed the date of my entry into this world in a small notebook in which he recorded village events. But he wrote down only the month and day, not the year.

My parents named me Wachira Ngaruri, and I was christened David Wachira Ngaruri. *Wachira* means "junior judge" or "people's representative." My father's sister Keru later told me that I was named Wachira because my mother had a dream when I was a few days old. In the dream, my great-uncle, who was a *muchiri*, or judge, appeared in his traditional judicial regalia. He wore a leopard skin and a headdress made of colobus monkey skin. His wrists, ankles, and neck were covered with colorful, bright cowry shell beads and braces, and he held a fly whisk and a walking stick. He told her that I would not die because I would be named after him and would become a judge. The next morning, frightened by the dream, my mother insisted on naming me Wachira, and I did not die.

There was a big age difference between me and my older brothers and sister. I grew up knowing the sheep and cows on our farm better than I knew these siblings. I didn't know then that we were only half-siblings. Even so, I didn't feel like their brother. They considered me a different generation, and, in Kikuyu tribal tradition, different generations don't customarily play or work with one another. Interaction is usually limited to "age mates," generations of male and female children, usually with a spread of at most five years, who have circumcision ceremonies at the same time. The oldest of my three half-brothers, Njogu, was about eighteen years older than I was. Mbacha was about fourteen when I was born, and Mugo was about eleven. Even my sister, Wangithi, was about ten years older than I was. To me, they were distant relatives.

Njogu and Mugo had violent temperaments. I don't recall ever playing with them. I remember only the beatings they gave me. My sister beat me too. Nobody tried to discipline her because she was the only girl in the family. My middle brother, Mbacha, wouldn't beat me, but he encouraged other children to beat me or told them that he would keep Mugo and Njogu from beating them if they attacked me instead. The sweetest moments in my childhood were those in which I played alone in the forest, safely hidden from these siblings and my mother.

During my earliest years, I loved to sing. I could make a song out of anything. In the evenings, my brothers and I would bring the animals from the forest to the farm, and while my father tended to them, my mother would cook and tell stories. We children would sit around the fire, and each of us would talk about our day. One evening, when I was singing about my day, Njogu smashed me in the face, saying that I made too much noise. My mother told me that I could keep Njogu from punching me if I stopped singing. I never sang again.

Every Easter, a motor rally drove through our village. During one of these rallies, a car broke down outside the village, and a helicopter landed to bring a replacement part. I had never seen or heard of a helicopter before. I was intrigued and amazed by the craft's ability to hover in the air above me like a bird. As it prepared to land, I felt the wind of its rotors and saw men with white skin come out of the helicopter. I had heard about white men, but this was the first time I had ever seen one close up. By the time the helicopter left, I had sketched a picture of it. I later built a detailed wooden model of the helicopter, even putting rotors on it. But my brothers found it and destroyed it before I could figure out how to make the rotors go around. From then on, I learned to hide my toys and my things in a clearing in the forest that my brothers did not know about. I also built a secret swimming pool in the forest, where I would play alone.

Once, when my family was growing tea bushes, I dreamed that we were all working on the farm, harvesting tea leaves with tea baskets on our backs. We were competing to see who could harvest the most tea leaves. Something caused my brothers to put all their tea leaves in my basket, so I won the competition. When we all were in the kitchen in my mother's hut, I told my family about my dream. Mugo dragged me outside and punched me repeatedly in the face. I ran back into the hut, blood gushing from my nose and mouth. My sister laughed, and my mother told me to shut up and stop crying. My father took me back to his hut and cleaned me up. He warned me that I should not tell my brothers about dreams like that, and he told me that they beat me up because they were afraid of me. He said that even though I had been born so small, I was growing very rapidly and would be bigger than they were. At that time, I wanted him to do something to make my brothers and sister stop hitting me; his words did not comfort me. But he taught me that although my brothers had to resort to physical force to get what they wanted, there were other ways to achieve my goals.

Our village consisted of traditional Kikuyu-style round huts, composed of mixtures of mud, nappier grass, cow dung, and white ash. The roofs were made of elephant grass tied from a central pole. Each hut had a fireplace in the middle. My mother and father lived in separate huts. Eventually I stopped sleeping in my mother's hut and moved to my father's residence, which was also the meeting place for the village council. His floor was covered with buffalo and goat skins. My first duty of the day was to start the fire in his hut so that the big pot of beer would brew throughout the day. Later in the morning, all the elders would sit around the fire, drink beer, and talk about everything that happened in the village, from who went to the bathroom that morning, and at what time, to whose cow had been left in the forest and who had gone looking for it. During these discussions, I would get beer or water or whatever one of the elders requested. I learned a lot by listening to the elders and helping to carry out their decisions.

For example, just outside the village was a pasture where, for most of the year, villagers were not allowed to graze their animals. It was a protected reserve, and it was opened for grazing animals only once a year, during the dry season. Whenever it opened, every family would take its animals into the pasture; and within days, there would be nothing left. Then everyone would start searching for any available grazing land, and those who owned large pastures made fortunes by leasing them to other farmers. My father and the village council discussed this problem for days. After three days of heated debate, they resolved to expand the size of the reserve, to divide it into five plots, and to allow only a certain number of animals to graze in each plot. To ensure that those resolutions were carried out, I was instructed to find a surveyor and a handyman to build the fence and to negotiate their terms of payment.

Every week, my father and I made the long walk across the hills to the district headquarters to meet with the regional council chief, Wamuri. He occupied a small stone office just outside the district market square. He was a decent man. Whenever we met him, he took us to a very nice restaurant and bought me sweet tea and fried sugar donuts. I was very comfortable with Wamuri, and I asked a lot of questions that I normally wouldn't have asked my father. Sometimes my father later cautioned me, saying, "Be careful about the way you question authority. The biggest tree in the forest is the first one to be cut down. You are a big tree, and if you don't learn how to interact respectfully with authority, you will be the first one to be cut down." Perhaps I did not learn this lesson well enough.

My mother was a physically strong woman. She may also have had some sort of undiagnosed emotional disability. She had little or no respect for any authority that challenged her will. She was the only woman I knew who could beat men into submission. Though she was a vicious protector of her children, my mother was not otherwise involved with me during my early childhood. She was, however, involved in all aspects of my brothers' upbringing. My older brothers would go around the village beating other boys, but if any boy dared to hit them back, my mother would attack that boy's family in public. Sometimes, when my mother went to the local market square, the slightest show of her anger would cause everyone in the market to disperse as if a wild animal had just escaped from its cage. To my mother, physical strength was power; whereas to my father, reason was power.

My father and my mother also fought frequently with each other. The fights were physical as well as emotional, and my father usually lost. He was about thirty-five years older than my mother, and my mother was a powerful figure, taller than all the Kikuyu men in our village. One day, over her opposition, my father planted on our farm the first pine trees ever seen in our region. My mother attempted to uproot them. My father attempted to replant them. She didn't like his response, and she scooped him off the ground and threw him down on his back. For a moment, I thought that she had killed him. He lay there, unmoving and unconscious, for a while. He didn't have any broken bones, but his health seemed to decline from that day until his death about seven years later.

When I was about eight years old, I began attending the local missionary school. I walked the two miles to school each day. The boys at school made fun of me because I was growing very tall and I was very skinny. My knees knocked against each other when I walked, and I looked gangly and weak. One day as I was walking home, the boys followed me and taunted me by calling me "giraffe," an English word they had just learned. I ran crying into my mother's hut. She demanded to know why I was crying. When I explained that the other boys were picking on me, she became furious. She took me outside, where the boys were playing together, and insisted that they tell her what they had done to make me cry. The boys were terrified of her, and one of them spoke up immediately. "We called him a 'giraffe,' " he squeaked, and he hid behind another boy. My mother did not speak English, and when she tried to repeat this word, her Kikuyu pronunciation distorted it. "Jioff?" she repeated slowly, squinting in confusion. The boys laughed despite their fear, because "Jioff" sounds even funnier to Kikuyu ears than "giraffe." When my mother let the boys go without a beating, they told the story to everyone in the village. By the next day, the entire village was calling me "Jeff." That nickname stuck, and I have been called Jeff ever since.

. . .

While my father was managing our small farm and serving as the chief elder of the village, he began tea farming on the additional five acres of land that the British had allocated to him. Years earlier, the British had created the Kenya Tea Development Agency (KTDA), a government corporation, to provide technical assistance to tea farmers and also to buy the harvested tea leaves from them. After Kenya became independent in 1963, the KTDA remained a state corporation, run and regulated by the Tea Board of Kenya.

In 1979, the tea harvest was good, and the KTDA made the largest payment in its history to the farmers. My father received 27,500 Kenyan shillings (about $300), more money than he had ever possessed. He needed to open a bank account because it wasn't safe to keep so much cash in his house. I remember going to the bank with him. He withdrew a large amount of money and asked me to carry it as we walked home. For the next several years, I was the family accountant, and we always had money when we needed it. Each month my father and I went to the local district headquarters, where the only bank was located. He withdrew money and gave it to me for safekeeping. I had to record all family expenses for my father. I was not allowed to spend the money without his authority, and I was not supposed to tell my older brothers or my mother where we kept the money. But my father's health was failing, and he worried that if he needed hospitalization, he would not be able to go to the bank to take out the money he would need. So eventually he signed papers allowing my mother to withdraw money. Once she had access to the account, her sisters and their children began spending all their time at my father's hut, living on his income. My parents' fights escalated.

The happiest day of my life in Kenya came in 1981, when my mother gave birth to my brother and sister, twins Njoka and Lucy. I fell in love with them as soon as I saw them, and I never left them even for a day until the government imprisoned me eleven years later. But that same year, my parents had a very big fight about money. My father questioned my mother's frequent withdrawals, and he revoked her authority over his bank account. In retaliation, my mother decided that she would no longer take care of the children. She never again prepared a meal for me or gave food to Njoka or Lucy. After she stopped feeding Njoka and Lucy, my father and I took care of the babies. About the same time, my mother started talking to herself, and one day I watched her burn all her clothes and belongings. Not long after, she left her hut and wandered the streets of the village, unwashed, wearing only filthy tattered clothes, and she assaulted people in the street.

My father's health continued to fail. He coughed all the time. After several visits to the hospital, he told me that he had a disease called tuberculosis. One day, I saw him weeping, and I asked him why. He said that he was not concerned about my older brothers and sisters, because they were grown, but he was worried about me and the twins. He told me that if anything happened to him, he wanted me to take care of the twins. I promised to do so. The next day, he called me and said that he needed to go to the hospital. A neighbor brought a car, and I watched it drive off. An hour later, my older brother came back in the company of two village elders and told me that my father had died.

Within a few days, my life changed forever. The second day after the funeral, my older brothers locked my father's hut, where I had been sleeping. I had to sleep in my mother's house, which was in very bad condition. It was January, and I was very cold. The next day, my older brothers went to the bank and withdrew a lot of money. They came back to the farm with a lot of building materials, which they locked in my father's house. Then they tore down my mother's house, leaving the twins and me with nowhere to stay. The twins were about two or three years old. I begged my brothers to let us into my father's house so that we would have a place to sleep. But they beat us and chased us away from the farm. Fortunately, I had about 100 shillings in my pocket, which my father had given me. This was a lot of money for a young person to have.

We went to my Aunt Keru's house. But Aunt Keru was elderly, and she had to look after her husband and his children from a previous marriage. Although she invited us to eat at her house, she advised us go back to our farm and stay there. But whenever we tried to move back there, my brothers refused to let us return. One day, Mugo found us sitting outside my father's house after we had returned from a day with Aunt Keru. He grabbed a dry branch from a nearby tree and whipped us with it, the three of us scattering and screaming at the top of our lungs. After that incident, we never returned to the farm.

My mother had moved away and rented a cheap shack in a large, dangerous slum about thirty miles east of the village. We never went there to see her. Instead, we lived on the streets for two years. Occasionally, we slept at the house of a sympathetic neighbor or at Aunt Keru's, but more often we slept under a tree. I worked on the neighbors' farms in exchange for food for the three of us. Despite the hardships, those were peaceful times, and I got to know my little brother and sister very well.

My best friend was David Kiguta, the son of a neighbor. He too had the middle name Wachira, or "judge," because his grandfather had been a very important traditional chief, who also had the powers of a judge. I gave him the nickname "Wash." When we were very young, before my father died, Wash and I hunted and fished together. We went into the forest to watch the elephants, and we sometimes played there, even sleeping inside a particularly large hollow tree. Later, when the twins and I had to live on the

Peaceful times: Wangithi, Njoka, Wangithi's son Duncan, Lucy, and myself

streets, Wash sometimes joined us. But most of the time, I was alone with the children. I became, in effect, their father; and I often went hungry so that they could eat. Despite our usually good spirits, living without shelter was unpleasant. Sometimes I went without food for six or seven days, and on winter nights we had to cope with the wet, chill climate.

By 1988, I could no longer tolerate homelessness. I met with one of the elders who had served on the council with my father to ask him whether the council could do something to allow us to go back to our farm. He told me that because my father had died without a will, his ten acres of land should have been divided among his five sons. Because he had been married to my mother when my three older brothers were born, they were presumed to be his sons and were entitled to share in his property. But Njoka and I had been denied our shares.

At about this time, my brothers Njogu and Mugo approached me because they wanted the district commissioner, as administrator of my father's estate, to release 21,000 shillings that were still in my father's bank

Mugo

account, and they needed my agreement. I agreed to join their petition to release the money if they would build a house for me and the twins on my father's land. My hope was that my mother would live in the house and that Njoka, Lucy, and I could go to school. My own education had stopped in middle school, when I had to start taking care of the twins. Njogu and Mugo agreed, and the district commissioner released the funds. But as soon as they received the money, my brothers started to build a house only for themselves.

I threatened to report them to the district commissioner, and a really big fight broke out. Up to this point, I had always lost fights with my brothers; but by this time I was pretty big, and I started winning. This made them very angry, and they tied me up, dragged me to my father's grave, put a rope around my neck, and beat me with rocks and choked me until I was unconscious.

I woke up in the hospital. Gathomi, the local chief, stood beside my bed. He had heard the noise of the beating and had saved my life. When I recovered, he convened the village council and invited me to address it. I had never spoken to the council before. After hearing my story, the council divided the land among the male children, just as it should have been divided after my father died. My brothers took the best part of the land, with my father's house, for themselves; but my part of the property included some of the tea bushes that my father had cultivated. As the land was being surveyed, my brothers told me that I would never make that part of the property profitable and that they would eventually take it back.

After the survey was completed, I built a shed for myself and the children. I worked on other people's farms until I had enough money to buy one cow. I sold the milk that we did not need to buy clothes and pay for school uniforms for the twins. I registered the twins at the local missionary school and began planting tea seedlings, beginning my brief career as a tea farmer. For the next three years, I cultivated these few acres of land, tending the tea bushes that my father had planted and clearing and planting more tea bushes.

· · ·

By 1991, my farm was producing as much tea as it could ever produce. As payment for the tea I sold that year, I received about 10,000 shillings (about $130), which was far less than I had spent to grow the tea. This was sobering, and it made me start to look into why I was losing money. I also began to evaluate the costs of producing and harvesting tea leaves. I realized that my loss had resulted from policies that the KTDA and the Kenyan government had imposed on tea farmers.

The government's tea-growing license prohibited farmers from planting, removing, or destroying any tea bushes without permission from the KTDA. This prohibition effectively prevented farmers from switching part of their land to more profitable crops. We were not allowed to process the tea ourselves or to grow vegetables for our own consumption on the plots where tea bushes were also growing. Violations of the terms of the license were punishable by imprisonment and a heavy fine.

Also, all farmers had to obey any instructions issued by the KTDA. Small-scale tea farmers like me were prohibited from selling our tea on the open market; we could sell our harvest only to the KTDA, a monopoly buyer, at the price it set. We could buy our fertilizer only from the KTDA, at steep prices. Every month, we sent our tea leaves to the local KTDA collection center, which had been built by the farmers but was managed by the KTDA. The entire raw product had to include two leaves and a bud; farmers whose tea deviated from that standard could lose their harvest. The roads between the villages and the collection center were so poor that the collection trucks often failed to arrive. Then the farmers had to carry twenty-five-pound bags of tea for two or three miles to a good road. When the tea reached the collection center, it was weighed. Then the KTDA processed the leaves in a factory and sold the processed tea on the international market.

We were paid monthly for the tea leaves we supplied, and we also received an annual bonus in November for the tea we had sold during the previous season. The amount of the bonus was unpredictable, but it never exceeded 3 shillings per kilogram.

In 1991, the KTDA paid farmers 3 shillings per kilogram for green (unprocessed) tea leaves, plus a November bonus of only 2 shillings more. After the 20 percent value-added tax was deducted, we ended up receiving only 4 shillings for each kilo of leaf tea. It took 4 kilos of leaf tea to produce 1 kilo of processed tea, so we earned 16 shillings for the leaves that made a kilo of processed tea. The government bragged that Kenyan tea was so well regarded that the international wholesale market price of processed tea was never less than 40 shillings per kilo and sometimes reached 140 shillings. I realized that processing and distribution accounted for some of the difference, but it seemed to me that the 16-shilling price we received for unprocessed tea was so far below the open market price as to raise questions about where the balance of at least 24 shillings per kilo had gone.

During the winter and spring of 1992, I had a large harvest. My farming costs were about 5 shillings per kilo of unprocessed green leaf tea, and therefore about 1 shilling per kilo higher than my income. Even after I received my bonus, my debt at the village grocery stall kept increasing. I began to discuss my frustrations with Wash and some of my other friends. I was angry; I felt that the KTDA was taking advantage of us. "We are all trapped," I complained, "because none of us can grow other crops along with or instead of the tea." I announced that I was going to stop farming tea because we were paid so little for our crop.

One night in early summer, a small group of us, tea farmers and tea pickers, walked and danced through the streets of Kangaita and the neighboring villages. As we danced, many of the farmers also sang a song that they had made up about how we were not going to grow or pick tea again.

To my surprise, at least five hundred farmers and pickers from the region gathered near our village the next day to find out why people had been singing and vowing to stop growing tea. This was an important subject for the people in Kangaita and the nearby villages, which were located in Kirinyaga District of Central Province, an important tea-producing region. Most of the residents had become engaged in the tea industry in one way or another as farmers, pickers, or processors.

Wash and I heard the commotion in the field near the village and wandered over. As the crowd grew, people debated with each other about whether to boycott the KTDA. The older farmers, resigned to poverty after years of tea growing, did not think that a few small-scale tea farmers could change the government's policies or prices. But those of us who were young and new to the tea industry couldn't see ourselves submitting to debt and subsistence conditions for our whole lives. One older farmer warned that it was foolish for us to demand more from the government. I surprised myself by blurting out that farming tea under the KTDA's rules made us no better than slaves. We were limited to tea farming and could not do what we wanted with our property.

Suddenly, everyone started to listen to me because of my strong language. As the crowd became more attentive, I grew more impassioned. I argued that if we could not change the KTDA policies, we would live as poorly as our parents had lived. I suggested that on the following day we should organize a march to the nearby KTDA tea-processing factory and that we should use peaceful means, such as a mass boycott, to prevent the factory from operating until the KTDA met our demands. Either it must raise the price that it paid for our tea, account for the difference between what we received and the market price of tea, or release us from the conditions of our tea licenses so that we could destroy our bushes and grow a profitable product.

The next day, the fields around our village were crowded with more than a thousand farmers from all the neighboring villages, who had gathered for the march on the factory. They looked to me to lead the march, because it had been my idea. So I was at the head of the procession. We marched to the factory, about two and a half miles from Kangaita, and gathered around the gates. I stood on the back of a flatbed truck and used a bullhorn to demand that the manager, Mr. Njuguna, speak to us. He emerged from the factory and saw people from every village staring at him. By this time, the police had arrived and were watching us. Tension grew as the crowd became fearful that the police would resort to violence to break up the protest.

Speaking through my bullhorn, I urged the farmers to remain calm and to avoid any violence that could provoke the police. I told them that if we remained peaceful, the police would ensure our security. Then I turned my attention to Njuguna and insisted that he close the factory until we received better prices or an explanation of where the profits were going.

As I spoke to him in front of the crowd, I became concerned that if he did close the factory, the people who worked there could lose their jobs. I therefore added the demand that he not fire any workers until our dispute with the KTDA was resolved. He looked at the huge crowd of people standing before him. After a short hesitation, he put a padlock on the factory door. Everyone cheered in celebration. We began to hope that things could change.

The tea-harvesting boycott quickly spread to all nine villages that had supplied tea to the factory. Only my brother Mugo and a few other farmers continued to harvest tea. My friends and I met every day to figure out what to do next. We discussed problems that the boycott would create. I worried that unemployment, idleness, and the absence of income from the sale of tea leaves would lead to hunger and crime and that the government would use any antisocial conduct as a basis for arresting us. Meeting in our homes and in the streets, we formed informal committees to take care of the villagers and keep order. We had a food committee to distribute food from those who had a little to those who had none, an intelligence committee to try to monitor what the police were doing, and a communications committee that set up a word-of-mouth network to relay messages among the villages. All committee members had to be tea farmers approved by those in their villages.

We conducted our planning meetings in secret because we knew that the government of Kenya did not tolerate challenges to its policies. Daniel arap Moi, the president of Kenya, had come to power in 1978 upon the death of Kenya's first president, Mzee Jomo Kenyatta. My father had greatly admired Kenyatta, who had been able to convince white settlers that they could remain in Kenya under a black president. When he heard about Kenyatta's death, my father looked as though he had lost a close friend. He told me, "Our Muthamaki [great leader] has died. We don't know what will happen. I hope that you will not have to see us return to the days of colonial rule."

Moi was a political nonentity when he served as Kenyatta's vice president. After Kenyatta died in his sleep, however, Moi was sworn in as president and eventually went on to become one of the longest-serving strongmen on the continent. He rapidly brought the state security forces under his personal control and used them to suppress dissent. In 1982, he crushed an air force mutiny against him. Immediately thereafter, he took leadership of the ruling party, the Kenya African National Union (KANU), and made Kenya a one-party state, passing new laws to outlaw other parties.

Using the machinery of government, President Moi censored the press and arrested opposition politicians. It soon became common knowledge among Kenyans that people who dared to challenge his power might disappear forever. Those who reemerged from arrest and imprisonment had broken bodies and spirits after enduring torture at the hands of Moi's security forces. In rural villages such as Kangaita, KANU recruited militant youths who conducted door-to-door searches for "seditious materials," which usually meant any book or magazine that the local KANU leadership could not understand. Students who happened to have contraband books—even books that had been purchased before they were proscribed—were ar-

Daniel arap Moi

rested and often disappeared. Sometimes, even illiterate citizens were charged with treason when banned books were found in their houses.

Despite a ban on opposition parties, several opposition leaders had emerged, forming political organizations such as the Forum for the Restoration of Democracy. In November 1991, Moi arrested several of those leaders to prevent them from holding a rally. Some of them died in prison. Western governments responded by discontinuing foreign aid to the Kenyan government.

Our boycott committee knew that we could become a target of Moi's police forces. We acted cautiously, but our fear did not dissuade us from boycotting or from holding a few public meetings to keep the farmers informed. We were not without enemies in the village, especially those who, like my brother Mugo, attended our public meetings with the chief of police and pointed out some of the organizers to him. Our boycott brought tea production in Central Province to a halt. That was a significant achievement, because Central Province was the heart of Kenya's tea industry, and tea had become the nation's most lucrative export crop. Only tourism brought in more foreign exchange. As a result, our protest made national news.

. . .

Flush with our growing success, we planned a longer-term reform: the creation of a farmers' union to work for structural changes in the tea industry. The goal of the union would be to advocate for the right to sell our tea to anyone who wanted to buy it. The best way to achieve this objective was to reform the structure of the KTDA so that small-scale farmers would have fair representation on its board of directors.

We decided to begin this next phase of our work by organizing a second march, this time to Kerugoya, about seven miles south of Kangaita. Although it was a dusty agricultural town, Kerugoya was also the center for the district's political administration and had a soccer stadium, an open-air market, several hardware stores, and an imposing government building where District Commissioner Francis Tiliitei, the highest-ranking official in our district, had his office.

On the day we picked for our march, the government planned a public political rally in Murang'a, a town about one hundred miles west of Kerugoya. Like Kerugoya, Murang'a was a district administrative center. There, too, most of the farmers were supporting the boycott. President Moi was scheduled to speak at this rally. The commissioners and other district administrators from the region, as well as all the farmers, were expected to go to the president's rally to hear what he had to say about our grievances. But if the farmers attended our march, they could not also hear the president. We therefore worried that the government would disperse our march to boost attendance in Murang'a and to prevent the district officials from listening to our grievances in Kerugoya. Nevertheless, we decided to proceed with the march, believing that if we drew a huge crowd of farmers on that day, it would demonstrate the depth and breadth of our protest.

Hundreds of farmers gathered at a junction where the feeder roads from the villages merged with the main highway to Kerugoya. Women wrapped their children around their shoulders with fabric slings and balanced them on their backs. Men wore tattered suits and working boots. Before we started marching, we sent a team of young men and women ahead to scout for police who might have been sent to disperse us. Another team of young men ran ahead to the nearby villages to help provide water to the marchers. At about 9:00 A.M., we started marching. We chanted antigovernment slogans and carried tea branches on our way to Kerugoya. Some of the farmers sang as we marched. As we passed through villages, thousands of farmers joined our march to the headquarters. I had never seen so many people coming to one place.

By the time we arrived in Kerugoya, all the businesses in town had closed their doors, and the owners were standing outside their shops watching the crowd. Some of them joined the march. As we proceeded toward the government offices, the police created a human chain and refused to allow us to enter the commissioner's compound to speak with Commissioner Tiliitei. But Tiliitei agreed to meet with us. He asked me and the other organizers to lead the crowd to the soccer stadium, where everyone could watch him listen to our grievances. Like all other stadiums across the country, the stadium was named after the president; it was known as Kerugoya Moi Stadium.

Commissioner Tiliitei set up a public address system so that everyone could hear us. The crowd numbered about thirty thousand. It was so large that many people could not find seats in the grandstand or even a place to stand on the field. Some stood outside the stadium, watching over a low fence. Inside the stadium, we asked the people to sit on the grass until the commissioner arrived. A few minutes later, he entered the stadium in a convoy of cars that resembled a presidential motorcade. Armed security personnel ran alongside the convoy and violently pushed people aside.

As his aides handed the commissioner a microphone, he said quietly to me, "I am impressed. I have been in this district for three years, and I have never been able to assemble such a large group." Then he turned to address the farmers. He told them that President Moi had originally wanted him to go to Murang'a, but after hearing about the march, the president had asked him to speak to the farmers in Kerugoya, to tell us to go home and listen to his address on the radio.

As I heard Commissioner Tiliitei speak these words, I feared that he was invoking his administrative power to order us to go home and that he would have the organizers arrested if we did not comply. But as he implored the crowd to disperse, the farmers began to heckle and shout at him. Frustrated, he stopped in mid-sentence and turned his attention to me. "I cannot talk to these people!" he said angrily. "You people did not come here because you wanted my help."

I told him, "I can calm them down. Let me have the microphone." The commissioner gave it to me.

I looked over the crowd. I had never thought of myself as a politician, and I was surprised and a little frightened to find myself the sole spokesman for all these farmers. The district's police chief and its intelligence officer sat just a few yards away from me. But I was pretty sure that no one would arrest me in front of tens of thousands of people, so I decided to speak my mind. I focused my full attention on the commissioner and on Wash, who was standing in front, as if they were the only people in the stadium.

I told the commissioner that we farmers had come to present our grievances to him. I asked the crowd, "How many of you agree that tea farming is so unprofitable that it is not worth our time? Raise your hand so that the commissioner can see." A sea of hands waved back, and the crowd chanted, "We won't go back, we won't go back!"

I had learned from my father that the best way to be understood is to tell a story, so I told the commissioner the story of a farmer's life. "A tea farmer," I explained, "spends three years preparing the land with his family. During that time, the farmer is compensated only by the hope that one

The speech at the stadium

day he will have a good harvest and be able to build a house, buy some clothes, and pay his children's school fees. For three years, the farmer tends the seedlings and weeds the bushes, sometimes surviving on only one meal a day. After three years, he must pay 50 shillings for a license that prohibits him from selling his leaves to anyone but the KTDA and from growing any other crops. In short, after three years of developing his farm, the farmer becomes subject to the direction of the KTDA."

Then I outlined the economics of tea farming. In front of all the farmers, I laid out the costs of growing tea, the taxes and charges that the government imposed, and the low price that the KTDA offered for tea leaves.

I explained that we had recently met with some local KTDA representatives to ask about the huge discrepancy between the market price for processed tea and the price we were paid for the leaves. The KTDA officials claimed that they did not know the reason and told us to ask the government.

I concluded by making a series of demands on behalf of the farmers. We wanted the KTDA board to be dissolved and restructured to include farmers. We called on the KTDA either to increase the basic price for a kilo of tea leaves from 3 shillings to 8 shillings or to allow us to sell our tea leaves to any buyer who wanted them. I wound up with a line that may have infuriated President Moi. "We demand that if this government cannot meet the needs of the people it claims to represent, it should resign and allow us to elect a democratic government that will let us sell our goods and services in an open market."

As I handed the microphone back to the commissioner, the crowd waved, cheered, and danced in agreement with my speech. Wash was in tears. Women began singing traditional songs. One sang a Kikuyu song whose lyrics mean, "Working together is easier than fighting each other. We work together to benefit our children." This became the slogan of the boycott.

I was surprised that I had been able to deliver this speech in front of so many people. It was as if I had been freed from some bond that I could feel but not touch.

As the farmers were dispersing to return to their villages, the commissioner told me that he wanted to meet with me in a week and that he wanted us to put our demands in writing. I agreed, but the boycott committee warned me that it was a trap, fearing that we would be taken from such a meeting and put in jail. However, we concluded that we could not get anywhere if we did not meet with the commissioner. As a precaution, we decided to send a delegation that would include me but would not include most of the boycott leaders.

Several days later, I went to the commissioner's office with a group of farmers chosen by the boycott committee. We brought a handwritten list of demands. He claimed that he could not read my handwriting and ordered us to have the demands typed. "Meanwhile," he said, "I want you to end this boycott so that we can have a healthy dialogue." I told him that we would type the list but that we would not end the boycott.

One night later that week, three armed police officers came to my home and ordered me to go with them to see Commissioner Tiliitei. I was afraid to leave with them, but I had no choice. We went in their Land Rover to Commissioner Tiliitei's house, where I alone met with him and one security officer. He ushered us into his living room. He told me that he was under great pressure from his superiors to end the boycott. He promised that they could make my life very comfortable if I ended the boycott and went back to tea farming. This was not a surprising response, as bribery had become a way of life in the government of Kenya. I rejected his offer and repeated our demands. I asked him, "If your friends in the government can make my life comfortable, why can't you distribute that money to the farmers who are dying of hunger and poverty? They are not boycotting to avoid hard work. They just cannot afford to farm tea anymore."

Commissioner Tiliitei became very angry. "I am not going to let a group of boys ruin my career," he retorted. "You are on your own, and don't say I did not warn you." He walked out of the room and gestured to the security officer to show me the door. I left his house and found a friend to drive me back to Kangaita.

· · ·

This meeting with Commissioner Tiliitei changed the tone of our dealings with the government. Now I began to fear that the government would arrest or kill me. I thought that I might lose my life in a freak "accident."

I decided that I had to reach out to opposition groups for their advice and help. One of the members of the organizing committee knew some politicians. He had met Mwai Kibaki, who had been Moi's vice president and minister of health but had recently broken with Moi and formed an opposition group called the Democratic Party. I had a late-night meeting with Kibaki and joined his Democratic Party. I was certain at the time that we were meeting in secret, but I later learned that the government had Kibaki under surveillance and that it spied on us.

My fear of government retaliation increased a few days later. The local newspapers reported a July 30 speech by President Moi in which he warned that the leaders of the tea boycott would face "dire consequences" if the boycott continued. He claimed, falsely, that we were forcing farmers to join the boycott by burning the farms of those who refused to cooperate with us. I was more afraid than before, but I couldn't let down the thousands of farmers by backing down in the face of a threat. I went into hiding, moving from village to village and sleeping in the homes of many friends.

Then I learned that the police were arresting innocent villagers and beating them to try to get them to reveal my whereabouts. They even arrested my oldest brother, Njogu. The police did not know about Njogu's animosity toward me, nor had they investigated enough to realize that he knew nothing and had nothing to do with the boycott. They knew only that he was my brother, which was enough to cause his arrest. I later learned that the police threatened to castrate him, but he was unable to lead them to me because he did not know where I was.

I felt ashamed to be hiding while others, who often had only minor connections with the boycott, were being arrested and beaten. I also knew that the police would find me sooner or later. I thought about trying to leave the country, as some dissident students had done. But I learned that those students had been able to get out because they had relatives in the countries to which they fled. I also learned that it was almost impossible to leave without a passport, and I did not have one. When I realized that I could not escape, I decided to turn myself in. I walked to the police headquarters in Kerugoya, with dozens of farmers following me in solidarity. Along the way, I heard that fires had been started on some farms and that, although the government was blaming the boycott committee for the arson, the fires had actually been started by the police as a pretext for the arrests.

I entered the police headquarters in Kerugoya and asked to speak with Chief Inspector Mosera, who was in charge. He owned a tea farm and had seemed sympathetic to the farmers. He and I knew each other and had exchanged some information during the boycott. He ushered me into his office, closed the door, and offered me a seat. "I have orders to arrest you," he informed me. "There is nothing I can do for you because Special Branch is now in charge."

Special Branch was the intelligence arm of the president's guards. "I have to lock you up, and I am sure you understand my position," Mosera said. He then picked up a red phone on his desk and told someone, "I've got him. He walked right into the station." He ordered me to remove my shoes, and he locked me in a cell without informing me of any charges.

The cell was dark. It was empty except for a dirty plastic container that smelled of urine. The walls were inscribed with messages from former occupants. One read, "This place is hell. Mutoto."

I thought that Mosera might throw away the keys and that I might die in that cell. I could hear the cries of people who were being interrogated and tortured. I knew that the security forces wanted statements that they could use against me, perhaps in a trial for treason. I thought that I could recognize the screams of my brother Njogu; later, I learned that he was tortured for three weeks before being released.

I thought about my little brother and sister, whom I had left in the care of my older sister, Wangithi, and my friend Wash. I had not spent very much time with them since the beginning of the boycott. I wanted them to know how much I loved and missed them. I imagined them sitting by the fire by themselves and wishing that I was there to prepare dinner.

I couldn't stand hearing the screams. I called to the guard and shouted that they could let everyone else go because I would tell them what they needed to know. An officer carrying a whip unlocked the cell and handcuffed me. He took me to a small office where another officer sat at a desk. He was writing something, and he continued to write as if no one else was in the room. On the desk next to him was a hedge clipper with blood-stained blades, dripping with small droplets of fresh blood. Bloodstains were smeared on the walls and on the floor. I became frightened as I imagined that I was about to be castrated. I wondered how much it would hurt. I thought to myself, "I will talk, but I will tell them only what they already know. I will be friendly, and they will not have to torture me."

Knowing that I was about to be tortured was unbearable. I turned to the officer who had taken me into the room and said, "You don't have to use this. I am ready to work with you and tell you what I know." The man at the desk suddenly stopped writing. He stared at me with a strange smile and said, "You'll talk when I want you to talk." Then he nodded to the officer: "Take him back. We've got a new team coming."

They came for me in the night, when, after several fitful hours, I was finally falling asleep. Very quickly, three officers took me out of my cell, blindfolded me, handcuffed both hands behind my back, pushed me outside, and forced me to sit on the floor of a van. The door of the van slammed behind me, and I flinched, thinking that I had been shot. The van started moving, and we drove for about three hours. The officers talked among themselves. One of the officers spoke only in Swahili, which I could understand. The other two spoke Swahili to me but talked to each other in Kalenjin, the language of President Moi's tribe. I recognized the language but could not understand it. I was frightened and tried to control my fear by focusing on breathing.

The van stopped. One of the officers grabbed my jacket collar and pulled me out of the van. I slipped and fell on the ground and blindly tried to catch my balance. Someone grabbed my shoulders and pulled me up so that I could stand. Another poked a sharp object into my lower back. "*Endelea mbere!*" he shouted in Swahili, ordering me to move forward.

I couldn't see through the blindfold, but I could hear birds chirping, so I knew that it would soon be dawn. The air was cold, and the ground was mushy. I could tell that I was in a forest, and I imagined that I would be buried in an unmarked grave where I would never be found. I expected that at any moment I might be shot in the back by these men, who would later claim that I tried to escape.

"I don't like wasting my valuable time with people like these," one of the officers screamed. I tensed, waiting for his shot. I had seen movies of people being executed and dying before they hit the ground. I hoped that it would be painless.

Someone grabbed me by the front of my collar and said, "Before I kill you, I need to know who told you to start this tea foolishness. We want to know names. Do you understand?" It was hard for me to speak, because his knuckles were cutting off my windpipe, but I told him that I had started the boycott and that no one had put me up to it. "We know you didn't start this by yourself," he scoffed. "Something like this can't be started by village people like you."

Another voice asked, "Do you know Kibaki?"

I lied to him, telling him that I had never spoken to Kibaki.

I complained to the officer that the handcuffs were digging into my skin and asked the officers to loosen them. One of them said, "You don't need to worry about that because I am going to blow your stupid brains away."

"Get on your knees," another officer bellowed. Before I could do so, he grabbed my shirt collar and pushed me, hard, against what felt like the trunk of a tree. My head felt like it would explode, and for a moment, I wished they would just get it over with. I felt a hard object being pressed into the back of my head, just above the hairline. I thought that it was a gun, and I expected and wanted to die at any second.

Moments passed. The officer pulled me away from the tree and turned me around so that my back and the back of my head were against the tree. I lowered myself and knelt on soft ground. He pressed the hard object to my forehead. From immediately in front of me, I heard a sound that seemed the cocking of a gun.

"Look at yourself," the officer demanded. It was a ridiculous command, because I was blindfolded. "You don't look as cool as you did when you were giving your speech in the stadium. I am going to kill you now. Do you think those farmers can help you now?" I continued to think that each second would be my last and that this nightmare would soon end.

The officer who spoke only in Swahili broke in: "It is stupid to kill him. He is just a small fish. He has a lot of information. If he is alive, he can lead us to the big fish."

Another officer replied in Swahili, "I have dealt with Kikuyus before. They don't know how to stop. When I release a Kikuyu, he comes back. The best thing to do with a Kikuyu is to kill him. Then you never have to deal with him again."

"But if we don't kill him," argued the first officer, "he could lead us to the head of the whole organization. Where did you get your training? *Mathura!*" This was an expression implying that his fellow officer was impulsive like a slum dweller.

A screaming argument ensued between two officers, in Kalenjin. I couldn't understand what they were saying. While they argued, the third officer said to me, in Swahili, "You stupid Kikuyus think you know everything. Do you know you can lose your life because of politics?"

I tried not to show how afraid I was. "If you shoot me," I replied, "I will not die for nothing. The farmers have heard my voice. Killing me will not stop the boycott. You can kill me, but you cannot kill the spirit of all those people."

Eventually the argument in Kalenjin ended. Without removing my blindfold or handcuffs, one of the officers grabbed my collar again and dragged me along the ground. Then another pulled me up and forced me to walk. They shut me in the van and began to drive. My hands were numb with cold. As the van sped through the night, I couldn't stop worrying about what would happen to Njoka and Lucy if Moi's officers killed me.

When the van stopped, the men dragged me out and led me through a building. When they took off the blindfold, the light blinded me. They made me remove my muddy clothing and threw me into the cold water torture chamber. For days, I knew nothing but darkness, cold, fear, hunger, thirst, and the belief that I had already died.

TWO

Basketball

In the water torture cell, I grew very weak from hunger and crazed from sensory deprivation. After about a week of this ordeal, two guards removed me from the cell. I could not walk. They dragged my limp, naked body by my ankles through the prison and left me lying on the floor of a small office. When I was able to adjust to the light, I saw my reflection in a mirror. My skin, which is normally very dark, had turned as white as a piece of paper.

Two men wearing black suits, crisply ironed white shirts, and ties were sitting next to a desk. Each was holding a pile of papers. "How have they been treating you here?" one politely asked. I tried to speak, but I could not make a sound. The men offered me a bowl of meat and rice, but I feared a trick and didn't eat it. They seemed upset by the treatment I had been given. One of them advised me, "You will be all right if you cooperate and tell us who was responsible for the boycott."

Since I was the responsible person, I didn't know what to tell them. I feared that if I told them the truth, they would return me to the water cell or do even worse things to me. One of them showed me a list of names and asked me to point out which people I knew. I recognized about half the people on the list as opposition leaders, but I lied and claimed that I did not recognize any of the names. I was afraid that anyone I named would be tortured the way I had been and that under torture they might accuse me of treason, an offense punishable by hanging. I knew that Moi's security forces often tortured false confessions out of people they arrested.

Either the two men believed me or they gave up on me, because they did not return me to the water cell. They gave me clothes and took me to a small cell lit by one electric lightbulb. The cell was warm enough. The next morning, a bowl of cornmeal was pushed through the one barred window. I grabbed the cornmeal and ate it as quickly as I could with both hands.

For months, I was in solitary confinement in this cell. Sometimes they took me for interrogation sessions. These sessions provided my only human contact, and therefore I looked forward to them. I often faced new interrogators, who asked the same questions as all the others, along with simple personal questions such as my name and height. There were times when I expected the officers to beat me, but they never did, even though I did not inform on the other leaders of the boycott.

After I had lived for several months in solitary confinement, two guards came into my cell, blindfolded and handcuffed me, and put me in a van. My mind flooded with images of my near-execution in the forest, and I could barely keep myself from screaming. This time, they transferred me to Kerugoya Prison Headquarters in my home district. The moment we entered the gates, I recognized familiar voices. Guards removed my blindfold and took me to the local commanding officer, a man I had met before. He sat behind a huge mahogany desk, a Kenyan flag dangling from a post beside him. "Welcome back," he said to me.

He dismissed the guard, closed the door, and stated that he had orders to keep me in his jail for an indefinite period. I would be confined to my own cell to keep me from communicating with other tea farmers who were still in the jail. This isolation would require me to share the officers' bathroom. The guard returned and led me away to a small, dark cell. He gave me two blankets, an empty plastic bowl, and a copy of the Bible. I asked for a newspaper, but he replied curtly, "This is not a hotel. Prisoners don't get newspapers."

Several days later, officers took me to the district court. It was late afternoon, and I was surprised that the court was still open. The judge was the only person in the room. He asked in Swahili, "What do I do with him?"

One of the officers declared, "He has committed treason. He tried to overthrow the government."

"What is the evidence?" the judge asked. "Did he have a gun?"

"No, Your Honor. He invaded the district commissioner's office with tea branches."

I tried to restrain myself from laughing as I imagined overwhelming President Moi's security forces by beating them with tea branches. The judge must have seen my expression. "Young man," he scolded, "the charges against you are very severe. I wouldn't be laughing, because a person can be hanged for treason. However, the police do not appear to have evidence to substantiate the claim that you tried to overthrow the government. So, for now, I have to let you go."

I seemed to be dreaming. After so much pain, freedom had suddenly emerged on the horizon, much sooner than I had expected. The judge dismissed the charges and ordered my release. I was overjoyed. But as I was about to leave the court, two officers abruptly seized me, pushed me back into the prison van, and drove me back to solitary confinement in my prison cell.

After a few days, the officers took me to court again. Again it was late afternoon, and the same judge questioned the officers. "What charge is it this time?" he asked.

I was now charged with being a threat to public peace, they replied. They asked that I be required to keep the public peace for a period of time to be determined by Special Branch.

The judge offered to release me if I posted a million-shilling "peace bond." This meant that I would have to deposit a million shillings in court, which I would forfeit if I did not "maintain public peace." The bond and its condition would be imposed for one year—a term that the police could extend indefinitely. The judge explained that I could not participate in any kind of political activity or meet with more than three

Kenyans at a time. I would also have to report to the district police station every two weeks and remain within the district unless the district commissioner or a senior police official allowed me to leave. If I violated any of these conditions, the million-shilling bond would be forfeited.

I agreed to the conditions. I would have agreed to anything in order to go home and see Lucy and Njoka. Of course, I did not have a million shillings, so the guards took me back to my cell. I hoped to see someone I knew while I was being put in the van, so that I could get word to my family. But I did not see anyone to whom I could give a message.

The next day, the guards brought me a bowl of sweet tea, and I tasted sugar for the first time in months. Later that morning, a guard took me outside and asked one of the prisoners to cut my hair. While the prisoner did so, he told me that the day after I was arrested, about five thousand farmers had gathered at the prison gates to demand my release. The guards had been very frightened. "You are a hero out there," he asserted. "Because of you, they had to increase the monthly tea payment rate to four and a half shillings to calm the people down. It was the first time they ever increased the rate."

After my haircut, the guards let me take a shower. There were no towels, so they told me to go into the courtyard and dry myself in the sun. It was a beautiful morning. I sat naked on the pavement leading from the main cell block to the commanding officer's office. One of the guards struck up a conversation with me and revealed that the tea farmers were raising money to post my bond.

Another guard emerged from the office. He seemed to outrank the guard to whom I had been talking. He shook my hand excitedly. "It's good to meet you. My parents own a tea farm, and I am a great fan of yours." He turned to the other guard. "Why are you letting this honorable man sit on the ground? This is wrong." He ran into an office and returned with a chair on his head. In retrospect, it is amusing to think about getting VIP treatment from a prison guard while I was stark naked. But at the time I felt humiliated by his attention. I sat on the chair and covered my private parts with my hands.

He continued, "Do you know what you did? You gave life to old men and women who had no hope. Families that didn't have enough to eat can afford to send their children to school."

I smiled and said, "Thank you, sir. This chair is very nice."

That afternoon, my mother brought Lucy and Njoka to see me in prison. I looked into my mother's eyes and felt an empathy I had never experienced before: finally I understood her fear and hatred of authority. Tears welled in my sister's eyes. "People said that you were dead," she told me. I asked her not to cry and promised that I would be coming home soon.

The boycott had ended after the police crackdown and the increase in the tea payment. The farmers of the district, grateful for their small gains, raised the money for my bond by borrowing it from their cooperative banks, putting up their farms as collateral. The fund-raising effort was led by Mwangi Mucira, who had been a Mau Mau leader and later a commanding officer in Jomo Kenyatta's security guard. After Kenyatta's death, Mwangi had retired to tea farming. I had met him briefly during the boycott, and he had become a leader in our organizing committee.

The people of the district responded strongly to Mwangi's efforts. They risked their farms to get me out of jail because I had suffered for my efforts to improve their lives. The 50 percent increase in the price paid for their tea leaves had been accompanied by other small reforms. For example, the KTDA now accepted the risk of loss after farmers delivered their tea leaves, and farmers were now allowed to purchase fertilizer on the open market as well as from the KTDA.

In early April 1993, the farmers deposited 1 million shillings with the court for my bond. Members of the boycott committee arranged for a local taxi driver to take me to my house. I went home for the first time in eight months.

· · ·

But I was not yet a free man. If the authorities caught me violating the strict conditions that the court had imposed, my supporters could lose their farms. I was often under police surveillance: armed officers periodically appeared in the village and inquired about my whereabouts. In addition, anyone who associated with me risked coming under surveillance themselves or being punished. If I visited someone, the police would later show up and ask about our conversation. Former friends were warned not to socialize with me, and some of them stopped seeing me, even within the terms of my bond, after they were harassed by the police. So I spent time with Wash, who became my constant companion, and with my little brother and sister, but not with my other friends or with the other people from the boycott committee. The police questioned Wash about me, but he portrayed himself as an insignificant village loser, and they lost interest in him.

I felt limited not only by the restrictions on my political freedom but also by my interrupted education. I knew that I needed more education to achieve anything. I had not gone to secondary school; worse, I had not even completed the middle school education necessary for admission to secondary school. But now I was too old to go back to middle school, or even to secondary school. I couldn't buy supplies to farm my own land, because the government had frozen my bank account. So I took a job as the manager of a farm owned by Matere Kerii, a former member of Parliament who was a close friend of Mwangi.

One day, Wash and I were making hooks from tree branches so that we could spread the tea bushes on Matere's farm. As we worked, he asked me, "Jeff, you know that house owned by Gituto?" I did know the house, a new one that a local tea farmer and businessman had built on his farm near the forest. "Someone told me yesterday that there is a white man living in it."

"Why would a white man live in our village?" I replied. I had not seen a white person in Kangaita since the helicopter landing when I was a boy.

"I don't know," he said. "But I heard he is an American, and he is living here with his wife."

Later that evening, when Wash and I were walking to the market square, a very short white man and a white woman sped past us on bicycles. Like everyone else in the village, I was curious about them and wanted to know who they were. We ran in the direction they went.

We caught up with them as they were leaving the local convenience store. I could read and write some English, but my ability to speak or understand it was quite poor. I tried using a few English words: "Are you the white people living here?"

The woman answered in Swahili: "We are not actually living here." The man added, in very poor Swahili, *"Habaari Yaako . . . Jina langu nii Fiu; na lako?"* (How are you? My name is Phil; what's yours?)

I was not surprised that he could speak Swahili, because most white people in East Africa could do so. Swahili was a widely used language that missionaries and, later, British colonial administrators had spread throughout the region.

"Hi, my name is Jeff," I countered in Swahili. "It's nice to meet you." The man replied that his name was Phil Chinnici, and he introduced the woman as Tracy Walbert.

Tracy asked whether the road to the east would take them to Kerugoya.

"Is that where you are staying?" I asked her.

Her Swahili was very good. She explained that she was staying in Kerugoya but that Phil was considering living in Kangaita. Phil was on his way to Gituto's store to find out whether he would be able to rent the house.

"If you rent the house," I said, "I would like to come there to visit you, because I would like you to help me learn English."

"He could teach you English, and you can teach him Kikuyu and Swahili," Tracy suggested. "He is going to need that."

As Phil and Tracy rode off, Wash and I speculated on why a white man from America would want to live in our village. "Maybe you have never looked around," Wash said, "but this is one of the most beautiful places there is. White people like to live in beautiful places."

The next day, I saw Phil riding his bicycle again. He had rented the house, and he invited me to visit him. As we walked to his house, he informed me that he was a member of the Peace Corps from the United States, and he tried to convey what that meant. He had studied how to plan the growth of towns, he explained, and had come to our district to work on regional planning with officials in Kerugoya.

I said that I understood that he was with the U.S. Army. "No," he corrected me. "The Peace Corps is a government agency, but it is not part of the military."

I had seen James Bond movies, so I understood what he was trying to tell me: that he was doing reconnaissance for the CIA.

"Look, man," he insisted, "I am not in the CIA. I am with the Peace Corps. We come here to engage in peaceful activities and cultural exchanges. We are not even allowed to work with the military."

As we walked a little farther, we worked out a system in which he would talk to me in English, to improve my English, and I would talk to him in Swahili, to improve his Swahili. He offered to let me bring one friend when I visited him.

That evening, I invited Wash to visit Phil with me. He was reluctant because his English was even more primitive than mine. "I don't want to be a spare wheel when you guys start talking *kimonmon* [a foreign language that cannot be understood]," he said.

I prevailed on him, and soon we walked to Phil's house, one of the few in the village that had electricity and hot water. At the house, we met another white man. In contrast to Phil, who was stocky with golden brown skin and a round face, this man was about six feet tall with a square jaw and eyes as blue as those of the cat who lived with us when I was five years old. He was much paler than Phil, pink with red marks around a sharp, pointed nose. For the first time, I noticed that there were physical differences among white people. Phil introduced him as Marc Cassidy, another Peace Corps worker, who was based in Nakuru, a city more than a hundred miles west of my village.

Marc asked whether I was a Masaai, and we started to talk about Kenyan tribes. But Phil suddenly interrupted, saying he had heard that there had been a big tea growers' boycott in our district, that the leader had been arrested, and that nobody seemed to know what had happened to that leader. He was wondering if the leader had been killed.

Wash and I exchanged glances. I wasn't sure about revealing my identity to Phil, so I offered to find out who that man was and let him know. To change the subject, I asked Marc to explain the Peace Corps.

"It's a branch of the CIA," Marc said in Swahili. "They sent us here to get you." I turned to Wash, looking for a possible exit from the situation.

"I'm just kidding," Marc laughed. "Phil told me that you thought he was CIA. I thought that was so funny that I wanted to make a joke of it. Americans make fun of everything around us. I didn't mean to scare you." Wash and I calmed down, and we all had dinner together.

Marc explained that he was in Kangaita because Peace Corps volunteers often spent their weekends visiting each other so that they could see the whole country. The two white men were looking for something to do. It was elephant migration season, so Wash and I suggested that we take a hike through the forest to see the elephants.

During the very long hike, I got to know Phil much better. I learned that he was the son of an Italian family that had immigrated to the United States. He had always loved geography and had joined the junior wing of the National Geographic Society when he was in high school. After graduating from Missouri State University, he had joined the Peace Corps so that he could see Africa.

As we walked, I trusted him more. I revealed that I had been the leader of the boycott and that I had recently been released from jail. Telling him my story cemented the relationship between us. Marc wanted to know if he and Phil could be arrested because I was with them. I told them that I could not associate with more than three Kenyans at the same time, but the court's conditions didn't say anything about being with Americans. I explained that what the government really wanted was to prevent me from speaking at any political gatherings. Then Phil revealed that the police chief in Kerugoya had told him about the troublemaker who had led the boycott and had warned him to stay away from that fellow. The warning had intrigued him and made him want to meet me.

We didn't see the elephants that day, because they had wandered to the other side of a valley. We could only listen to them breaking tree branches as they ate.

On the way back, Marc asked me what I was going to do in the future. I didn't know what I could do, I admitted, because my bank would not release my savings account and because I had been forbidden to congregate with Kenyans at least for a year. I mentioned that I would like to go back to school, but I wasn't sure that the government would allow that either.

Marc asked, "Well, how about going to school in the United States?"

I didn't speak much English, had received only a few months of middle-school education, and had no money. "That would be a good idea," I laughed. "But I don't think that I could afford it."

Marc was a visionary, and he ignored my laughter. "I've got an idea for you. You speak English, and you are very tall, like a Maasai. Let's tell a basketball program in the United States about you. You can become a great basketball player and get a basketball scholarship."

I asked, "What is basketball?" Marc and Phil both burst out laughing.

"Basketball is one of the greatest games of all time," Marc informed me, still chuckling. "It's every American's dream game. People who play basketball make a lot of money. Michael Jordan is a millionaire."

"Who is Michael Jordan?" I inquired.

This made Marc laugh more. Then he tried to explain basketball to me. We continued to joke about the idea of my going to play basketball in the United States, but he was quite serious. At the end of the conversation, he promised to ask the other Americans back in Nakuru whether any of them knew anyone who was involved with basketball in the United States. In particular, Marc had a friend in the Peace Corps named Grant Ingram, who might have some connections in the world of basketball.

·   ·   ·

During the next few weeks, Phil and I spent most evenings discussing life in my village. I helped him to interpret the culture and etiquette he observed. During some of the weekends, I went with him to visit Peace

Corps volunteers in other towns. I started to feel very comfortable with Americans. When I made my weekly reports to the police, they asked about the Americans, but they didn't try to stop us from associating.

One evening, as I was preparing to milk a cow on my farm, one of the local elders approached the gate with two more white people. They were looking for Phil's house, and the elder knew that I had been hanging out with him. I invited them to have dinner with me and the twins while they waited for Phil to return from a trip to Nairobi. One of the white men was Grant Ingram, the Peace Corps volunteer Marc had mentioned. The other was Mike Ramelot, Grant's former high school buddy, who had come to visit Grant in Kenya. Grant and Mike had heard about the tea boycott from other Peace Corps volunteers in Kenya. But Mike admitted that he was surprised when he met me; in his mind, he had pictured the boycott leader as a dissident politician or an intellectual, not a peasant farmer milking a cow.

My sister Lucy brought over freshly cooked fried vegetables and boiled corn, and we all started eating. Marc had told Grant and Mike about my interest in going to America. Mike mentioned that he knew the basketball coach at the University of San Francisco, and he offered to try to interest the coach in recruiting me when he returned to the United States. The conversation seemed far-fetched to me, like the talk with Marc during the hike.

The next evening, we all had dinner at Phil's house. They again brought up the idea of a basketball scholarship. I told them that I had never even seen a basketball and that I had no idea how the game was played.

Grant invited me to visit him in Nakuru. "I have a basketball. The high school near my house has a basketball court, and you could see what basketball is all about."

I explained that I was prohibited from leaving my district without police permission, which was not likely to be granted, and that I had no accessible money, so I could not even take a bus to Nakuru. But Grant said that if I could figure out a way to leave, he would give me money for transportation.

Phil Chinnici and Jay Sugnet

In the late spring of 1994, a year after my release, another group of Peace Corps volunteers arrived in Kenya. As part of their cultural training, they visited other Peace Corps volunteers in various locations to learn more about the country. Phil organized a party for some members of this new group and invited me. This was the largest gathering of white people that I had ever attended. I was a little worried about being there, but they were very friendly. Some of them had heard about me from other volunteers, and they asked me about the boycott. We talked about the political climate in Kenya and in America.

At the party, I met Jay and Kathy Sugnet. Kathy was a naturally beautiful woman who spoke quickly, but with a soft voice. Although she wore tennis shoes, she walked on her toes as if she were wearing high heels. Whenever she saw that I did not understand her English, she spoke more slowly but with the highest degree of sincerity; and she smiled whenever our eyes met. She was from Oregon, a state in the northwest part of the United States; she drew a map of her country to show me where it was.

Jay and Kathy Sugnet

Soon she introduced me to her husband, Jay, a tall man with rimless glasses who had been assigned to work as an agroforester with the Ministry of Environment.

During our first conversation, Jay mentioned that both he and Kathy had gone to the University of Colorado. I described how Grant had encouraged me to learn basketball and go to America on an athletic scholarship. Jay had once worked for Joyce Aschenbrenner, one of Colorado's assistant athletic directors. Through her, he had met Ricardo Patton, the assistant basketball coach. When Patton learned that the Sugnets were going to Kenya with the Peace Corps, he had taken them to a new movie called *The Air Up There*, about an American basketball coach who goes to a remote Kenyan village and recruits a superstar player. Patton had told the Sugnets, "There are a lot of tall guys in Kenya who can speak English. If you can find one, call me, and we'll see if we can recruit him to play basketball for Colorado."

As I listened to Jay, Mike Ramelot's idea of my going to America to play basketball began to sound less far-fetched. At the same time, I was becoming more eager to get out of Kenya. I was still unable to socialize with Kenyans. The restriction imposed by the court had been for one year only, but the police refused to let it expire, and now it had been extended for another year. Local farmers who were seen with me were being harassed by the police. The bank manager refused to allow me to withdraw funds from my account without written authorization from the police, and the local police chief would not grant authorization unless I paid him half of each withdrawal. I was unable to continue providing money to my little brother and sister. And I could not speak of my discontent to most of the people in my village, because I did not know which of them I could still trust, other than Wash. My social life was centering more and more on the visiting Americans, several of whom had been enabling me to survive by giving me small amounts of money.

I told Jay that I was really interested in his coach's idea. "Call the coach and tell him that you have found your man," I declared.

I still thought that my chance of going to America was approximately zero. But several weeks later, I received a letter from Jay. He had called Aschenbrenner and related my story. He had told her not only about my height but also about the boycott, my arrest, and my desire to leave Kenya. Aschenbrenner had agreed that I would be the perfect catch for the University of Colorado.

The next day, I told Phil about the letter. He was skeptical. "These guys can tell you anything," he advised. "But don't put your hopes in it until it happens."

A week later, another letter from Jay alerted me that Ricardo Patton, the assistant basketball coach, was coming to Kenya in a few weeks to meet me and to see how well I could play basketball! He was planning to make a videotape of me playing basketball, to take back to Colorado.

I had to read this letter many times. An American coach was coming to tape me playing basketball. My American friends had described a basketball and a basketball court to me, but I still had never seen either one.

Phil was as astonished by this letter as I was. "I think this is a good time to accept Grant's offer to visit him," he said. "It's time for you to learn basketball."

I still didn't have funds for bus fare to Nakuru, but Phil gave me some money that Grant had left with him. I told Wash about the invitation and asked his advice about getting police permission to leave the district and go to Grant's house.

Wash doubted that I could quickly become skilled enough at basketball to impress an American coach. He was also doubtful that the police would let me travel. "They will never give you permission," he warned. "But I do have an idea. Go to Nakuru. I will remain here and try to make the police think that you are here as well. There are police informers everywhere. I know most of them. Every evening, I will talk to people about where you and I have been during the day and what we have done. The informers will continuously report your presence in the district. However, I can't keep up this ruse for more than two weeks. You will have to come back and be seen after that."

The next day, I began my preparations to leave Kangaita for the first time since my release from prison. I wrote to Jay and Kathy and asked them to meet me in Nairobi. I arranged with Wash to watch the animals and take care of the twins while I was away. For a week, Wash and I showed ourselves frequently in the village square, sometimes together and sometimes separately. He began talking to people about what we had done each day.

I could not risk being observed taking a bus out of the area, so at the end of that week, I walked thirty miles to board a bus and head for Nairobi. In the city, I disguised myself as a tourist guide for Jay and Kathy, who looked like tourists. I carried Kathy's backpack and spoke only Swahili. The three of us took a bus from Nairobi to Nakuru.

Grant welcomed us and immediately pushed me to start getting in shape to play basketball. But he looked questioningly at the tattered shoes on my feet. I didn't know that you needed certain kinds of shoes to play basketball.

Kathy pulled me aside and said that I could not practice in my worn-out shoes. She asked me my shoe size. "Size seventeen," I told her. She realized that she would not be able to find the proper shoes in size seventeen in Nakuru and conceded that I would just have to train in the shoes I was wearing.

Grant joined us outside, holding a big red ball. "This is a basketball," he said. "You bounce it on the floor and throw it to someone else on your team, and then someone throws it into a basket." Jay and Grant ran around tossing the ball to each other. "This ball can change your life," Grant claimed. "It can bring you money, fame, pride . . ."

". . . and all the women in the world," added Marc Cassidy, who appeared suddenly in a doorway. He greeted me with a hug before heading back to his work.

That evening, I went with the Americans to the local high school's basketball court, where a few people were playing. As we got closer, they all gaped. I thought it was because they had never seen white people, but in fact they were staring at me.

One of them, a man with a shaved head, approached me. *"Wewe ni Mmassai?"* (Are you Maasai?)

I replied that I was not.

"Are you Kenyan?"

"Yes, I am," I responded.

"You must be more than two meters tall!" he exclaimed. "I am the captain of the post office employees' basketball team. We would like you to join our team."

"I have never played basketball before," I revealed.

"That's all right," he said reassuringly. "It's not a hard game to learn. I learned by watching other people play."

Grant handed me the ball and told me to throw it through a round ring hanging on a flat board about ten feet above the court. I looked at the ring, which seemed pretty close to me. I thought the task would be easy, so I aimed at the center of the ring and threw the ball. It hit the board and bounced back at me. I was embarrassed to have failed at something so trivial. I ran after the ball and tried again. This time, I moved closer and aimed at the ring. The ball bounced back at me from the edge of the ring. It hit me flat on the face, and I stumbled. My American friends were keenly aware of my frustration.

"I would have been shocked if you had put it through the ring on your first try," Grant said.

"You have the will," Kathy insisted. "You'll get better with time." She grabbed the ball and threw it at the ring as she walked toward me. It landed on top of the ring, spun around, and went through it, landing right where I was standing. "It's not easy if you've never done it before, but these guys and I all grew up playing basketball. Everyone in America plays this game. But most people are not good enough to be on Patton's team. He understands the situation. All you have to do for now is to show some interest."

Marc later joined us. He organized a game that included the local team and the Peace Corps volunteers. I watched intently. After the game, we went with some of the local players for beef and beer. "If you can play like these guys, Patton will take you to America," Kathy said.

Later that evening, Jay told me that he had asked Joyce Aschenbrenner to write to me about the University of Colorado. I was to reply to her in English, and Grant would edit my letters to help me improve my ability to write in English.

My training began at once. I had to get into better physical shape as well as learn basketball skills. Grant also declared that I would have to learn about managing time, but I didn't understand what he meant.

"We're going to divide your day into specific activity periods," he explained. "In America, people are very serious about time. Here in Kenya, when I arrange to meet someone at a particular time, they are always an hour or two late, and they don't see that as a big deal. I've gotten used to that since I've been here. But in America, if you say you will be somewhere at one o'clock and you are even a few minutes late, people will be very upset with you and will not take you seriously. So you'll have to get used to living on a precise schedule."

Every day for two weeks, Grant had me get up at 5:00 A.M. and run for three miles while he rode his bicycle beside me. Then I had to make breakfast, read and discuss the local newspaper, work on my basketball skills at the court, and so on, through the late morning. In the afternoon, I read *Newsweek* magazine, discussed the articles, and then wrote letters to Phil, Jay, and Kathy to practice my English. Later, we would go to a local gym to lift weights. In the evening, we returned to the court for more basketball.

. . .

During the second week, Jay sent me a letter saying that Patton, the basketball coach, was coming in three days. I had been practicing, but I had never played in an actual game. Fortunately, Jay had advised Patton that I was just learning to play basketball, so that he would not be shocked to learn that I was new to the game.

When Patton arrived, I was waiting for him on the court. Jay drove up in a Suzuki Sierra, with Patton next to him in the front seat. I had expected a very tall white guy, but Jay's passenger was a small, muscular black man with a sharply defined moustache and a grin. As they got out of the car, Jay towered over Patton, who was about five foot three.

Kathy emerged from the rear seat. She introduced Patton to me. "We are here only briefly," Patton announced, "so let's see what you can do." He aggressively seized the ball that I was holding, dribbled it around me, and hurled it right at my face. It bounced off my nose and disappeared behind a shrub.

I had no idea how to react. Jay and Grant seemed amused. I wondered why someone would come all the way from America just to smash my face with a basketball.

Patton looked at me and sensed that I was confused. He retrieved the ball and said, "When I throw the ball at you, I want you to grab the ball."

"Okay," I said. I stepped away from him. Patton pretended to aim the ball to my left side. I reached in that direction, but he threw it straight at me again. It smashed into my chest and bounced off, again rolling into the bushes. Patton sighed deeply.

Full of frustration, I said to Jay, "This guy is trying to humiliate me."

"I don't think so," Jay replied. Kathy told me, "He's trying to find out how responsive you are. Just relax and try to get the ball." In a whisper, she added, "Just show him that you can handle the ball, and you will get out of Kenya before you know it."

Patton threw the ball again. I sprinted, grabbed the ball in the air, and put it into the basket.

"If you can do that every time I throw the ball at you, you'll be fine," he announced. Then he bounced the ball off the rim and shouted, "Get it before it hits the ground!" I jumped and grabbed it in mid-air.

"Okay, I've seen enough," he told Jay and Kathy. "He hasn't had much practice, but he's willing to work. Even if he doesn't get good enough to play for Colorado, I know his story, and I'd like to help him get out of the country. But I can't do anything for him unless he gets at least a combined score of 700 on the SAT so that he can be admitted to Colorado. So you'll have to work with him on that."

I had no idea what he was talking about. I thought he meant that he was not impressed and would not help me.

Jay explained to me that the SAT was a standard college admission test of English and mathematics. I had not taken a test since the fourth grade, but if this was my ticket out of Kenya, I was willing to try it. "I've been trained as an engineer, but I'm temporarily underemployed by the Peace Corps, so I can spend time tutoring you in math while Jay helps you with your English," Kathy offered.

Because I had to be seen in Kirinyaga District, I returned to Kangaita the next day. During the next few weeks, I showed myself whenever possible in the community while preparing to return to Nakuru. By this time, however, life in the village was changing. Some of the farmers were beginning to abandon tea farming and instead were opening small businesses in the village. Others were focusing on raising animals rather than crops. Women were organizing themselves into small business cooperatives. These changes meant that tea was now less central to the district's economy, which led the police to reduce their surveillance of me. I was therefore able to leave the village regularly, and I returned to study for three months with Jay and Kathy in Mai-mahiu, the field site where they were stationed.

We collected SAT registration materials and study guides at the American cultural center in Nairobi. For ten hours a day, Jay taught me written English. He required me to send letters to Ricardo Patton explaining Kenyan history, culture, and current events. Kathy tutored me in math, working up from elementary arithmetic to algebra and geometry, which I would need for the test. She created large wall charts with formulas that I rehearsed each day, and she encouraged me to apply the formulas in our daily activities. For example, when she and Jay had to drive to Nairobi, I had to use my formulas to figure out how long their trip would be and when they would return.

Every two weeks, I returned to my village for a few days to show my face. On one of these days, the district police chief visited me and reminded me that, in his view, I was still confined to his district. He invited me to confer with him if I needed to go to other parts of Kenya. Perhaps, I feared, he had heard that I was rarely in Kangaita. I told him that I hardly ever left my house. Slowly, however, I was disappearing from my village and from his district.

The time came for me to take the SAT, which was administered at the Nairobi Technical Teachers Institute. As usual, I had to evade the police. By this time, however, Joyce Aschenbrenner had sent me a University of Colorado sweat suit, and Grant's parents had bought me a pair of Air Jordans to wear when I practiced basketball. When I got to Nairobi for the SAT, I did not look like a local political activist. Instead, I seemed to be a sporty American tourist on holiday, wearing clothing and shoes that few Kenyans could afford.

The wait for the test results made me anxious. I knew that if I hadn't scored at least 700, the whole process would end. One night, Wash and I sat at our favorite spot on the farm smoking cigarettes after dinner.

"You look much better," Wash said. "You have gained some weight. I never thought you could be yourself again."

"Have I changed that much?" I asked.

"Did you ever see yourself in the mirror after you got out of prison? You were just a bunch of bones. But those white guys are taking good care of you. And it's becoming clear that you really might be going to America."

"We won't know until I really leave," I cautioned. "This whole thing can fall apart, and you and I will continue with life as we have always known it."

After about two months, Jay came to the village. He handed me a white envelope, which he had already opened. "Jeff, you passed," he smiled. "You can go to America." I had gotten a score of 710.

· · ·

The next step was to apply for admission to the University of Colorado. Patton had explained that I had to be accepted there before the university could send me a certificate of admission on Form I-20, as required by the U.S. Immigration and Naturalization Service.[1] Because I had achieved the necessary minimum SAT score, the university would take care of my admission, athletic scholarship, and I-20 certificate.

But a new hurdle loomed. In order to get a visa, Kathy reported, I would need not only the I-20 certificate but also an airplane ticket and, still more challenging, a passport from the government of Kenya.[2] I told her that she and the other Americans had done a great job, but that the government of Kenya would never give me a passport.

"Jay and I will buy you the airplane ticket," she said. "But you will have to figure out how to get a passport."

They asked me what the options were. I told them that although I was very much opposed to bribery and corruption, the only way to get a passport at this stage would be to bribe someone in Kenya's Department of Immigration. Aside from my scruples, I had no money for a bribe.

Jay and Kathy promised, "You find someone who can do the job, and we'll find the money."

First I tried to go through the regular channels. I filled out a passport application, which my Peace Corps friends took to the passport office in Nairobi to file. Officials there insisted that the application be accompanied by an airline ticket. The Americans bought the ticket and submitted it to the passport office. But the officials denied the passport and held on to the ticket, which Jay and Kathy then had to cancel.

We tried again. Jay and Kathy bought me another ticket. This time, to prevent the officials from seizing it, they submitted only the printed itinerary, rather than the paper ticket, to the passport office. But the officials demanded a paper ticket.

Then Wash and I talked to everyone we knew about any remaining options for getting a passport. Some of those we talked to were former members of Parliament who had been detained for opposing Moi. One of them told me to stop wasting my time because even he, a politician with plenty of money available for bribery, couldn't get a passport so that he and his family could leave the country.

Many people around Kangaita wanted to help me, however, because they knew that I had tried to help them and had suffered for it. During my search, I came across Mama Murage, a woman in my village whose brother worked at the immigration department at a border post between Kenya and Ethiopia. "My brother could issue you a temporary passport for the border crossing where he works," she suggested. "You could then take it to Nairobi and convert it into a permanent passport."

"How much would I have to pay your brother?" I asked.

"Nothing," she replied. "Given what you did, we are going to get this done for you."

"But that could be dangerous for your brother. He could be fired or even arrested."

"You took risks to help us," she said. "It is time for some of us to pay you back."

Two days later, her brother met me in Kangaita. He took my passport application and told me to wait two weeks. Two weeks later, he called his sister, who told me to meet him at a restaurant in Nairobi. I was instructed to bring with me a police certificate of good conduct, showing that I was not a criminal, because no passport could be issued without it.

That evening, at a local restaurant, I met with Inspector Mosera, the man who had arrested me two years earlier. "I shouldn't be seen with you," he said. "They would roast me like a cow if they knew about this meeting. Grab a beer and look the other way." He sat on the opposite side of the table and pretended to be drunk. We both continued to sip our beers.

"I need a certificate of good conduct," I explained. He laughed so hard that he sprayed a mouthful of beer all over the table.

"You are worse than a criminal and you want what?"

"I need a passport, and I can't get it without the certificate."

"If you are trying to get out of here, I will help you. But it will cost you a lot of money. And I can't get it at all if you have committed a crime. No amount of bribery can produce a false clean record. But I'll tell you something. Political arrests are not recorded in police files, so if you haven't done anything else, you will actually have a clean record. And I respect you a lot, so if you haven't committed any ordinary crimes, I will be able to get you a certificate."

"What do I have to do?"

"Tomorrow morning I will come to your village," he whispered. "Make sure you are at home." He left by the back door.

The next morning, he left a small envelope with my sister Lucy. Inside was a note with the name of a person I should see at police headquarters in Nairobi. The note continued, "If it wasn't for you, I would have wasted my whole life in the force." He had been promoted after arresting me in 1992.

The next day, I went to Nairobi. Mosera's contact fingerprinted me. One hour later, he gave me a police certificate showing no criminal conduct. I paid him a few hundred shillings and went to meet with Mama Murage's brother at a restaurant. I handed over the certificate, and he gave me an envelope. "Take this to the main passport office. Be sure that your American friends accompany you. Someone will ask you what team you play for. Tell him that you are going to play for the Bulls. Give him the envelope and your airline ticket. He will go into a back room. If he doesn't return within fifteen minutes, leave the building immediately and do not return."

There were evident risks. But this man's plan seemed feasible, because although my name must have been on certain police or security lists, the government of Kenya did not yet have interconnected computer systems. Presented with paperwork from their co-workers, including a temporary passport issued by one of their own border officials, the officials who issued regular passports in Nairobi might routinely issue one to me without scrutinizing their files of typewritten lists from various police agencies.

I offered to pay him, but he refused to take any money. "I don't know whether this will even work," he said. "But if it works, get your visa the same day, if you can, and get out of the country in two or three days."

The next day, Jay, Kathy, and I went to the main passport office. I was dressed again in my university sweat suit and Air Jordans. The Americans stood outside while I entered. The man was apparently waiting for me. He asked what team I would be playing for.

"The Bulls," I responded.

"We don't want you to miss the game," he said. "We have to get you a passport soon. Come with me." He directed me to sit on a dirty bench in the middle of a crowded hallway. "Give me your papers and wait here."

He took the envelope from me and said quietly, "If I am not back in twenty minutes, leave and don't come back."

Just a few minutes later, he returned, grabbed my hand, and walked me out of the building. He handed me an envelope. "Here is your passport. Get out of here." I tried to give him another envelope with money, but he just looked at me with a puzzled expression. "A passport does not mean that they will actually let you leave. When you get to America, mail me a tie to let me know that you made it." He walked up the stairs before disappearing into the building. That was the last I ever saw of him. Later, I learned from Inspector Mosera that this official had helped other political dissidents leave the country. The security forces discovered his activities and arrested him. Nobody knew what had happened to him.

Although I now had a passport, a new problem arose: I had never graduated from secondary school. When we met in Kenya, Coach Patton had not regarded this as a big issue; he indicated that I could take a test and get a GED certificate, for high school equivalency, after I got to the United States. But when he returned to Colorado, he learned that the National Collegiate Athletic Association (NCAA) required recipients of athletic scholarships at Division I schools to have taken certain high school courses.[3] A GED would not have satisfied that requirement. So it turned out that although I had received a sufficiently high SAT score, Colorado could not give me an athletic scholarship. Therefore, it could not accept me or release an I-20 certificate after all. And, despite my passport, I could not get a student visa without an I-20 certificate from an American college.

Grant solved this problem. He had completed his Peace Corps service a few months earlier and returned to his home in Los Altos, California. He contacted Jim Forkum, the basketball coach at Hartnell Community College in Salinas and told him what had been happening. He asked whether Hartnell could issue an I-20. Forkum arranged not only my admission to his college but also an athletic scholarship there, on the condition that I play basketball for at least one year for Hartnell.

A few days after I received the I-20 from Hartnell, Jay, Kathy, and I went to the U.S. embassy. When they had first arrived in Kenya, Jay and Kathy had stayed briefly at the home of the chief consular officer, Marsha Von Duerckheim, who had been very hospitable. After they started helping me, Jay and Kathy contacted her and told her my story. She was extremely sympathetic, and once I had a passport, she rushed my U.S. visa. I applied on May 8, 1995, and received the visa the next day. The consular officer even wrote her home number on a piece of paper for Jay and said, "Tell Mr. Ngaruri to call me at any hour if he has any problems leaving the country."

Bon voyage

Meanwhile, Grant had taken a temporary job in Chicago. Weeks earlier, we had made a plan that if I ever received a passport and visa, I would fly to Chicago and meet him there.

That night, I went home and told my fourteen-year-old brother and sister how sad I was to be leaving them. Lucy reassured me, "I know how you feel. But this is great. My big brother is going to America, and I am so happy about that."

Njoka said to her, "You don't understand. He is not coming back."

"I know that," she replied. "But if he stays here, he will die. What good is he to us if he is dead?"

Njoka tried hard not to cry. This was one of the most difficult moments I ever had to share with the twins. We hugged and held each other tightly, as if we would never let go.

"I want you to go," Njoka insisted. "But I am very afraid."

"Your sister will take good care of you," I told him. "I will write to you every week, and if anything happens to you, I will do everything I can to come back for you. I promise." We hugged some more.

Later that night, Wash and I again smoked cigarettes under the stars. I told him how much I would miss him. "Just don't forget where you came from," he advised me.

I went to see my mother and told her that I was about to leave to study in America. Her mental condition was not good, and she knew very little about the turn that my life had taken. "You don't even have shoes," she exclaimed. "How are you going to afford an airline ticket?"

"My friends have helped me," I explained, but she could not believe that I was really leaving Kenya. Nevertheless, on May 17, 1995, after the Peace Corps volunteers threw a bon voyage party for me, I took a bus to Nairobi. Wash brought my mother, Lucy, and Njoka to the city, where I had a final meal with those who were closest to me. Then I got into a car with Jay and Kathy and drove to the airport. For the first time in my life, I boarded an airplane. My life had changed a lot in the three years since I had protested the government's tea policy. But on the other side of the Atlantic Ocean, it was about to change even more dramatically.

THREE

Temporary Safety

The airplane left Nairobi a few minutes after midnight. I had escaped from Kenya without being rearrested, but I was anxious about my first flight, and I already missed my little sister and brother. I felt as though my intestines were floating inside my abdomen. I found myself waving my arms to try to maintain my balance, though the seat belt held me firmly to my seat. Below me, as the lights of Nairobi vanished in a cloudy mist, I imagined Lucy and Njoka waving at the plane. My heart pounded, and my eyes swelled with tears.

We headed north, toward Rome. There, I would change planes before continuing to Chicago, where I expected to meet Grant. When we landed in Rome, the airport officials separated the continuing passengers by race or nationality. We Africans were put in a lounge that was devoid of furniture. Looking through a large glass panel, we could see the white passengers in a separate lounge, which had comfortable couches and chairs.

An attendant processed all the white passengers first and then came to issue our boarding passes. Another attendant asked whether we wanted to see the Coliseum. I had never heard of the Coliseum, but I said that I would like to go. Airline personnel ushered five or six of us into a waiting bus.

The driver took us into the city of Rome. The narrow streets were lined with brown buildings. Cultivated lilies hung from pots neatly arranged on the sills of the apartment windows. After we stopped for pizza, we drove through another narrow street and arrived at a large structure that looked like a mostly destroyed stadium. I wondered why the Italians had left such a large ruined building for so long in the middle of their capital city. The driver explained that this Coliseum had been built during the Roman Empire. Years passed, however, before I understood the historical significance of this huge ruin. The driver said that we did not have time to enter it, but we could take pictures from the windows of the bus. I wanted to take pictures, but I didn't have a camera.

Soon I was on another plane, and eventually we landed in Chicago. I followed the other passengers, who were lining up in front of the immigration counter. While I was in line, a tall, white police officer approached me, a big smile on his face. I smiled back at him.

"Where are you from?" he asked.

"Kenya," I told him.

"Are you a long-distance runner?"

"No, I used to run when I was small, but not anymore. I will be playing college basketball."

"Where?" he inquired.

"In a year or two, I hope to play for the University of Colorado."

"That is a great school," he said. "They have great football, too."

I thought he was referring to soccer, which is called football in most of the world. "I play football, too," I added. This information seemed to impress him. He shook my hand and escorted me to the head of the line, in front of a booth where an official was stamping passports.

The passport-stamping official surveyed my height, took my passport, had me sign a form, stamped it, stapled it to my passport, and said, "Welcome to America. You are surely going to love it here."

I retrieved my luggage, which contained Grant's Chicago telephone number, proceeded through customs, and followed everyone else through a door. Suddenly I was outside, at a curb. In front of me and above me, highways piled on top of each other, and I felt like I was in a space station on some other planet. Nearly everyone around me was white, and everyone seemed to be in a hurry to get somewhere. Those who were not hurrying were pacing around nervously and glancing repeatedly at their watches. Hundreds of cars, including long, gleaming limousines, drove past in constant motion. Some of the cars pulled over. Drivers emerged to hug and kiss people on the sidewalk and help them into the cars. I knew that Grant was not at the airport, but I wished that he would come for me and pick me up.

I was surrounded by more white people than I had ever seen in one place, and I felt overwhelmed. I thought that perhaps the black people had been segregated in a different part of the airport, as we had been in Rome, and that I had mistakenly gone to the white part of the airport. I wondered how strange I looked to all these white people, as I stood wearing the unmatching, African-style kitenge shirt that I had put on in Kenya and my Air Jordans.

A middle-aged white woman seemed to be observing me very carefully. She slowly approached me and asked, "Are you stranded or something?"

"Yes," I admitted, "I am stranded."

"I saw you on the plane from Nairobi," she told me, "and later I saw you in Rome."

I felt a little better. At least someone recognized me.

"We were on the same flights. I was visiting my son, who is in the Peace Corps." She offered to shake my hand. "My name is Danielle."

I understood this woman's English perfectly, and especially the magic words "Peace Corps." But I could barely converse with her because my ability to speak the language was still very limited. I told her my name and shook her hand.

"My son's name is Peter," she volunteered. "Can you tell me something? Before I left him a few days ago, he told me about this young man that his friends had been trying to help. This man had been a political prisoner, and he was trying to leave Kenya, but the government had denied his application for a passport, and he didn't have the money for an airplane ticket. Peter and his friends were very worried about him, and nobody knew whether he managed to leave the country. Do you know who I am talking about, and whether he got out of Kenya?"

I thought that I knew a Peace Corps volunteer named Peter, but I wasn't sure. In any event, I knew that almost everyone in the Peace Corps in Kenya had heard about me, and I was certain that she was talking about me. I hesitated to tell this stranger that I was the person she had heard about. But I couldn't see any harm in it, and I was pleased that she had spoken to me.

"That man was me," I said to her. Suddenly she became ecstatic. She began hugging me, and she became very emotional.

"I'm so happy," she cried. "Peter is going to be so happy to hear about this. By the way, where are you going now?"

I didn't really know where to go. Several weeks earlier, I had called Grant in Chicago from the international telephone office in Nairobi. In America, I thought, I'd have to find some sort of telephone company office from which to call him. I didn't know where the office was, and I didn't know how much a telephone call would cost. I had only $5, and I was hesitant to spend it on a call. Before leaving Kenya, I had concentrated on all the problems involved in getting out of the country rather than on collecting money for my stay in America. Coach Patton had also told me to call him if I ever got to the United States, so I assumed that Grant and Patton would take care of my needs once I managed to cross the ocean.

"I have a Peace Corps friend who is living in Chicago," I told Danielle. "But I don't know how to reach him. I have his number in my suitcase, but I don't know where to find a telephone office or how to use an American phone. If you can help me find my friend, I will be okay."

"My other son, Peter's older brother, is picking me up. You should come to our house, and you can call your friend from there," she offered.

We sat on a bench waiting for her son, and she told me more about herself. She was a widow who had lost her husband in a motorcycle accident five years earlier. Partly in response to his grief at losing his father, Peter had joined the Peace Corps immediately after his college graduation. She showed me a picture of Peter, and I recognized him as someone I had met at a party in Kenya.

A converted passenger van pulled up, driven by a middle-aged man. It was the biggest car I had ever seen, looking even more massive than the passing limousines. She introduced the driver as her son, and she directed him to load my luggage into the van.

We drove to her townhouse. After we unloaded the luggage, she said, "We are both very tired from the trip from Nairobi, and now it's too late in the evening to call your friend. So I will take you to our guest room, where you can sleep, and in the morning we'll call him."

She led me to a room with a big bed. I was in fact more than very tired, and I fell asleep at once.

I awoke early in the morning. The room was still quite dark, and I did not know where I was. The first thing I saw was a wall of guns, rifles, and pistols that were neatly lined up on racks, in some sort of glass cabinet. I became frightened. For a moment, I thought that I was back in Kenya, that I had been arrested, that I was being held in a secret military facility, and that I was going to be shot. I got out of bed and observed the guns carefully, without attempting to touch them. I had seen similar models in movies, but I had never seen guns like these in Kenya. I got back into bed, utterly disoriented.

Suddenly a man entered the room. He was holding a large handgun. His face was slightly familiar, but I couldn't place it. I thought that he had come to kill me. I raised my hands high and bowed my head to avoid looking down the barrel of the gun. "Please don't shoot me," I pleaded. "You don't really have to kill me."

"Mother!" he yelled, running out of the room and closing the door behind him. None of this made any sense to me. I recalled that I was in America and that the intruder was a white man. I had seen American gangster movies in which the criminals shoot their victims without discussion. I realized that when he came back with his murderous "mother,"

I would have to persuade them that I didn't have any money, so that they would have no reason to kill me.

The door opened again. This time, Danielle entered and spoke sweetly: "How did you sleep?" She was followed almost immediately by her gun-toting son, whom I now recognized as the driver who had picked us up at the airport. He apologized for barging into my room. He explained that he was a gun collector, like his late father, and that he had entered the room to return one of the guns to the showcase that lined one wall.

"I was confused," I told him. "In Kenya, ordinary people are not allowed to keep guns in their houses."

"Most of these guns belonged to my father," he explained. He opened the cabinet and pointed to one short gun and an assault rifle. "This is a Civil War pistol, and this is the type of gun that my father used in Vietnam."

I was still afraid of being near all these guns, and I began to believe that I would not feel safe and comfortable in Chicago until I could find Grant. I dug my address book out of my bag and asked Peter's brother how I could call Grant.

He took the address book and disappeared. Danielle explained that they had a telephone in their house. He returned to tell me that nobody had answered but that he had left a message on an answering machine. He asked whether I wanted to call anyone else. I gave him Ricardo Patton's number in Colorado. He, too, was not immediately available.

After an hour or two, Grant called back. He explained that his work in Chicago had ended and that he had moved back to his home in California. He had not been able to wait long enough for me to manage to get a Kenyan passport. Although he had left town, his girlfriend, Stacey, was still in Chicago and knew about my possible arrival. She and Grant had planned that if I showed up in Chicago, I would stay with her briefly, and then both of us would join Grant in San Francisco. He gave me Stacey's number, and Danielle called her. Danielle drove me to Stacey's apartment, where we said our farewells.

Stacey was happy to have me stay with her until we could leave for California. That evening, she took me to dinner at a Chicago restaurant with Joe, a friend of hers who was a consultant for a small business. Before dinner, Joe drove us to the John Hancock Building, one of the tallest buildings in the world, where we ascended to the observation deck. I saw the enormous city laid out in front of me.

When we sat down to dinner, a waitress came and gave us menus. I had been in restaurants in Nairobi, but I had never seen a menu that offered so many choices. "Do they cook all these things here?" I asked Stacey.

"Are you guys ready to order?" The waitress had arrived, and she looked straight at me. I stared back at her, unable to tell her what I wanted.

"Meat," I said. "I would like to have meat."

"What kind of meat?" The waitress recited a list: "We have beef, pork, chicken, ostrich, moose, lamb, and buffalo."

"I will have buffalo."

"How would you like it cooked?" Again I felt on the spot. But I remembered that meat could be either boiled or fried.

"I would like it cooked on the top of the stove."

Everyone at the table burst out in laughter. I felt embarrassed. "In America," Stacey explained, "there are many choices about everything, and you have to be very specific. That's why we're laughing." She then told the waitress, "Bring him the baby back ribs. He'll like that."

During dinner, I asked Joe a question that had been on my mind since my arrival in Chicago: "I have never seen so many white people before; doesn't Chicago have black people?"

Joe and Stacey exchanged knowing glances. "Okay," Joe said. "If you want to see black people, I'll show you black people. We'll take a drive over to the South Side." Stacey laughed nervously, and I didn't know why.

After dinner, Joe drove us to a region that apparently was called South Side Chicago. As we passed through it, Stacey told me, "This is where black people live. Look around and you'll see them."

We came to an intersection and stopped for the red light. As we waited, I saw three muscular black men standing on the street corner.

One of them saw me and stared back at me with a strange, angry expression on his face. I had never seen him before, so I couldn't imagine why he would be angry at me. I started to open the door to ask him what he was angry about.

"Don't open the door!" Stacey screamed at me. I didn't understand her concerns, but I quickly shut the door and rolled down the window instead. The big man came up to the window and leaned down, his face in the window. He asked, in a very threatening way, "What are you doing in a white man's car?"

At first, the question didn't make any sense to me. Then I thought that perhaps he suspected these white people of kidnapping me and that he wanted to know whether I needed help. "No, no," I assured him, "these are my friends."

Suddenly he pulled a gun out of his waist pocket and pointed it at me. I was starting to get used to the idea that everyone in Chicago had a gun.

"Drive, Joe . . . drive!" Stacey yelled. Joe hit the gas pedal, and we drove through the red light, missing a passing motorist by inches.

"What's happening?" I asked.

Stacey replied, "Jeff, just don't go into neighborhoods like the South Side, okay?" I never did understand why that man was so angry about my presence in a car full of white people.

The next day, Stacey introduced me to her friend Marcelle, a woman who had been in the Peace Corps in Kenya and could speak Kikuyu. The three of us decided to run to the Lake Michigan shore and then run along the beach. Not long after we started, it became obvious that I was a much faster runner than they were. Since they were holding me back, Stacey advised me to run ahead. I could run along the beach, and on my way back, we would meet and head back to Stacey's apartment together. Given my height, Stacey assumed that it would be impossible for them to miss me. I ran toward the beach and left them behind.

It was a glorious late spring day in Chicago. The beach was crowded with bicyclists, roller bladers, runners, and tourists, all wearing t-shirts, dark sunglasses, and sneakers. The skyline was visible with great clarity.

I ran for about an hour and then turned back to meet Stacey and her friend. But I did not see them on the way back.

I wasn't concerned. I had noticed that in America every house had a number and street names were posted at each intersection. I could read English well enough, and I knew Stacey's address. I had also read all the billboards and street signs and had identified the shapes and types of buildings between her apartment and the beach. Memorizing a route marked with writing and buildings was much easier than memorizing a return route through a forest by attending to the shapes of particular trees. I knew that I could find my way. I assumed that Stacey had gone home, so I ran back to her apartment. Neither woman was there, so I relaxed and waited for them.

Later, I learned that Stacey and her friend had become very worried when they could not find me. They assumed that I could not find my way around the city and that I was lost. After they asked many people at the beach whether they had seen a very tall black runner, they called the beach police and reported that they had lost a friend. "He has just come from Africa, and he has very limited urban skills," Stacey told the officer.

"What does he look like?" the police officer asked.

"He is more than seven feet tall and—"

"Wait a minute!" the officer interrupted. "How do you lose a seven-foot-tall guy?"

Nevertheless, he alerted other beach patrol units to watch out for a seven-foot-tall guy in running shorts.

Meanwhile, after waiting three hours for Stacey and Marcelle, I decided to head back to the beach to search for them. When I neared the beach, a policeman stopped me and inquired, "Excuse me, sir. Are you Jeff?"

"Yes, I am," I responded hesitantly.

"And you are from Kenya, aren't you?"

I wondered how he knew so much about me, but I admitted to being from Kenya.

He pulled out his walkie-talkie and announced, "I have him." I wondered whether he was going to arrest me. I did not understand what I had done wrong in this strange country.

"Your friends have reported you as lost," he said.

"But I am not lost," I told him. "They are the ones who are lost."

The officer laughed. Soon he reunited me with Stacey and Marcelle.

· · ·

The next day, Grant sent me an airplane ticket; and a few days later, in late May or early June 1995, I flew to San Francisco. Grant met me at the airport. Jim Forkum, a basketball coach from Hartnell Community College in Salinas, California, the school that had issued my I-20 form, accompanied him. Grant took me to his parents' house in Los Altos. The next day, we drove to Hartnell to see Forkum. During that meeting, he informed me that there had been a change of circumstances—and that we had a problem.

"I've been offered a job as head basketball coach at the University of Hawaii at Hilo," he told me.

"Why is that a problem?" I asked.

"Hawaii is an island that is very far away from here," he explained. He pointed it out on a large map on his wall. "I don't know whether you would like living there. Also, I can't guarantee your admission to the University of Hawaii, and your visa is valid only if you remain a student. However, you can certainly remain in Salinas. If you do that, your only obligation would be to attend Hartnell for one semester. After that, you can transfer to any school that accepts you. You won't need my permission, because I won't be here anymore."

Back in Los Altos, Grant and his parents helped me to evaluate my choices. We decided that I should remain in Salinas and take English courses during the summer, since my spoken English still needed a lot of work. I would also study for the GED exam, because if I passed certain courses to fulfill the NCAA Division I requirements and received a GED certificate, I might still be admitted to the University of Colorado or some other good school that could offer me a basketball scholarship.

Grant's family offered to pay for my tuition and housing at Hartnell. They also introduced me to a wealthy industrialist whose many charitable ventures included providing financial assistance for indigent students who seemed promising. He assured me that I did not have to play college basketball; he offered to help with my tuition if I preferred to spend my time studying. I told him that if I could pay my own way by playing ball, I would prefer to do so rather than taking his money.

The following day, I called Coach Patton at the University of Colorado to ask about the prospects of admission there if I took some junior college courses first and then tried to transfer. He informed me that because Colorado was an NCAA Division I school, I would have to complete at least one full year of junior college, and preferably two years, before I could transfer. This new information confirmed the decision to start at the junior college level.

That summer, I studied English at Hartnell. When I registered for my classes, one of the registration clerks misspelled my last name, Ngaruri, as "Ngarurih." Like some communicable disease, this error was transmitted from document to document for a decade. All of my academic records, and later my legal documents, would bear this new terminal *h*.

I later informed Coach Patton about my decision to attend Hartnell, with the hope of transferring to Colorado when I became eligible to do so. A couple of weeks later, he flew to California to see me. He still wanted me to play basketball for Colorado, and he explained how he hoped to make it happen. I was glad that he had a plan, but by this time, I had become skeptical about the promises of these American coaches. I still had very limited basketball skills, and I had seen that coaches moved around. Because I feared that his oral promises of a basketball scholarship might never become a reality, I asked him for a written commitment.

Patton's response was surprisingly positive, and it alleviated my fears. He gave me a letter from Bill Marolt, the University of Colorado's athletic director, guaranteeing me a great deal. I would go to St. Gregory's College, a two-year college in Shawnee, Oklahoma, where I would receive an athletic scholarship and would begin by "redshirting" on the basketball team (sitting on the bench and watching). In my second year, I would play on the St. Gregory's team. At the end of that year, I would transfer to Colorado on a full athletic scholarship "regardless of your basketball development at St. Gregory's" and "even if in the unforeseen future you become injured and cannot play basketball."

It sounded like an excellent offer, so after I completed my summer at Hartnell, I became a student at St. Gregory's. It was a small but prestigious Catholic college in the heart of the Oklahoma plains, about forty miles east of Oklahoma City on Highway 44, which extends from North Carolina to California. St. Gregory's had been started as a seminary, more than a hundred years earlier, by Benedictine monks who wanted to educate Native Americans. It gradually evolved into a high school and later into a two-year college. Most of the students came from Texas, Arkansas, Kansas, and other midwestern states. Initially, I was the only student from Africa.

When I arrived at St. Gregory's, my only contact was the college basketball coach, Kelly Bass. He had coached high school basketball in Colorado, where he had become friendly with Patton. He had just taken the coaching job at St. Gregory's and was eager to advance his college coaching career. Also, he was proud that his advancement to a college coaching position impressed his father, who was an assistant basketball coach with a professional team, the Charlotte Hornets, part of the National Basketball Association (NBA).

Kelly picked me up at the airport in Oklahoma and drove me to his house. During dinner that evening, he told me about his father and how excited he was about introducing the two of us. I ate dinner with Kelly often. Strangely, however, he neither showed nor expressed any interest in where I had come from or about my feelings about living in a foreign land. He talked only about basketball, a subject about which I knew very little. He asked about me only when he wanted to verify my height and my potential to become a great basketball player.

A few weeks later, he invited his father to meet me. As soon as the older man saw me, he offered to sign me to play for an NBA team. I was baffled by this proposal.

"Are you sure you want to do that?" I asked.

"Why wouldn't I want to? You're tall, you're black, and that's all it takes," he exclaimed.

"But, sir, I have very little experience with basketball. I wouldn't want to disappoint you."

"Dad, don't worry about him," Kelly interjected. "I'll be working with him, and I'll get his skills where they need to be."

"Wait a minute," I stated. "I am here to get an education. I am interested in basketball, but basketball has to be my second priority, after getting an education."

Kelly ignored me and continued to explain his plan to his father. He kept referring to me as if I were an absent third party, even though I was sitting across the table from him.

As the semester started, Kelly developed a basketball practice schedule for me, but it conflicted with my academic courses. On three occasions, he interrupted a class and asked me to leave the classroom to practice basketball. When I asked him to stop coming to my classes, he insisted that I must cooperate with him without questioning his authority. He threatened to terminate my athletic scholarship if I did not obey him. "Don't forget," he added, "that the only way a black man like you can be anyone in this country is to play basketball. You better listen to me, or I'll have your ass shipped back to Kenya."

"You can terminate my scholarship," I said, "but first I am going to talk to Colorado. Coach Patton sent me here so that I could play basketball for Colorado."

"I don't argue with people like you," he replied. "Your scholarship is terminated as of today."

I quickly put in a call to the University of Colorado. But, to my surprise, nobody returned my call. In desperation, I called Grant in California and asked him to inquire on my behalf. The Colorado athletic officials told him that if I could not play basketball for St. Gregory's, Colorado would not give me an athletic scholarship. My letter from Bill Marolt wouldn't help me; although it didn't require me to excel at basketball, it did require me to stick with the St. Gregory's team for two years.

I explained my problem to Brother Nicholas, a Benedictine monk who was my American history teacher. I explained the pressure from the coach and the loss of my scholarship.

I had been doing very well in my classes, and my teachers did not want to see me forced to leave the school. Brother Nicholas arranged a position for me as a resident student assistant during the school year and a job in the Benedictine monastery during the summer. In return, the monastery would provide an academic scholarship, which allowed me to remain at St. Gregory's for two years without having to play basketball.

Before I went to St. Gregory's, Grant's industrialist friend had given me about $3,000 to assist with college living expenses. I had not spent this money, and I had sought his guidance on how to invest it until I needed it. He referred me to Dave Sutch, an investment banking advisor in San Francisco, who suggested that I open a money market and securities account with him. I consulted frequently with Dave, who sent me monthly newsletters, which I studied with care. I learned how to trade stocks and bonds and started investing in the stock market. I also learned how to borrow investment capital on margin. Grant's industrialist friend gave me additional investment advice. The late 1990s turned out to be a good period in which to be a beginner in the market. Within a year, my $3,000 had become $15,000, far more money than I had ever had.

Even though life in America was going very well for me, I missed the twins, my younger siblings. No matter how much we wrote to each other, nothing could fill the space in my heart that was reserved for them. I could not visit them because if I returned to Kenya, my life would again be in danger. I was also aware that my student visa would not last forever and that when I finished my studies, I would have to return.

I enjoyed both my studies and my work at St. Gregory's, and I was very involved in the student community. My contact with large numbers of students taught me a lot about American culture. During my second year, I was elected president of the student body.

I worked part time in a group house that the monastery ran for troubled adolescents from the community. One evening, this house was the setting for a strange intercultural encounter. I had organized a weekly "movie night" for the boys, who were allowed to pick the videotape for the night. They decided that we should watch *Return of the Jedi*. I had never seen this movie, or any *Star Wars* movie, and I did not know what it was about.

One of the scenes includes a conversation between the main characters and some creatures called Ewoks, who inhabit the moon of Endor. When the Ewoks started talking, I realized that I could understand them because they were speaking in Kikuyu. They were speaking the very stage directions that they were following, such as "take a few steps forward and then go to the left."

I blurted out, "I know what they are saying."

The boys looked at me strangely. Their jaws dropped.

"What is the problem?" I asked.

"You speak Ewok?"

"That is not Ewok. It is my native language."

I later learned that during the editing, the director had asked some Kenyan extras from the studio to dub Ewok conversation into the movie. But to the boys at the group house, I was the guy who could speak Ewok, and that made me their great hero. After that, they referred to me as "the Ewok guy."

In my second year at St. Gregory's, I worried that the University of Colorado was not going to accept me because I hadn't played college basketball for St. Gregory's. I knew that if I did not remain in school, I would no longer have a right to remain in the United States. My time at St. Gregory's was nearly over, because it was a two-year college. There was no four-year Catholic college in the state. But I noticed that other Christian denominations, such as the Baptists and the Lutherans, had four-year colleges in Oklahoma. So I approached the president of the university, Dr. Frank Pfaff, with the idea of converting the college to a four-year institution.

It turned out that he had been thinking along the same lines, although he doubted that a sufficient number of students would continue for an additional two years. I asked how many students he would need in order to make the conversion. He calculated that two hundred of the six hundred students would need to remain, and he offered to keep me at St. Gregory's on a four-year scholarship if I could assist in persuading two hundred students to pursue four-year degrees at the school. I worked on this project with the student government and other student organizations. We obtained written pledges from three hundred students. The conversion was approved, and St. Gregory's University became the only four-year Catholic university in Oklahoma. In part for my work, the administration gave me its Distinguished Sophomore Award.

During that process, I was concerned that the school's conversion would come too late for me because of the amount of time required for planning. I needed another way to remain in school. I consulted Father Theodore, another monk who had become a good friend and counselor. He was a graduate of Santa Clara University. He asked what I would like to study at a four-year college. Because I had been successful in the stock market, I had developed an interest in business finance and hoped to advance my study of that field. He suggested three schools with very good business programs that might accept me as a transfer student: Santa Clara, the University of San Francisco, and Stanford. He warned that they might not award scholarships, but he offered to recommend me for admission and financial support.

To my surprise, Santa Clara turned me down, but I was accepted at both Stanford and the University of San Francisco. I would have liked to attend Stanford, but I chose the University of San Francisco because it also offered me scholarship support. I graduated from St. Gregory's with an associate degree in business administration and made arrangements to move to San Francisco.

• • •

As I was preparing to leave Oklahoma, I received a shocking letter from one of my older brothers, Mbacha. My little brother Njoka, who was then sixteen years old, had purchased a television set. Mugo wanted the television and demanded that Njoka surrender it. Njoka refused, and Mugo threatened to make Njoka's life miserable if he did not relent. Njoka continued to defy him. A couple of weeks later, Mugo persuaded his seven-year-old daughter Mary and one of Mary's friends to accuse Njoka of raping them. The police arrested Njoka and beat him until he confessed to the crime.

I called Mbacha to find out what had happened since his letter. He reported that Mugo had visited Njoka in his jail cell and told him that if he pled guilty, he would withdraw the charges. Under the influence of Mugo's promise and the fear of more torture, Njoka entered a guilty plea, expecting to be released. But Mugo had double-crossed him. Working with corrupt police officials and judges, he had Njoka sentenced to an eight-year prison term.

According to Mbacha, no one had told me about these events while they were happening because they didn't want to interrupt my studies or encourage me to return to Kenya, where I too might be arrested.

Mugo's ferocious aggression toward his own brother was crazy, and I have never forgiven him for it. But it was consistent with his past actions toward me, such as nearly killing me when I demanded my share of my father's property. I knew that Njoka would not have raped anyone, much less his own niece. Even if he had, he was still a juvenile and should not have been sentenced to prison as an adult.

I was distraught when I heard that Mugo had destroyed Njoka's life. I recalled vividly how Njoka had worried about my impending departure and how I had promised to return to help him if he was ever in trouble. I could not remain aloof in America and pretend that I was helpless to assist him. Early in June, as soon as I completed my exams at St. Gregory's, I got on a plane for Kenya. I did not inform anyone about my trip because I did not want the authorities to be watching for my arrival. In Nairobi, I immediately boarded a bus and went to my village.

As soon as I got there, I ran into the district chief of police. I bent my head and hoped that he would not recognize me. But I had not lost any height, and my huge backpack also drew attention. He approached me immediately.

"When did you get back?" he asked.

"I just got back today," I told him.

"We will be watching you every moment," he said.

Despite this warning, I met with some of the members of the 1992 boycott committee. They advised me to keep a very low profile and avoid engaging in any political activities. One of them suspected that the police had cooperated with Mugo because they wanted to use Njoka as bait to get me back in Kenya, where they would eventually characterize some action of mine as political and send me back to jail. I wanted to return to America to continue my education, and I certainly wanted to avoid detention or any restriction on my departure. I therefore agreed to avoid all political activity. I always dressed in shorts and sneakers rather than business clothes, so that I could present myself as a visitor, not a political activist. I made no political speeches.

Although I hate corruption, the only way to visit Njoka in prison was to bribe some police officers. They allowed us to meet in an office where we could have physical contact and more privacy, rather than in the visitors' room, where prisoners and visitors are separated.

Njoka was miserable. He had been beaten severely and repeatedly, and he looked weak. He was broken in spirit because he had already been in jail for several months with no visitors allowed other than his accuser, Mugo, and he faced a long prison term. In addition, as soon as Njoka was jailed, Mugo had seized his television and all the property I had left for him. Lucy had tried to protect some of the property, but Mugo had assaulted her as well. Mugo had not been prosecuted because he continued to serve as a police informer.

I spoke with Njoka at length and wrote down notes of our conversation. I gathered enough information to file a formal request with the court for the transcript of his plea and sentencing. For about $4,000, I hired a lawyer who requested the pleadings and filed an appeal for Njoka, relying mainly on the fact that Njoka had been improperly

Njoka after his release
from jail

charged as an adult. The process of interviewing Njoka, obtaining the transcript, hiring the lawyer, cajoling him to file the appeal quickly, and waiting for the court's decision took about two months.

At the end of that time, the appeals court agreed that Njoka had been charged improperly, and it ordered a new trial. In the meantime, Njoka could be released on bail. I paid the $7,000 for his bail. The day after he was released, I boarded a bus for Nairobi and immediately flew back to the United States to start my studies in San Francisco.

.   .   .

The last two years of my undergraduate education passed quickly, and, except for worrying about Njoka, I had a great time. While at the University of San Francisco, I met people from all over the world. Some other foreign students and I started an association for international business students. We became involved in the life of the city, too. Through the association, I was able to meet San Francisco's mayor, Willie Brown; the founder of Apple Computers, Steve Jobs; and a future governor of California, Gray Davis. I worked in the university's development office and learned about networking and business development skills.

During my senior year, I was a research assistant for Dr. Hartmut Fischer, one of my professors, who also worked in the university's Center for the Pacific Rim. In addition, I was recruited by some major corporations. My student visa allowed me to remain in the United States for one year of postgraduate practical training. Because of this limit, no corporation would offer me a permanent job, but several wanted me for a one-year term. I accepted a position with the Hertz Corporation, to become the manager of the Hertz rental station at the San Jose airport.

But shortly after I began working for Hertz, I received a call from an MCI executive whom I had met during one of his recruiting visits to the university. He was working for MCI's government markets office in McLean, Virginia, near Washington, D.C. MCI had been awarded a large government contract to provide services to certain federal agencies. The contract was expected to last for ten years, and he was part of the team that would develop a new division to administer it. He urged me to leave Hertz and move to the Washington area, where he would give me a job in his division. He also offered to support me in pursuing an advanced degree in business management.

I quickly accepted his offer, packed everything into my car, and drove to Virginia. But when I arrived, he told me that as a result of the recent

WorldCom/MCI merger, he had been transferred to the corporation's office in Jackson, Mississippi.

MCI hired me anyway. My new supervisor did not know about the promises that the executive had made to me. She also did not realize that my student visa would allow me only one year of practical training. I soon told her about this limitation and explained that if the company wanted to retain me, it would have to sponsor me for a work visa. She said that I should not worry about this because the company valued my services.

Several months went by, during which I did not hear from anyone from the human resources office about my expiring visa. Two months before the end of my year of practical training, I went to see the human resources director. She told me that MCI did not sponsor employees for work visas.

This new revelation presented a very serious problem. I could not return to Kenya because President Moi was still in power. If I did return, I would remain under police surveillance and restriction. Furthermore, the security forces would realize that, with an American business education, I was now a far greater threat to Moi's domination of the farmers of Central Province. If I complained about political or economic conditions, I could easily end up, once again, in jail or in a torture cell, or perhaps even dead.

My friends suggested that I apply for asylum. I was very resistant to this idea. Applying for asylum meant that I would have to revisit my experiences of torture in Kenya and recount them to American officials in great detail. I would have to mentally relive my near-execution in the forest, my fearful days in the water cell, and the months in solitary confinement. This was something that I had not done and was not prepared to do. I hoped for an alternative that would let me avoid applying for asylum.

But the only two other choices were even worse. I could return to Kenya and live under Moi's thumb, trying to exist at a subsistence level, without complaining about the subjugation of Kenyan farm labor. Or I could remain in the United States by marrying an American woman I had dated in Oklahoma. Her father had encouraged the prospect of marriage and had advised me that if I married his daughter, I could remain in America. I had thought about it, but I had decided not to marry her because I was not willing to marry someone I did not love. Another woman, whom I had dated in San Francisco, had moved to Virginia and proposed to me, but I didn't love her either. I feared returning to Kenya, but marrying for the sake of remaining in America was morally wrong.

In May 2000, only one month before my visa expired, I decided that seeking asylum represented my only chance to remain safely in the United States.

I began my quest for asylum by obtaining an application form. Its length and the accompanying set of instructions astonished me. In addition to its many standard biographical questions, the form asked me to thoroughly explain the basis for my asylum claim, attaching as many additional pages as I needed. It required a detailed explanation of my involvement in any political party, student group, ethnic group, or human rights group, again suggesting additional pages. I had to describe all the ways in which I or any member of my family had been mistreated or threatened by the authorities of my country and provide details of any charges against me and the conditions of any imprisonment. To prove that these events had occurred, I was told to "attach documents referring to these incidents, if they are available."[1]

When I left Kenya, I had not taken with me any documents about my arrest and imprisonment. The security forces provided no records showing that they had jailed and tortured me. Even if they had done so, I would have left them behind because they would have reminded me of the pain, fear, and suffering I had endured. All I had from Kenya was my old tea license. Even my copy of the receipt for the bond money that had bought my freedom was in my closet back in Kenya.

On another part of the asylum application, I had to explain what I thought would happen to me if I returned to Kenya—and once again I was expected to provide documents to support my statements. The application form also asked whether I had ever returned to Kenya after I had come to the United States and required details about any such visit. In response, I described my brief visit in 1997 to help Njoka get out of jail.

I worked very hard on this application. With the completed form, I submitted thirty-six pages of documents, including a copy of my birth certificate and a copy of the tea license that had so restricted my right to work on my own farm.

Shortly after I mailed the form, I was summoned to the Asylum Office in Arlington, Virginia, to be fingerprinted and to be interviewed by an asylum officer, Patricia Craddock. In retrospect, I should have found a lawyer to prepare me for this interview and to accompany me to the appointment, but I didn't think I would need a lawyer. It simply never occurred to me that the American government would doubt my story.

When I arrived at the Asylum Office, I was glad to see that Patricia Craddock was black. Her skin was as dark as my own, so dark that it was difficult to see the line that separated her face from her dark, wavy hair. Her large eyes stood out and seemed to scrutinize my every expression and gesture. She was tall but seemed quite delicate.

She greeted me nicely and asked whether I had a lawyer. She explained that most people preferred to have a lawyer present during asylum interviews, and she asked me whether I would like to get one and reschedule our appointment for a later date. Her race, her gentleness, and her professional demeanor made me feel sure that she would grant me asylum. I replied that I knew my story and didn't need a lawyer to help me explain it to her. She asked me to raise my right hand and had me swear to tell the truth.

She asked me dozens of questions, perhaps probing for inconsistencies in my tale that would indicate I was lying about the boycott and about my incarceration in Kenya. Her insistence on detail, my lack of preparation, and my inability to recall numbers and dates made the atmosphere tense. I told my story as best I could, but I was relating events that had occurred eight years earlier and dredging up memories that I had worked hard to suppress. I got some of the details wrong.

At one point, she asked how many people had initially organized the boycott and how many had participated in the protest. I said that four of us had started it, that about one hundred thousand farmers had eventually participated, and that we had brought Kenya's tea production to a halt. As it turned out, my estimate was off by a factor of three; I later realized that about thirty thousand farmers had participated actively in the protest. But my answer made her doubt me. Maybe she thought that she would have heard about a protest involving a hundred thousand people. When she asked for the date of my arrest, I erroneously stated it as May 1992. Later, I was able to reconstruct the timeline and realized that the protest had occurred in July and that I had first been incarcerated in early August.

She also asked whether the newspapers had reported the protest and my participation. When I replied that the story had indeed been carried in the newspapers, she inquired whether I had a copy. I did not, because I had not brought a newspaper with me from Kenya. I did not think that anyone in America would ever be interested in the tea farmers' boycott in Kenya.

At the end of the interview, Craddock instructed me to return in two weeks to receive her decision. When I went back, I was handed her written decision and was not allowed to see her again. The moment I tore open the envelope and read the decision, I felt that my period of temporary safety in America had come to an end.

Craddock had declined to grant asylum, and she had placed me in deportation proceedings in an immigration court. The reason was that she thought I was lying. According to her, I "couldn't establish" that I had ever started a tea farmers' association or that I "was the leader of such a powerful organization." She had reviewed the State Department's annual human rights report on Kenya for 1992 and found that it "showed no information about the group the applicant claims caused a boycott that stopped most of the country from working in support of the farmers." She noted that I had "no documents" to support my claim that there had been an organized protest. She cited what she termed "inconsistent testimony": I had first claimed that I "was arrested in 1992 because of inciting a boycott," she wrote, but then had stated that I was arrested after I "participated in a march"—as if the boycott and march were somehow completely unrelated events rather than two aspects of our protest. She concluded that the discrepancy she perceived "goes to the materiality of his claim, calling into question whether the events described by the applicant ever took place . . . or whether any acts of persecution were committed."

I was upset about not being believed, but I could also see Craddock's point of view. She had to make judgments on hundreds of asylum applications every year, and some of the people she interviewed were probably frauds. It must have been very difficult for her to imagine that a protest dreamed up by Wash and me, two peasant farmers with no organizing experience, could mushroom to the point of threatening a major export crop of an entire nation. Such a thing probably could not happen in the United States.

A staff member at the Asylum Office gave me a copy of the decision, along with a legal notice summoning me to immigration court a month later, on July 19, 2000. The charge against me was very peculiar. The summons said that I should be deported because I had been admitted to the United States on a student visa to attend Hartnell College in California, but that I "did not attend Hartnell College from June 17 to June 18, 1997." In fact, by June 17, 1997, I had transferred first to St. Gregory's and then to the University of San Francisco, and both those schools had sent the Immigration Service the necessary I-20 forms certifying my transfer. Furthermore, neither St. Gregory's nor the University of San Francisco was in session on June 17 or June 18, 1997, as both were on summer break, and I was not required to attend school during summer breaks.

Noting the obvious errors both in Craddock's decision and in the summons, I asked to see her to straighten them out. The staff member refused this request, but a supervisor came to see me in the lobby of the office. He looked at the summons and agreed that it was erroneous, as no one would have expected me to be in school on those dates. He told me to go home and promised to send me a corrected notice.

Two weeks before the scheduled July 19 court hearing, I began to get worried because I hadn't heard from him. In addition, I was increasingly sobered by the realization that Patricia Craddock hadn't believed me. I began to think that the judge might not believe me either.

On July 19, I still had not received a revised summons, but I went to the courthouse. Four judges were presiding in four different courtrooms, and I didn't know which one to see. I entered one of the courtrooms, where a male judge was scheduling hearings in several other cases. After he finished with those cases, I approached him to say that I was supposed to be in court. I showed him the original summons the Asylum Office had given me, with that day's date. After checking with the court clerk, he said that the court did not have my file, perhaps because the Asylum Office had realized its error but had never issued a corrected statement of its allegations or filed a copy of my summons with the court. Therefore, there was no case, and he could not listen to my story.

"So what should I do?" I asked the judge.

"If you can find your file somewhere in this court, bring it to me, and I will be happy to hear your case," he replied. "I'm sure that you have a very interesting story to tell. But if you don't find the file, return to the Asylum Office and remind them to file the allegations with the court so that we have a case to decide."

I had no way to locate my file in the courthouse; probably it was never there. I returned to the Asylum Office. A supervisor explained that none of the documents from my case had been sent to the court yet. He assured me that the office would now do so and that I would receive a new court date. However, another two months went by before I heard from the Asylum Office again. During that time, I was not allowed to work in the United States, because my permitted year of practical training had ended.

Late in September, the new summons arrived, requiring me to go to court on November 21. To my surprise, however, the new summons had exactly the same error as the old one, charging me with not being at Hartnell on two days in June 1997.

During the summer, I had been warned that I might have to wait a long time to get a trial in immigration court. Since I couldn't work, I decided to spend my time learning about the American legal system in which I was becoming enmeshed. I began to explore going to law school. Perhaps with a legal education, I thought, I might be able to handle my own case. I hadn't yet heard the American adage that "a lawyer who represents himself has a fool for a client." I researched all the local law schools and learned that their application processes would require me to take the Law School Admission Test and obtain numerous letters of recommendation. But law school studies began in the fall, so even if I did well on the test, I could not enter an American law school for almost a year.

My research also persuaded me that I would need help in court. An acquaintance from MCI recommended a lawyer, whom I engaged and paid a consultation fee. But before my court date, I became dissatisfied: this lawyer didn't interview me in any depth, nor did he show any interest in the details of my case.

As I looked more deeply into the idea of going to law school, I studied the web site of the Georgetown University Law Center (www.law .georgetown.edu). Everett Bellamy, an assistant dean for academic affairs, was listed on the site, and I made an appointment to see him.

Dean Bellamy advised me to apply to several schools, because it was difficult to win admission to Georgetown. When I told him that I no longer had a student visa and had been summoned to appear in immigration court, he emphasized that I needed to win my asylum case more urgently than I needed a law degree. Dean Bellamy understood my dissatisfaction with the lawyer I had engaged, but he also disparaged my idea of representing myself in court. In fact, he laughed at my notion that I could learn enough law to handle my own case. "Trust me," he chuckled, "you do not want to represent yourself in an immigration case."

Then he became more serious. "Georgetown has a clinic that deals with asylum cases," he informed me. "If it accepts your case, it will not charge any money."

I did not know what a law school clinic was. Dean Bellamy explained that it was a law school course in which students learned how to practice law and earned academic credit by representing actual clients in court. "Just walk around this corner," he directed. "Talk to the people at the Center for Applied Legal Studies; we call it CALS for short. The students might be able to help you. They are very able, and they are supervised by the clinic's two directors, Professors David Koplow and Philip Schrag."

I had nothing to lose. I left his office and walked around the corner.

FOUR

Bernie and Dave

A short woman with a round face sat behind the desk in the small law clinic office. Large, silver-rimmed glasses balanced on the bridge of her nose. She looked up at me, removed the glasses, and let them hang from their cord. She smiled, but I had the sense that my towering size frightened her. "I'm Karen Bouton, and I'm the office manager here," she said. "Can I help you?"

I felt the need to justify my presence in what was obviously her domain. "Is this the law clinic? Dean Bellamy suggested that I come here because I need legal help with my asylum case."

"You are in the right place then. Do you have a court appearance notice?"

I scrabbled through the pile of papers in the folder I was holding and found the notice.

She looked at it, consulted her desk diary, and slowly shook her head. "No . . . they can't do it. Our fall semester calendar is full, and the spring semester students won't be ready to handle hearings until April."

I started to walk out of her office, discouraged, when she suddenly added, "Unless the immigration judge is willing to schedule your hearing in the spring."

I looked at her, encouraging her to continue.

"Professor Philip Schrag will be the director of our program for the spring semester. If you want, he can consult with the other two lawyers who supervise cases in this office. If they approve, and if the judge is willing to postpone your hearing until April, we might take your case. So tell me the basic facts, and I'll provide the information to the clinic's directors. Then I'll call you and let you know." She smiled and offered me a chair. "Please be as detailed as you can about your experiences in your country."

So, once again, someone was asking me to describe what had happened to me. I had never discussed my imprisonment in detail with anyone but Wash. Even in my asylum interview with Patricia Craddock, I had not been able to discuss in any depth what happened after I surrendered to the police. I grew anxious about the prospect of talking to the woman behind the desk about the night in the forest and the jail cells. How could a stranger who had never lived in my country understand my experience? I imagined her listening to my story for a while and interrupting me to say, "You know, enough of the lies—you can't possibly have lived through all that. I have another appointment."

But instead, Karen grew very attentive as I explained my case. She asked a lot of questions and wrote down my responses. Although she seemed very sympathetic, I realized that I was avoiding answering her questions about aspects of my imprisonment. Karen just glanced at me blankly and kept writing. I hoped she would realize that my discomfort reflected the truth of my story, not an effort to lie. After we concluded this preliminary interview, I was happy to leave the office, and I didn't want to talk to her again. At the same time, I was relieved when she promised to call me in a few days to let me know whether the clinic would take my case.

A few days later, she did call, to tell me that I could indeed become a client of the legal clinic. According to Karen, the November date on my hearing notice was the day when the judge would schedule a full hearing in my case. Professor Schrag would meet with me the evening before this scheduling hearing.

Professor Schrag surprised me. In Kenya, barristers are formal, remote figures. The American lawyer whom I had hired briefly had been somewhat formal as well. Schrag did not fit that mold at all. He was older than I was, in his late fifties, and short, perhaps five foot seven if he stretched a bit. He wore neither a jacket nor a tie, and his thick glasses suggested that when he was a child, he had spent too much time reading in the dark. I saw untamed graying hair and a bushy mustache. He looked exactly like history's most famous physicist, and I blurted out, "Are you Albert Einstein?"

"A lot of people say that I look like Einstein," he replied. "But we were not related. By the way, please call me Phil."

After listening to a short summary of my experiences in Kenya, Phil explained that he didn't need to know all the details for the calendar hearing. When the clinic's spring semester students arrived in January, they would interview me in much greater depth, he indicated. I was relieved that I did not have to tell the whole story again, at least not now.

Through that first conversation with Phil, and in later conversations with him and his students, I found out a lot about why the American Congress had passed an asylum law and how it worked. (Actually, although I understood many of the explanations that Phil and his students provided as the case progressed, I didn't fully comprehend all the legal standards and procedures until much later, when we were writing this book.) I learned that in response to the Holocaust in Europe, and to the cold war that began in the late 1940s, many countries signed an international treaty concerning the treatment of refugees, known as the Convention Relating to the Status of Refugees. The countries that signed this treaty pledged that they would not return certain people to nations where their lives or freedoms were threatened. The protection offered by the treaty is temporary, however, because it does not require any country to give permanent refuge or resettlement rights to anyone. Furthermore, the nonreturn obligation does not apply to people fleeing from wars, famines, earthquakes, or other natural disasters; it protects only a person who, "owing to well-founded fear of being persecuted for reasons of race, religion, nationality, membership in a particular social group or political opinion," is outside his or her own country and is "unable, or *refugee def.*

owing to such fear, unwilling to avail himself of the protection" of the home country.[1]

The United States was not an original adherent to the treaty and did not agree to become bound by its terms until late in the administration of President Lyndon B. Johnson. The U.S. Congress did not pass legislation to implement the convention until 1980. But when it finally did so—in the Refugee Act, which amended the Immigration and Nationality Act—it gave refugees even better protection than the international convention required.

First, rather than offering only a temporary shelter, Congress provided asylum as a long-lasting protection for refugees. One year after being granted asylum, a refugee may apply to become a lawful permanent resident of the United States; eventually, that person can become a U.S. citizen. This provision of the law recognizes that brutal autocrats such as Moi often do not disappear quickly from the world scene and that refugees should be able to get on with their lives and not be held in suspension indefinitely.

Second, Congress made asylum available to people who had been persecuted in the past as well as those who had a well-founded fear of persecution in the future. Such persecution, however, had to be based on one of the five grounds listed in the convention: race, religion, nationality, membership in a particular social group, or political opinion. Phil explained that I could fit within the protection created by Congress because I had reason to fear continued persecution in Kenya on account of my political opinion.

In the Department of Justice, two agencies handled tens of thousands of asylum applications every year. The Immigration and Naturalization Service (INS) consisted of a professional asylum corps with officers who worked out of eight regional offices. Patricia Craddock, who had interviewed me and referred my case to the court, was a member of this corps. According to Phil, this group of professionals had won the grudging respect of the immigration bar, which found the INS generally insufferable but regarded the asylum corps as the best unit in the agency.

The other agency was the Executive Office for Immigration Review, known by the acronym EOIR, pronounced like A. A. Milne's famously depressed donkey. EOIR included several dozen immigration courts, spread around the country, with several hundred immigration judges, each of whom heard several cases every day. These judges decided whether foreign nationals in the United States, including certain asylum applicants, should be allowed to remain or should be deported. My case would be decided by the immigration court in Arlington, Virginia.

Three categories of people can apply for asylum. The first category consists of those who are apprehended at border crossings, airports, or seaports because they arrive in the United States lacking passports or U.S. visas or because officials discover that their travel documents have been forged or purchased on the black market. These individuals are jailed (or sometimes released on bond) and are put into deportation proceedings in the immigration court, where they may apply for asylum. Persons in the second category are apprehended in raids on restaurants or other establishments that employ undocumented immigrants. These individuals are usually jailed, and they too may apply for asylum during deportation proceedings.

My situation placed me into the third and largest category of asylum seekers, called "affirmative asylum applicants." These are people who arrive with lawful travel documents (such as tourist or student visas), people who enter the United States by crossing the Mexican or Canadian border without being detected, and people who persuade immigration inspectors that their false passports are genuine. We affirmative asylum applicants come forward voluntarily, identify ourselves to the U.S. government, and take our chances on the asylum process. We are evaluated initially by asylum officers such as Patricia Craddock and are then either granted asylum or referred to immigration court for deportation proceedings.[2]

Those who are granted asylum either by the Asylum Office or in immigration court have the right to remain in the United States. But those who are denied asylum are worse off than before they applied, because an immigration court orders them to be deported. Although Phil believed

that America had a pretty good system, he acknowledged that asylum lawyers always worry about every case because a mistaken denial of asylum can result in an applicant being escorted onto a plane, in shackles, and sent to a country where he or she will face the loss of freedom or even death.

Phil looked over the documents that I had submitted with my application. He wasn't surprised that Craddock had not granted me asylum; persuading an asylum officer often required many more corroborating documents than I had filed, he explained, as well as testimony that was consistent with those documents in every respect. According to Phil, when an applicant was lucky or wealthy enough to have a lawyer, a well-documented asylum application might include two hundred to five hundred pages of supporting evidence, some of it gathered at great cost from the applicant's home country. He added that although the government must provide a lawyer for indigent defendants in criminal cases, the government does not furnish legal representation to indigent asylum applicants, even though in nearly all cases the consequence of losing is deportation.

Asylum officers grant asylum to only about 40 percent of the applicants they interview, Phil told me. The other cases, like mine, are "referred" to an immigration court. This referral is a euphemism for rejection by the INS Asylum Office.

Now that my case was in immigration court in Arlington, one of the four judges of that court would hold a hearing and make a new decision on my application. Winning asylum at this stage would be easier in some ways and more difficult in others. It would be easier because I would have a lot of help from two of Phil's students, who would be assigned to my case in January for what would probably be an April hearing. Having representation was very important: in court, the two-thirds of applicants who had representatives won 37 percent of the time, whereas unrepresented applicants won only 6 percent of the time.[3] The success rate of applicants represented by CALS was much greater, more than 85 percent, because the students put so much time into each case.

For three months, the students assigned to me would spend most of their time gathering evidence and preparing me for my hearing. The clinic could not afford to send the students to Kenya to collect evidence (not to mention the danger such a trip would pose for them and for my family). But as a result of university support and fundraising from alumni, the clinic had the funds necessary for international phone calls, faxes, and mail delivery services, which made it possible to collect a lot of evidence without international travel.

Even with student representatives, however, winning would be very difficult. Unlike the interviews in the Asylum Office, immigration court proceedings were formal. Furthermore, the Justice Department would assign a lawyer to cross-examine me, challenge my evidence, and try to defeat my asylum claim.

I asked what would happen if I lost in immigration court. Phil soberly told me that if I lost, I would face a deportation order. I could challenge the ruling at the Board of Immigration Appeals and, if I lost with the board, in a federal court of appeals. Appeals were expensive, however, and they were usually fruitless.

Phil told me that I could not work or receive welfare while going through this process. Like other applicants, I would have to subsist for several months on whatever money I had and any private charity from friends, relatives, or community organizations. Fortunately, I had been investing for some time and had money to live on, but I asked why the United States prohibited asylum applicants from working. Phil explained that in 1994, the rules were changed to discourage people from filing groundless applications just so that they could earn a few months' pay. Under these new rules, an applicant who appealed after losing in immigration court was barred from working during the entire appeal, even though the appellate process could take years.

Then Phil informed me that the greatest problem in my case was not the lack of corroborating documentation. In fact, he was confident that the students would be able to collect much more evidence. The really big problem was that my case had been assigned, at random, to Judge Joan

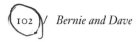

Churchill. CALS tried cases before eight different judges in Arlington and Baltimore, and most of the cases that the clinic had lost were those heard by Judge Churchill.

"Who is this Judge Churchill?" I wondered.

"She's been on the immigration court for twenty years," Phil said. "Other than that, we don't know very much about her. She went to Michigan Law School and graduated in 1965. She spent a year in private practice and then joined the Immigration and Naturalization Service. After six years, she became a staff lawyer for the Board of Immigration Appeals. Then she was appointed as an immigration judge, and she's been on the court ever since. We've won some cases from her, but we know that she has the lowest rate of granting asylum in the Baltimore-Washington area. In fact, a California reporter studied the asylum grant rates of all the immigration judges, and he discovered that hers was only 14 percent, though other judges in our area had grant rates as high as 51 percent during the same period."[4]

"What is your clinic's record with her?" I asked.

"It's better than 14 percent, probably about 40 percent," he replied. "But that's less than half of our success rate with any of the other judges. So I have to tell you that however strong your case looks after the students have worked with you, we are never going to be able to be very optimistic about the outcome. Also Judge Churchill will probably give you no clue about what she is thinking until she announces her decision orally, at the end of your hearing in April."

"Will she be in court tomorrow?"

"Yes, so now let's talk about what will happen in the morning. Usually, one of the clinic's fellows attends these scheduling hearings with our clients, but neither of them is available, so I'm going to go with you. In April, we'll be in court for several hours, including an hour or more for your testimony. The students will prepare you for that. But tomorrow we'll be there only for a few minutes. I will speak for you. The judge will ask how the respondent—that's you—pleads to the charges. We'll admit that you no longer have a valid visa, and we'll say that you are asking for asylum. Judge Churchill may ask you to confirm that you understand that law students will represent you. And we'll agree on a date in April for the hearing."

. . .

The next morning, during the twenty-minute drive from downtown Washington to the court across the Potomac River in Arlington, Phil inquired, "Do you play a lot of basketball?"

He must have seen me grimace, because he encouraged me to explain.

"Everyone asks me that question," I said. "Everyone looks at a seven-foot black guy and expects me to be a good basketball player. But the fact of the matter is that I have tried to play the game, and I am terrible at it. So I hate it when people ask me."

We arrived at the Arlington court, which consisted of several rooms on the top floor of a thirteen-story high-rise office building in the central business district. The building housed a metro station, upscale shops, and a hotel. In the lobby, people were rushing to and fro. Most of them wore dark suits and brightly colored ties, and I guessed that they were government officials. Mixed among them were military officers in crisp, starched uniforms who appeared to be hurrying to the metro station to catch the train to the Pentagon. I realized that this building was not merely a business center; it was also a bureaucratic hub of governmental and military activities. On the top floor, where I was going, federal officials sat in judgment on the futures of asylum applicants who had fled from dozens of countries around the world.

The court suite had a metal detector at the elevator entrance. In a large waiting room, people sat in uncomfortable plastic chairs. There was a window through which lawyers could talk to a clerk by yelling through a pane of glass. Each judge had a separate courtroom, and a private area was set aside for the INS lawyers.

We entered Judge Churchill's courtroom and sat in the audience section. The walls were covered with brilliantly colored pictures of house facades and flowers. Phil whispered that Judge Churchill's husband had painted all of them.

Wearing a black robe, Judge Churchill entered the room, with a smile that made her look younger than her nearly sixty years. Her thin red hair, barely graying, rested on her shoulders. Her skin was pale, and her eyes seemed watery.

She scheduled hearings in several other cases before she got to mine. Then Phil and I walked through a little gate, moving up to a table in the front of the courtroom.

Phil began the scheduling hearing by complaining about the weird error in the summons I had received, which alleged only that I had been issued a student visa to attend Hartnell College but had not been present there for two days in June 1997, after Hartnell's semester was over. The government should have charged simply that as of the present time, I was no longer a student. The Asylum Office had promised to correct this error when I brought it to their attention, but instead they had reissued the defective summons, changing only the date of the court's scheduling hearing.

Phil had explained to me earlier that this error was both irrelevant and significant. It was irrelevant because my status as a student had in fact ended on June 30, 2000, when my postgraduate year of practical training came to a close. I was subject to deportation regardless of whether my status had lapsed in 1997 or just a few months before the scheduling hearing.

The error was significant, however, for two reasons. First, a person who wants asylum in the United States must apply for it within one year of entering the country, unless he or she can prove that filing after that date was justified by a changed circumstance (such as a coup in the applicant's home country) or some other extraordinary occurrence. But the INS had published a policy stating that if a person applies for asylum while holding a valid student status, or within a reasonable time after that status expires, the existence of the valid status is considered an extraordinary circumstance, and the one-year deadline for asylum application does not apply. I had applied on May 10, 2000, while still holding lawful student status. Thus, if no one disagreed that my student status remained valid through June 2000, we should have no problem with the one-year deadline.

The second reason why the error was important had to do with timing. If the government did not correct its formal charge soon, its lawyers might come to the April hearing asking for permission to amend the charges and return to court months later. Alternatively, if the government's lawyers failed to amend the charge, we might be able to win the case by proving that Hartnell was out of session in June 1997—but the government could immediately file new charges against me. Either of these scenarios could delay the hearing by several months. By then, the spring semester law students would have completed their work in the clinic and thus could not represent me at the hearing, even though we had worked together for months. That would be bad for me and bad for the students.

At the scheduling hearing, Phil offered to concede that I was subject to removal for overstaying my student visa, provided that the government amend the charge. Judge Churchill agreed that the summons seemed to be in error. She noted that the INS would have to amend the charge in writing. She told the government, "If you are going to make a change, that needs to get done soon because I will not be able to go forward on the date of the hearing. It does seem unusual that a charge would relate to just one day of absence." The government's lawyer promised to file an amended charge within a week.[5]

The next step was for me to ask for "relief" from deportation. Phil told Judge Churchill that I wanted asylum, but he also asked for two other types of relief as alternatives if necessary: "withholding of removal" and "voluntary departure." The first of these alternatives was not very important in my case. Withholding is something like asylum, because the respondent who wins it is not deported. However, it is not as good as asylum, because the person whose removal is withheld may not become a permanent resident or a citizen. If conditions ever change for the better in the respondent's country, even decades later, after the person has established a new life in the United States, he or she can be deported at that time.

Curiously, however, American law makes it more difficult to win withholding than to win asylum. To win asylum, the respondent need prove only a well-founded fear of persecution. The Supreme Court has ruled that if a reasonable person in the respondent's circumstances would be afraid to return, the fear is well founded; the respondent does not need to prove that persecution is more likely than not. To win withholding, a respondent must show that it is more likely than not that he or she will be persecuted—in other words, the respondent must demonstrate that there is at least a 51 percent chance of persecution. By contrast, a much lower probability of harm, perhaps a 10 percent chance of being jailed or killed, is enough for the government to grant asylum.[6]

Lawyers often ask for withholding as an alternative to asylum, because if respondents have committed nonpolitical crimes or have applied for asylum too late, they are ineligible for asylum but might still win withholding. I had assured Phil that I had never committed a nonpolitical crime, and he knew that I had applied on time. But Phil said that many refugees are so fearful that they don't tell their lawyers the whole story during intake interviews. Thus lawyers routinely request withholding in case they later learn of a bar to asylum that a client didn't reveal at the outset.

Phil's alternative request for voluntary departure was more important.[7] If Judge Churchill denied asylum but granted voluntary departure, I could leave the United States voluntarily, at my own expense, rather than being deported at the government's expense. Obviously, this alternative was less desirable than either asylum or withholding, both because I would have to leave the country and because of the expense. But it had two potential benefits. First, if I lost my case after being ordered deported, I would not be allowed to enter the United States again for ten years, even if I won the annual lottery for U.S. immigrant visas. I could not return as a tourist or for more education. But if I left under voluntary departure, I would not be stuck with the ten-year prohibition. Second, if the government deported me, INS officials would put me on a plane to Kenya under guard and in shackles. I was terrified of being sent back to Kenya, and arriving in handcuffs with INS guards would make my situation much worse. But if Judge Churchill granted voluntary departure, I could leave on my own initiative and try to obtain a visa to live and work in some other country—which both Phil and I agreed would be a better alternative.

When Phil finished telling Judge Churchill that I wanted asylum and, in the alternative, withholding or voluntary departure, she asked, "Does he fear torture?" This was a shorthand reference to the Convention Against Torture, which the United States had recently signed and ratified.[8] This agreement provides still another possibility for avoiding deportation. The United States, as a signatory of this convention, cannot force any persons to go to a country whose government would probably torture them. Individuals can be deported to some other country that will take them, or they can be jailed if they are criminals or security risks; but under the provisions of this convention, the United States cannot facilitate torture. According to Phil, however, it is exceedingly difficult to win a torture case because of the standard of proof: there must be at least a 51 percent chance that the person trying to avoid deportation would be tortured by government officials. This is a high hurdle because all governments deny that they torture people, and they conceal any acts of torture that they commit. Furthermore, even when government officials have tortured someone in the past, it is difficult, if not impossible, to prove that they will probably do so again.

As I later learned, Phil had not planned to make a claim based on the torture convention, for two reasons. One was the high burden of proof. The other was that I had downplayed torture in the asylum application I had filed before my interview with Patricia Craddock. In response to the question asking whether I feared being subjected to torture, I had responded that "people who oppose government views are still subjected to harassment and in some cases, opposition figures in Kenya have been beaten in public meetings by government controlled groups. [A 1999 State Department human rights report had noted that] security forces . . . continued to torture and beat detainees." I had not revealed that Kenyan security officials had tortured me. Nor had I discussed any physical torture in my initial screening interview with Karen Bouton. In my brief discussion with Phil the night before the scheduling hearing, I had talked about being detained for months, but not about torture.

For these reasons, Phil thought that it would be good strategy to focus on the stronger asylum claim. So when Judge Churchill raised the issue of torture, Phil started to say that I was not asking for protection under the Convention Against Torture.

But I had been tortured, and I was afraid that I might be tortured again. So before Phil could finish his sentence, I told Judge Churchill, "Yes, I am afraid that I will be tortured." Phil changed his plan and told Judge Churchill that I did indeed want protection under the torture convention as well.

The last item on the agenda that day was to set a date for the hearing at which I would testify. Phil requested that the court set a date for the following April, because by then the students, who would begin their clinic work in January, would have had about two and a half months in which to collect evidence and prepare for the hearing. Judge Churchill set the hearing for April 20.

The scheduling hearing was drawing to an end when Judge Churchill asked whether I had any other ways in which I might lawfully remain in the United States. Did I have a close family member who was an American citizen, for example, who might sponsor me for permanent residence? Phil replied that I did not have any relatives in the United States.

"Okay," she noted. "How about a basketball offer? Do you play basketball?"

"I played basketball in college, Your Honor."

I could see that Phil was embarrassed for me, as I had just told him how much I hated being asked about basketball.

"In college," she repeated. "No professional possibilities?"

"I wasn't that good," I confessed.

"Okay. The reason I asked is because you are so tall. How tall are you?"

"I'm seven foot one, Your Honor."

Judge Churchill seemed satisfied that I was not going to be able to immigrate as a skilled professional basketball player, and she adjourned the hearing until April. Phil promised that the students would be in touch with me in the middle of January. Meanwhile, he would file a request under the Freedom of Information Act for a copy of the government's file on me. That would enable us to see the notes that Craddock had taken when she interviewed me.[9] Any contradictions between my statements to her and my statements during Judge Churchill's hearing could cast doubt on my credibility unless I could explain them.

Phil drove me back to the law school and mentioned that I would not see him again until he played the role of judge in a mock hearing in April, a week or so before the real hearing. At the April 20 hearing, the students who had been working with me would sit with me at the lawyers' table, and Phil would be watching from the audience section of the courtroom. After being trained for a whole semester, the students would be my representatives for all practical purposes.[10]

. . .

A month and a half passed. I was still hoping to become a law student, so I spent the time managing my investments, which continued to be successful, and preparing to take the Law School Admission Test. A law student from George Mason University was offering tutoring for this test at a high school near my apartment. I registered for his course and attended the lessons about twice a week.

One evening in January, my telephone rang as I was about to leave for one of those lessons. I hesitated because I didn't want to be late for the class.

"My name is Bernie Huang," said the female voice on the telephone. "I'm a law student at Georgetown University Law Center. I got your number from Professor Phil Schrag, who directs our law school clinic. I'm one of the students assigned to your case. My partner and I would like to meet with you at the law school so that we can start to prepare you for your asylum hearing. Would you be able to come and meet with us this week?"

"Sure," I replied casually, without much thought.

"Great. How about meeting at the law clinic at ten tomorrow morning then? Do you know where Georgetown Law Center is located?"

"I do. I have been there before. That is where I met Phil," I told her.

"I'll see you then. And my partner, Dave, will be with me."

The following day, I arrived at Karen Bouton's office fifteen minutes before my appointment. She was typing on the keyboard below the edge of her desk. Her large glasses were again perched on the bridge of her nose. She kept typing as if no one had walked into her office. Staring at her computer monitor and without moving her body or even turning to look at me, she calmly asked, "Did any of our students talk to you yesterday?"

She no longer seemed frightened by or even conscious of my height. Perhaps I had simply imagined that in our first encounter she had felt me taking up all her space. In any event, I now felt relieved that she was apparently comfortable with my presence.

"Yes . . ." I replied. She turned around to look at me, took off her glasses, and leaned forward on her desk. "I am here to meet with one of the students who will be handling my case," I added.

"Good." She gestured toward an empty seat near the door. "Have a seat and wait for them. They are probably preparing the interview room. They should be here shortly." She went straight back to her typing, staring at the monitor.

A few minutes later, a petite woman with Asian features entered Karen's office. Though smiling, she appeared tired and disoriented, a bit uncertain of herself. She was a little younger than I was, probably in her late twenties, and she seemed only about five feet tall. Her straight, shiny black hair flowed stylishly toward her neck. Her square, black-rimmed glasses made her look like an eyeglasses model who was worn out by too many hours without sleep or food. She gazed around the room as if she expected someone to recognize her.

I thought she might be an asylum seeker hoping to be represented by the law school clinic. I considered suggesting that she speak with Karen. I was about to do so when she turned toward me and stared straight into my eyes. "Jeff!" she said confidently. Her sudden shift from uncertainty to control startled me.

"Yes, I am Jeff," I stammered. She smiled.

"We talked last night. I am one of the law students who will be handling your case."

I had been seated, so I stood up to shake her hand, dwarfing her. She stared straight up and down at me and glanced at my huge hands. She grinned. "You didn't seem so tall when you were sitting down. Phil told me you are tall, but I wasn't expecting you to be this tall." She grabbed my hand and shook it firmly. "By the way, I'm Bernie."

I thought of telling her that I had mistaken her for a refugee, but I buttoned my mouth, because telling this to the student who would be handling my case didn't seem polite.

"Come with me. We're going to have the interview in one of the rooms downstairs, on the first floor," she said as she motioned me to follow her. "My partner and I are going to need to learn all the details of what happened to you in your country. Do you think you are prepared to tell us what happened?"

"I have never been prepared to talk about it, but I will try," I responded. I was getting nervous, and I didn't like it. She seemed just as nervous.

"You will try . . . uh?" she giggled. "That's funny. I mean, it's good that you are willing to try. I'm sure it's not easy to talk about experiences that evoke stressful memories."

I wondered what she knew about the agonies of recalling the darkest period of your life. "How do you know about that?" I asked her. She glanced at me again and smiled.

"I've studied these issues. Before I came to law school, I did human rights work in Hong Kong. Some of the people I worked with had been imprisoned by the Chinese government. They had gone through horrible times, and none of them liked talking about their experiences. That's why I thought it was funny when you said you would try," she explained.

"How tall are you by the way?" she inquired as we reached the bottom of the stairs and turned toward a long hallway.

"I am just over seven feet."

"I've never met anyone who is seven feet tall. Do people always ask you whether you play basketball? I would be so annoyed by that. I would just hate it."

"I do hate it. How did you know?" I asked.

She laughed again. "You're the tallest person I've ever seen. Most people would think you're a basketball player. It's obvious." We reached the end of the hallway and stood before a door marked "Interview Room."

She knocked, and a white man with blond hair opened the door. He was about the same age as Bernie, or perhaps a bit younger, and was nicely dressed. He wore rimless glasses and stood about five feet seven. His shirt sleeves were rolled up, exposing muscular, hairy arms.

"Hi, I'm Dave Herzog," he said as he offered me a chair next to a small conference table. The room was bare, except for a small tape recorder.

"I used to think *you* were tall, but you don't look that tall anymore," Bernie said to Dave. Dave turned to look at me and, with admiration, ran his eyes over me all the way up and then down. "You are pretty tall," Dave agreed. "How tall are you?"

"I wonder how many times he gets asked that question in a day—I just asked him the same thing a couple minutes ago," Bernie laughed. Then she became serious. "I would be annoyed if every time I met someone they asked me how tall I was."

"I didn't mean to embarrass him, but seriously, he must be like . . . six nine? Seven feet?" Dave spoke to Bernie as if I were not there. Though I didn't find it strange that Dave was interested in my height, I was put off that he seemed more interested in my height than in my legal case. It didn't occur to me until much later that he was trying to make me comfortable by not jumping right into the work. I thought of telling Dave, "Get over it, and let's get into the business that brought us here." But I kept silent, because I knew that I would have to spend a lot of time working with these students.

"All right," I said softly. "I am seven feet tall. And I don't play basketball."

Dave was more surprised by this admission than by my height. "You are kidding me," he blurted out.

"I really don't. I play miniature golf," I said sarcastically.

"I can see why you would be a good golfer," he chuckled.

Bernie burst out laughing. "Oh, my God . . . this is extreme!" Dave was startled, and we both turned to look at Bernie. She couldn't stop herself from laughing. "Dave," she said finally, "he is messing with you. . . . Can you imagine him playing miniature golf?"

Dave was completely embarrassed, and he became serious. "I know you get that question all the time. I'm sorry, but I had to ask you. I wish I was as tall as you. Here in America, being tall is a good thing. A lot of people admire your height, and that's probably why they ask you how tall you are."

"It's a good way to start a conversation, too," I said.

"But I'm sure it can get annoying," Dave responded apologetically.

"Yes, it can," I replied, "but I have learned to deal with it."

As we continued to talk, I realized that Dave had a mercurial personality. He spoke articulately but very quickly. Often during our conversations, he rose from his chair to attend to something else. The next minute, he would be bouncing around the room like a loose ball, deeply immersed in a thought process. Sometimes as he asked me a question, he would stop in mid-sentence and say, "I need to check on something—Can you hold on to that thought for a minute?" before rushing out of the room. Working with Dave sometimes felt like dancing with a huge chipmunk.

Bernie was the opposite in both character and personality. The way she treated me strengthened my desire to become a lawyer. Everything meant something to her, and she was aware of even the smallest detail in a casual conversation. For example, during the interview, I kept doodling pictures of cubes on sheets of paper as I responded to her questions. This was something I had done for years whenever I was nervous. At the end of the interview session, Bernie wanted me to explain what those images meant and why I drew them during the interview.

"I don't know" I said.

"Can I make copies of your drawings?" she asked.

"You can have them. They don't mean anything to me," I told her.

"Thank you. I'll keep them in your file." I was dazzled. I couldn't see the importance of it. It wasn't until months later, after numerous hours of counseling, that I came to learn why I unconsciously drew those images—and discovered that obsessively drawn cubes could be evidence that a person had spent months in solitary confinement.

Bernie spoke in short sentences, each of which communicated one specific fact or idea. She could be laughing one moment and then turn stone-cold serious in a matter of seconds.

It was amusing to watch the interaction between Dave and Bernie. Early in our first interview, Dave said, "This is what we are going to do. Bernie may have explained this to you . . ." He stopped in mid-sentence and looked at Bernie. "Have you guys already gone through this?"

But before either of us could respond, he continued, "Here is what we are going to do. . . . I know you have already spoken with Professor Schrag, but we're going to need more details than what you told him. . . . That's why we're here, right?" Both Bernie and I stared at him, confused.

"We've already talked about that," Bernie stated calmly. Indicating the tape recorder, she said to me, "We're going to spend some time with you talking about what happened to you in Kenya. We will tape these sessions so that we don't forget what we discuss. Dave and I will listen to these tapes and come up with more questions regarding the specific details that we need to build a strong case for you. If you feel uncomfortable talking about something, we need to know that. We can stop if we have to. If you can't remember a detail, don't worry about it. I think that's what Dave is trying to say. Is that right, Dave?"

"Oh . . . yeah . . . that was it. You said it . . ." Dave acknowledged. Then he turned to me and added, "We are going to do what she said." I just smiled.

During our weekly interviews, Dave and Bernie learned a lot about me, but I also learned about them. After going to college in Los Angeles, Dave had been accepted into a graduate program in English literature at the University of Glasgow. In the summer before starting his graduate studies, he worked on a kibbutz in Israel. One day that summer, he went to a barbecue in Gaza with a friend who worked for the British consulate there. At the barbecue, he talked with a Palestinian man who said that he

Bernie Huang and Dave Herzog (standing on chairs) with me

could tolerate a great deal—living under the guns of the Israeli army, knowing that Israel controlled Gaza's drinking water and electricity, and often being unable to get to his job in Israel because of border controls. But what truly upset this man was that when Palestinians took their chances in rafts on the open sea, seeking a land in which they would not be doomed to poverty, some of them died of thirst because they were refused entry, and even drinking water, at every port. After learning more about the plight of Palestinians, Dave found the study of Renaissance emblem books too disconnected from reality, and he left the study of literature for the study of law. He applied to work in the law school clinic with the words of the man from Gaza still ringing in his mind.

Bernie had entered Georgetown Law School with a strong background in public service work, having spent four summers as a group leader in a camp for children of families living with HIV and AIDS. After attending college at Columbia University, she had become an assistant to Wei Jing Sheng, China's most prominent dissident in exile. Then, as she had mentioned in our first meeting, she took a job as the coordinator of the Hong Kong office of Human Rights Watch, where she monitored human rights developments in China and represented Human Rights Watch in meetings with Chinese officials.

Over several months, Bernie and Dave interviewed me repeatedly about the initial events leading to the tea boycott and my role in those events. Leading the boycott was one of the high points of my life, so I enjoyed reminiscing and talking about the protest and my actions. I became animated when explaining these events.

But then we came to my arrest and imprisonment, and the tone of our interviews changed. I became morose and hesitant to discuss my prison experiences. I had frequent nightmares and headaches, and even occasional hallucinations. In particular, there was a moment during one of the sessions when the students asked me to recall the darkest days from my past. I had just explained the events following my arrest when Bernie asked, "How did it feel to be in a cell full of water?"

From the time of my release until that interview, I had never thought about how I felt while I was in the water cell. In that moment, I was transported to another place, a brightly lit room. Suddenly Dave and Bernie became my interrogators. I looked at them and saw two Kenyan security officers I knew. They were conniving and elusive; all they wanted from me was information. I had some awareness that I was hallucinating, but I couldn't make the vision go away. I tried to convince myself that it was not real. But I moved my feet and felt water splash under them. The interview room became really cold, and the walls began to close in on me. Dave's face changed. I could see through his skin, and I recognized him. Under white, hairy skin, a kind of mask, Dave was really the security officer who had pulled me out of the cell in the middle of the night and placed a blindfold around my face.

"How could I have been stupid enough to believe that these guys would never find me in the United States?" I thought. "Governments are like elephants—they work with each other, and they never forget. . . . I should have known that it was just a matter of time before they caught up with me."

The security officer seemed impatient and eager to act tough. I could only guess at the enormous resources at his disposal that had enabled him to follow me to the United States and wait for so long to have me in his grasp again. He must have known that my visa would expire some day and that my choices would be limited. All he had to do was sit and wait for me to present myself. He had permission from higher-ups to do whatever he liked, including killing me.

I could see him taking his time before charging at me. He would break the leg of one of the chairs and hit me with it. I would probably fall on the ground and pretend to faint, but he would step on my groin and slowly try to crush my testicles. I would hide them between my thighs and pretend to be having a seizure, in the hope that he would leave me alone for a short time.

Suddenly everything changed. I saw Bernie again, looking at me with puzzlement. "How long have we been in this interview?" I asked.

"About two hours," she replied. I wondered how much of my past I had revealed. I couldn't tell them anything more that day. "Who was Bernie?" I wondered. I should have found out more about her before submitting to the interviews. She could have been a Kenyan agent pretending to be a law student. A voice in the back of my head warned me not to trust her.

"Can we get out of this room?" I asked Bernie.

"Why? What's wrong with the room?" Dave interjected.

"I am really cold, and I don't want to continue with this interview. I am also tired and haven't eaten."

"Can I get you something?" Bernie offered.

"No, I need to get outside. I need some fresh air, and I am not sure whether I want to do this anymore," I told her. "There are parts of the story that I can't talk about."

"Let's go outside," Bernie suggested. "I'll come with you because I need some fresh air, too." We ended the interview, and Bernie and I walked outside, into the law school courtyard. The day was beautiful, and the sky was a perfect blue. I couldn't remember ever feeling so good just to be outside. I wanted to run and not come back, but Bernie sensed that something wasn't right about me.

"Jeff, I want you to go home and watch a movie or do something you love. Dave and I are going to review our materials, and I will call you tomorrow. But you must promise me that you will continue to try to work with us."

Bernie called me the following morning. "How did you sleep?" she inquired. I did not want to tell her that I had been afraid to sleep and that I had watched TV all night. "I slept okay," I murmured.

"Why did you stop the interview yesterday?"

"It was weird. Maybe it was the windowless room. I can't explain it."

"But you have to explain your prison experiences to the judge, or you will lose your case," she warned.

"I don't want to continue with this asylum case then. I will just drop this case and forget it ever happened," I declared.

"No," Bernie argued. "You can drop your case if you want, but before you make such a serious decision, I think you should sit down with someone who specializes in counseling torture victims. Then you can decide whether to drop the asylum claim. Would you be willing to do that?"

"I will think about it," I told her. But I really did not want to meet with a counselor.

·   ·   ·

Each time I told Dave and Bernie my story, some of the facts changed. I realized, for example, that I had erroneously recalled the dates of the protest and my arrests. On my asylum application and in my sworn testimony to Patricia Craddock, I reported that the protest rally where I had addressed the farmers in Kerugoya Moi Stadium had occurred on May 15, 1992, and that I had been arrested on May 18. But as I worked with the two students, I recalled picking avocados to eat on the way to the protest, and I knew that avocado season did not start until July. Therefore, the protest must have occurred no earlier than July, and I must have been arrested in July or August.

I told Dave and Bernie, "Being in America, I can tell you that in almost everything I do, I am thinking of dates and times. But in rural Kenya, you don't refer to the day by the date. For example, you might say, 'Let's meet on Tuesday,' but you wouldn't know that Tuesday was June 24 or even that it was in June. When you think of time in Kenya, you think more of the seasons."

Besides dates, other small points in my original application were also wrong. In fact, the more I worked with Dave and Bernie, the more I recalled details of what had happened to me—and as I recalled more details, I had to correct what I had said before. Sometimes when I met with the two students, I would have to change what I had told them just a few days earlier.

The students described a clinic class they had taken in which a psychologist gave a lecture on cultural differences and on the effects of trauma on memory. They told me that it was normal for CALS clients to recall some of the facts differently from one telling of the story to another, but that Judge Churchill might interpret variation as lying. Therefore, they would have to work hard with me, over many weeks, to get a complete and accurate picture of what had happened in Kenya nine years earlier.

In our meetings, Dave and Bernie kept me informed of their thinking about the case. Phil required them to write a lengthy "case plan," a statement of what they knew about the facts and law of my case, what they needed to find out, how they might acquire the knowledge they were missing, how they might obtain evidence to corroborate each fact of my story, and what strategic, ethical, or practical problems they expected to encounter. Their plan was fifty pages long, much of it in the form of a chart, in a bacteria-size font, listing every fact in my history and brainstorming all the possible evidence, in addition to my own testimony, that might prove that the fact was true.

In their case plan, Dave and Bernie identified both the strong points in my case and the many major problems that the three of us would have to address. They believed that corroborating Kenya's miserable human rights record under President Moi would be no challenge at all; in fact, they argued that I had understated the brutality of Moi's security forces. They showed me the State Department's annual reports on Kenya's human rights violations.[11] Because these reports are written by the U.S. government itself (which is sometimes criticized for downplaying or not reporting the human rights failures of its allies or potential allies), they are given great credence by immigration judges, the Board of Immigration Appeals, and federal courts.[12] In the State Department's report on human rights in Kenya in 1992, the year of my protest and imprisonment, Kenya's violations were strongly condemned in these stark terms:

> The government continued seriously to abridge human rights in 1992. . . . Former political prisoners consistently and credibly reported abuses in prison. Methods of torture used in past years, including flooded cells and beatings, continued to be employed. . . . the government used the assets of the State, including the judicial system, to clamp down on dissent. There were many incidents of arrest on grounds of rumormongering, sedition, incitement to violence, and the like, which were political in nature. . . . The government and the security forces were generally hostile to demonstrations, and police often broke up unapproved (and some approved) rallies brutally.[13]

Human rights observers confirmed that little had changed between 1992 and 2000. The State Department report for 2000 noted that President Moi's government continued to commit extrajudicial killings and to detain political dissidents. In March 2000, the U.N. Special Rapporteur on Torture, Sir Nigel Rodley, stated that in Kenya torture was "inflicted to intimidate detainees, to dissuade them from engaging in political activities and to extract bribes."[14] With these documents, and similar reports from Amnesty International and Human Rights Watch, included in the evidence they would submit, Dave and Bernie were reasonably confident that Judge Churchill would not disbelieve my claims of harsh treatment out of some erroneous supposition that Kenya's government tolerated political dissent. When I saw these reports, I wished that I had been able to show them to the asylum officer who had interviewed me initially.

But the students predicted that it would be much more difficult to prove my personal history to Judge Churchill's satisfaction than to establish the political facts of life in Kenya. There was the matter of my prior sworn testimony that contained incorrect dates and other erroneous details. Dave and Bernie would have to correct those errors and also explain how I made them. They needed to persuade Judge Churchill that the changes in my story represented more accurate recollections and that I had not deliberately lied in my previous statements.

They were also concerned that key facts in my story, particularly the details of my incarceration, remained vague. Although I remembered events in most of my life with precision and detail, my memory grew cloudy when I described the time between my near-execution in the forest and my transfer, months later, to the jail in my home district. For example, I recalled that I ate nothing while imprisoned in the water cell. Yet I also remembered that after those days of starvation, when an interrogator offered me rice with meat as I sat trapped in an interrogation room, I refused to eat it. When my captors threw me into solitary confinement, I again refused to eat because I expected to die anyway. I told Dave and Bernie that not eating seemed to make me stronger. I had decided that if my interrogators were not going to kill me, I would starve myself to end my ordeal. But after three days in isolation, I began to feel badly for the guard who brought me porridge, who said that I was getting him in trouble because he had to explain every day why I was not eating. Because of him, I decided to eat again. Dave and Bernie understood that this made a certain amount of sense, but they doubted that Judge Churchill would think it plausible that a starving man would refuse to eat because he expected to die or that he would finally start eating so that his jailer would not get in trouble.

The two students were also worried that I might not be giving them the entire story because it was so painful and that, for the same reason, I might remember these obviously troubling events differently when I was on the witness stand, creating further contradictions in the record.

They explained that American judges regarded plausible time sequences as important indicators of truthfulness, and I was very confused about how much time I had spent in prison. At first I recalled being released in time for Christmas in 1992, but later I realized that the holiday I finally celebrated at home was Easter of 1993. This meant that I had been in jail for months longer than I had earlier remembered.

Another problem Dave and Bernie faced was that I continued to be ambivalent about pursuing my asylum case. I had failed to convince Craddock; I had doubts that Judge Churchill would believe me; and I didn't want to go through the ordeal of dredging up all my memories of prison, only to be told by still another American official that I was a liar. In addition, I felt guilty for having escaped to America, while other tea farmers were still struggling with the oppression that I had left behind. I told Dave and Bernie, "Nelson Mandela spent twenty-seven years in South African prisons. If Nelson Mandela could have left prison and received political asylum in America, where he would probably have lived very comfortably, I don't think he would have done that. When those guys were in prison, they were free, and they knew exactly what freedom meant."

Dave and Bernie worried that keeping up my spirits and getting my story straight were problems enough, but corroborating my history with independent evidence would be even more difficult. I had no records of my arrest, no documentation of President Moi's prior warning of harsh treatment for the protest leaders. No one had witnessed my ordeal in the forest. No one outside the government of Kenya had seen me in the water torture cell—and I didn't even have any proof that such a cell existed in Kenya. I had no record of spending months in jail or being charged with treason. Because the water torture had left no marks on my body, and I had never been beaten, I had no scars, unlike many of the clinic's other clients. None of my Peace Corps friends had been in Kenya during the farmers' protest or my imprisonment; they had all arrived after my release.

My case also involved some problems of legal theory. If the students could prove the facts of my arrest, near-execution, torture, and detention, that would be enough to show "persecution" as that term was understood in refugee law. And because I had suffered persecution already, the law would presume that I had a well-founded fear of future persecution. Thus I should be eligible for asylum unless the government's lawyer proved that the Kenyan government had so much improved its human rights record since 1993 that my fears were groundless. But had Moi persecuted me on account of one of the five grounds listed in the law? According to Dave and Bernie, I did not appear to have suffered persecution on account of my race, religion, nationality, or membership in the Kikuyu tribe; although one of my captors had shown anti-Kikuyu bias, Kikuyus were the largest tribe in the country, and most of its members were not persecuted. The legal category that best fit my situation was persecution on the basis of my political opinion. But was the farmers' boycott an expression of political opinion, or was it merely an instrument of economic leverage? I was jailed because I had tried to improve economic circumstances for the farmers. Did that count as a political action?

The circumstances of my departure from Kenya and my activities in the United States presented further legal problems. Individuals are eligible for asylum only if their reason for coming to the United States is to flee from persecution. But I had arrived on a student visa, and I had made the most of it, earning a bachelor's degree from a U.S. college and going on for a year of practical training. Those actions might convince Judge Churchill that I left Kenya for education, not out of fear of persecution. Furthermore, I still wanted to go to law school in the United States. That was why I had landed in the office of Dean Bellamy, who had sent me to the asylum clinic. Also, just before I met Dave and Bernie, I had filled out an application for admission to the University of Baltimore Law School. I hadn't mailed it yet, and I wanted Dave and Bernie to advise me whether filing it would jeopardize my asylum bid.

Finally, there was the problem of my 1997 return to Kenya to help get Njoka released from jail. In a previous clinic case, Judge Churchill had denied asylum because the applicant returned to his own country briefly. Would she decide that my 1997 return somehow rendered me ineligible for asylum?

I felt grateful that Dave and Bernie talked to me about the problems in my case. I was also happy that as we kept working together, they shared their plans for solving each problem. But the more I heard about asylum law and about the upcoming immigration court hearing, the more I doubted that Judge Churchill would believe me or care about me. As the weeks passed, I grew more despondent and ambivalent about even trying to remain in the United States.

FIVE

My Day in Court

For the first three months of 2001, I talked almost daily with Dave and Bernie, and I met with them every week as they addressed each of the many issues that my case presented. Bernie realized that the very first problems she and Dave needed to handle were my increasingly depressed and alienated mood and my inability or unwillingness to dredge up the details of my confinement and torture.

As I worked with the two students, my sleep became increasingly disturbed. Since my release from prison in Kenya, I had dreaded sleep, because I often dreamed that familiar yet hostile people were trying to kill me. When I tried to fight back in the dream, I would be unable to move my body either to defend myself or to escape from the threat. I would awaken only at the moment when someone was about to kill me.

Over the years, after I left Kenya and began my life in the United States, the nightmares had become somewhat less frequent, but they never went away. They reminded me that I was always in danger. To make myself feel better, I challenged myself to succeed and not to succumb to the fears that lived within me. But even when I was successful, as I was in school and in my financial affairs, I never achieved a sense of satisfaction. In fact, with each accomplishment, I felt a greater threat to my own stability.

I lived in constant fear of falling asleep. When I was awake, I often felt pressure above the back of my neck, as if my brain was swelling and would ooze out of my head. I would sometimes knock my head repeatedly against a wall, which seemed to relieve the pressure. I could also relieve the pressure temporarily by exercising or running. If I did not exercise for a couple of weeks, I would resume the pattern of sitting with my back to the wall and knocking my head against the wall for hours at a time. My friends would ask me why I was hurting myself. I didn't understand why, and I was embarrassed by my inability to explain it. So I just exercised a lot, and I avoided sleep so that I would not dream.

For a few weeks before I started to work with Dave and Bernie, I had not consistently maintained my regular exercise routine. Furthermore, I was living in a basement apartment in a very quiet suburban neighborhood in Virginia. In my apartment, I could bang my head against the wall as much as I wanted. Nobody noticed, and I didn't have to explain my conduct. Banging my head made me feel better, but Dave and Bernie's questions about my months in prison brought back the memories of my ordeal in a terrible way, and I felt worse again.

In one of our meetings, when the law students insisted that I reveal the details of what had happened after I turned myself in to the police, I had to fight the urge to bang my head against the wall of the interview room. I placed both hands behind my head and pressed hard in an effort to relieve the pressure. For a while, the pressure subsided, and I went into a mental state in which everything around me started to change. I began to dream with my eyes open. It was painful and awkward, and I did not know how to explain the situation to Bernie and Dave, so I kept it to myself, hoping they would not notice.

After that meeting, I contemplated killing myself. I thought of different ways to make my death as painless and as quick as possible. I considered parking my car on the train tracks, but I was concerned that a crash might derail the train and cause unnecessary deaths. I considered driving off a cliff but feared that I might not die and would have to live with the pain of a broken body. I also considered jumping off a building but could not come up with the perfect building. I looked around my apartment and saw an electrical extension cord that connected the television to the outlet on the wall. I thought of using the cord to hang myself in my apartment, but I realized that the basement's ceiling was not tall enough to hold both the rope and the length of my body.

I was psychologically and physically devastated. I could no longer sleep. Nightmares and fear invaded my nights; in the daytime, migraines and horrible images haunted me. I couldn't imagine being able to explain these things in a manner that someone else could understand.

One night, I went to my desk and impulsively booked a one-way ticket to Vancouver. I packed my clothes and sat down on the bed. I don't know why, but I started to cry. I banged my head against the wall as hard as I could. Curled into a fetal position in the corner of my bedroom, I tried to go to sleep on the floor, but sleep would not come. I thought about my father and wondered what he would say to me at that moment.

I remembered the day when the head teacher at the primary missionary school had come to my classroom, asked me an arithmetic question, and struck me in the face because I asked him to repeat it instead of answering it quickly. He knocked me against a wall, and I became unconscious. After regaining consciousness, I went home, hoping that my father would forbid me to go back to school. Instead, he insisted that I return and find a way to avoid conflict with that teacher.

"It doesn't matter what it takes," he told me. "If you run away from him, you'll never get what you need from school, and that is what he wants. Running away only makes you weaker and makes him stronger. You are better than that." Then he grabbed my hand and led me straight back to the school. He didn't say another word to me during the long walk. That silent walk to the school was as painful as my fear of being left in school with the head teacher.

When we got to the school, he went straight to the head teacher's office. He did not even knock as the head teacher required. This was very much out of character for my father. He told the teacher, "If my son can't learn, kill him; but don't beat him and then send him back to me because you can't teach him." Then he turned around as quickly as he had entered and walked out of the office, closing the door behind him.

I was shaking with fear, convinced that my father had just handed the teacher my death warrant. I couldn't tell whether my father was angry because I had run away from the teacher or because the teacher had hit me. Regardless, both the head teacher and I understood that he was not happy with either of us and that the situation must be handled in a different fashion. I waited for the head teacher to kill me, but instead he stared at me for a moment and said softly, "Go to your class." I always avoided any conflict with him, and he never hit me again. In fact, he was very diplomatic with me after that. We both understood that he could hit me again, but that if he ever did, my father would do something drastic. Neither of us knew what he would do.

As I recalled that day, it seemed as though I heard my father talking to me again. I could feel his presence in my apartment with me. I thought, "If I allow myself to run or die, those who imprisoned me will get stronger." I canceled the ticket to Canada, resolving to stay and seek the freedom that I hoped to find in America, without running away from the difficulties of telling my story to Judge Churchill.

The next morning, when I saw the law students, Bernie renewed her request that I see a mental health counselor. "I know someone who can help you," she said. "I want us to go together to see her. Her name is Judy Okawa. She is a psychologist, and she is highly experienced in dealing with people who have gone through experiences like yours. We want to ask her to counsel you and help us prepare you for the trial."

I took in the name Okawa and thought that she was probably African, from the Luo tribe. "How much does it cost?" I asked.

"You don't have to worry about money," she replied. "She works for a nonprofit organization that pays her from grants it receives. She won't charge you anything."

"I don't need a psychologist. I am not crazy," I insisted.

"Jeff, I've seen and worked with many people like you. You are not crazy, but you are having a lot of emotional problems because you went through stuff that was so scary that you haven't even been able to talk to us about it. We need to know the details of what happened to you so that we can help you, and that is why you and I are going to see Dr. Okawa. You will not be able to go through this trial without her help. She's the best you can get when it comes to working with people who have gone through what you did. I don't want to hear you say you aren't going, because we won't be able to help you with your case if you don't see her. If you don't like her, you can tell me, and we'll decide what to do. But right now, you must come with me to see her."

Bernie was so insistent that I agreed. We went to the third floor of a downtown Falls Church high-rise. According to the sign on the office door, this was the Center for Multicultural Human Services. We were greeted by a short man with a shaved head and a soft mustache. He had an Ethiopian accent and very strong Ethiopian features. After a few minutes, a middle-aged lady entered the room, smiling. In a very soft voice, she introduced herself. Contrary to my expectations, she was a white American.

"This is Jeff Ngarurih, the client I was telling you about," Bernie said.

"Great. Please come to my office." She led us into a corner office from which we could see the traffic slowly snaking its way across the main street of Falls Church. Dr. Okawa noticed that I was staring at the traditionally African art pieces that covered her walls.

"Some of my former clients gave those to me," she explained. She pointed to a small statue of male figures joined together in a circle. "This is my favorite. It was given to me by a client from central Africa. To me, it represents the unity of the earth."

"I like it," I told her.

"Is it familiar?" she asked.

"Not really, but it reminds me of something familiar."

"Tell us about it."

"Well, this is a council of elders, and the ball in the middle is a beer pot. Each of these elders should be holding a straw and sucking the beer from the pot."

Both Dr. Okawa and Bernie laughed. "What's familiar about that?" Bernie asked.

"It reminds me of my father's village council. The elders would come and sit around a huge pot of beer and talk about everything that was going around the village while I filled the pot with beer. They would all be bundled into a circle like that."

"That's very intuitive. I have never thought of it like that," Dr. Okawa replied. She then turned her attention to Bernie and inquired, "So, what's going on?"

"Well, we need your help to help Jeff. We hope that you can spend some time with him and let us know whether you can help him. He's been through a lot, and he's having trouble relating the details to us and to the government," Bernie explained.

"I can squeeze him into my calendar, but I will be pushing myself. I have people on my waiting list, but since his trial is coming up, I can spare some time. However, I cannot promise anything," she told us.

"That's great. I think we can work with that," Bernie responded.

The following day, I went to Dr. Okawa's office in the morning as we had scheduled. She asked me to call her Judy. I talked to her for about two hours.

A few days later, Bernie called me to share what Judy had told her. "Jeff," she said, "according to Judy, you have been handling your situation better than anyone could imagine. It's amazing that you have not killed yourself, become a drug addict, or gone insane. But working with her is going to take more time than she had expected. She's offering to spend the extra time with you so that you can explain your memory problems and your experiences to the judge. But before she starts working with you, she recommends that you be medically treated for depression. Can you work with her on that?"

"Is it that bad?" I asked.

"You experienced trauma that was more serious than anything she's seen in her career, and your symptoms are the most interesting she's come across. Your severe water torture has impaired your ability to recall the events of your imprisonment easily or accurately. Judy thinks that you're dealing with your memories of torture and imprisonment by repressing them. It's so bad that it will probably take longer than she had hoped before you start feeling like a normal person again. But she's willing to take the extra time with you if you'll take some antidepressant medicine. It will help you work with her and prepare for your hearing." Bernie was very frank with me, and I began to realize how much I needed her on my side.

Judy proposed that I meet with a psychiatrist who would prescribe the medications. I had never imagined myself as a mentally unstable person, and at first I objected. But Judy told me that my resistance was a normal reaction. "You have a strong ability to suppress your emotions, and you react to stress by ignoring it. You are able to do that better than most of us. But it won't work in the long run. I would like you to try the medication and let me know what you think after that." I agreed, and a few days later, I met with the psychiatrist.

After several weeks of taking antidepressants, I no longer had the urge to bang my head against the wall. My energy level increased dramatically, because I was able to sleep without nightmares. I no longer felt a need to scout the landscape for threats and escape routes. I was more focused. However, I lost my appetite and was unable to eat. I spoke with Judy about it, and the psychiatrist gave me a different type of antidepressant.

Judy is creatively methodical yet sensitive. She is the gentlest person I have ever met. During our sessions, she struggled to help me understand the emotional impact of my past experiences, including those dating back to my early life with my parents and brothers. She used a very simple but effective method that involved a sandbox in which I could re-create my childhood using models of action figures such as dolls, trucks, and toys. Each figure triggered a specific memory. Judy walked me through the memories, and together we explored how the emotions they evoked had influenced my decisions and how those decisions had affected my life. At some point, I started to appreciate my own willingness and determination to survive and thrive even when my chance of survival was diminished.

Judy consistently advised me to think of the sandbox as my past, my present, and my future. In it, I could re-create positive images of my life.

The sandbox

In the process, I constructed a model of my village using small huts that I found in her cabinet. I even re-created the cows and the fire pit where my father and I used to sit in the evenings after I brought the animals home from the forest. Later, Judy said to me, "I want you to remove anything you don't like in that model village, and I want you to tell me why."

Without even giving it a thought, I quickly removed the image of my older brother Mugo. "Why did you do that?" Judy asked.

"Because I hate him. He used to find pleasure in beating me up for no reason."

"See," Judy said, "you have the power to remove from your life anything that hurts you, and you don't have to be afraid of it anymore. Here in America, it is acceptable to avoid anything that threatens your life. Fear is accepted as a reason for avoidance."

Judy's remark provided the most enlightening and empowering moment I had ever known. I had the ability to remove or escape from anything that threatened my life. I had always known this in some intuitive way, but I had never been able to put it into words.

As we continued to work together, I realized my own power to remove the elements of my life that inhibited my desires and dreams. Just as I could physically remove from the sandbox a character that I did not like, I could overcome my fear of being hunted like an animal or killed by enemies. And just as I could create new models in the sandbox, I could create elements of a new life. I could imagine a future without fear.

After several sessions, Judy told Bernie that she might be able to help make progress on three of the problems with my case. She could explain to the court why my original application and testimony included chronological and other errors. She could help me recall the details of my incarceration so that I did not seem to be fabricating a story. And she could talk with me about my feelings of guilt for having left Kenya.

. . .

I met with Judy for about eleven hours over the course of two months, and I also kept meeting with Dave and Bernie, who tackled what they called the corroboration problem. Asylum applicants can lose otherwise good cases if they do not supply sufficient documentation to back up their stories.[1] This difficulty had to be approached on multiple levels.

One approach suggested by Dave and Bernie was to contact my Peace Corps friends. Although they were not in Kenya while I was in prison, some of them had heard about my detention even before we met in Kangaita, which would tend to prove that I had not made up the story for their benefit. These same friends could also corroborate the events of my story from shortly after my release until some time after my arrival in the United States. I could see that Judge Churchill might be skeptical that an American university would offer a basketball scholarship to someone who had never played basketball, so corroboration of this part of my story by independent American witnesses might help to dispel doubts about my credibility. I quickly gave Dave and Bernie permission to contact the former Peace Corps volunteers, who by now were scattered across the country and the world, and the students started tracking them down. I spoke with each of the former volunteers first and asked them to help me by cooperating with the law students. I told them that the students would need their written statements or, more likely, their sworn affidavits.

Because my Peace Corps friends could not directly corroborate my imprisonment, Bernie and Dave also needed affidavits from people in Kenya who knew that my story was true. These witnesses included my mother, who had visited me in jail after I was transferred to my home province; my little brother, Njoka, whose release from jail I had engineered; my best friend, Wash, who had gone through the boycott with me; and other farmers and members of the boycott committee.

There were two problems with getting affidavits from the people in Kenya. First, asking them to supply evidence for my court case could endanger them. If the Kenyan government intercepted the communications and found out that I was defending myself in court by criticizing Kenya's human rights practices, it could retaliate by arresting my friends or members of my family. Second, even if my friends and relatives were unafraid and willing to cooperate, physically obtaining their affidavits in time for the court hearing would be challenging. By the time Bernie and Dave identified all the corroborating testimony they wanted, it was mid-February, and the court required them to file all evidence at least ten days before the April 20 hearing. My friends and family did not have computers or access to email or faxes. The man who had the only telephone in Kangaita did not like to let other people use it. The only fax machine in the area was in the post office in the district headquarters, where incoming faxes could be read by the police. Federal Express delivery would be the most secure method of getting documents to or from Kenya. We could send packages to a FedEx office in Kerugoya, and that office would eventually send a messenger to Kangaita to request that the recipient pick up the package. But FedEx service between Washington and Kenya took five days one way and cost about $80 per package.

Furthermore, several of the witnesses, including my mother, spoke only Kikuyu or Swahili. They could draft affidavits in one of those languages, and the students could have them translated into English. But inviting my friends and relatives to write their own statements without help from the law students would risk the possibility that the statements would be riddled with irrelevancies and not focused on the particular facts that needed corroboration. My mother, in particular, was not well enough to draft an affidavit without help. According to Dave and Bernie, American lawyers usually interview their witnesses, draft statements for them, have the witnesses correct the drafts, redraft the statements to reflect the corrections, send them to the witnesses, have the witnesses sign and notarize them, and collect the statements for submission to the court. Following that procedure with witnesses who did not speak English, and with long delays in transmission time, would be a daunting and expensive task.

Nevertheless, the students wanted to obtain as much corroborating documentation as possible. For example, I had one piece of paper related to my imprisonment, a copy of the receipt for the funds that the farmers had put up as bond to obtain my release. But I didn't know whether it could be located—I had probably left that "peace bond" in my closet in Kangaita, and my older brothers might have discarded or destroyed the contents of my closet during the four years since I last left Kenya. Newspapers had carried reports of the farmers' boycott and President Moi's threats against the organizers, but I did not know where I had put the clippings. Other possible pieces of corroborating evidence included a copy, if one could be found, of the typed list of farmers' demands that I had presented to District Commissioner Tiliitei in 1992 and a copy of the draft constitution of the Kenya Tea Farmers Association, the farmers' union that I had tried to organize in the midst of the boycott. These papers, too, might never be found. I suspected that the man who wrote the constitution still had a copy, but I doubted that he would give it to anyone but me, fearing that if the government obtained it, he would land in jail.

With some misgivings, I agreed to write letters in Kikuyu to my friends and family in Kenya to ask for their help in obtaining documents and affidavits. I worried that the police might intercept our communications, putting these people in jeopardy. I also warned the students that Kenyans would not understand the urgency of an American court calendar and that it might take them months to find documents or write affidavits.

Nevertheless, Bernie and Dave began the long, slow process of gathering the necessary evidence. They also came up with an alternative plan for finding the newspaper articles about the boycott. They ascertained that the Library of Congress had microfiche copies of Kenya's *Daily Nation*, an English-language paper. They took me to the reading room of the Library of Congress, where the three of us spent hours scanning microfiche newspaper records from the summer of 1992. One afternoon, our eye strain was rewarded: I spotted the articles that could provide key elements of corroboration. One article, published on July 18, 1992, reported that "thousands of angry tea farmers" had staged a demonstration at the stadium in Kerugoya and that "their spokesman, Mr. David Wachira . . . accused the government of failing to expose the reason behind the refusal of the KTDA to review tea prices."[2] A second article, thirteen days later, reported that "President Moi yesterday warned those inciting farmers to stop picking tea that they will face dire consequences for their action."[3]

Unfortunately, the first article, about the boycott's spokesman, referred to me as "David Wachira," not "David Wachira Ngaruri," so even with the article in hand, we would need other evidence tying me to the boycott. I did, however, have the photographs that I had brought to the United States, which showed me addressing the rally with District Commissioner Tiliitei just behind me. Dave and Bernie believed that, together, the newspaper article and the photographs were probably sufficient to corroborate my claim that the protest and boycott had occurred and that I had been a leader. If they could get affidavits from Kenya in time, they would be able to show that I was not only a leader but the principal instigator of the boycott.

To equate violent suppression of the economic boycott with persecution on account of political opinion, the students decided to call Judge Churchill's attention to an event in colonial American history. They told me that the famous Boston Tea Party had been a precursor to the American Revolution and that it was a quintessentially political event, even though, like my protest, it arose from economic distress. The founders of the

United States had organized a nonviolent protest and boycott involving the very same product that I had grown in Kenya. Dave and Bernie hoped that this appeal to Judge Churchill's patriotism would help her see that an economic protest against a government policy was at root a political act.

The students had several ideas for addressing my motivation for emigrating. Apparently, it is not unusual for refugees to travel to the United States both to flee a persecuting government and to improve their economic prospects. This issue had come up a few years earlier, and the Board of Immigration Appeals had established that such a person qualified as a refugee, despite the mixed motivations, as long as a well-founded fear of persecution was one of the reasons for fleeing.[4] In my case, the students could show that my pursuit of an American education was my method of escape, not a separate reason for my flight from Kenya. I knew nothing about asylum in 1994 and 1995, and I had sought a student visa primarily as a means of avoiding new danger and the restrictions that Moi's government had placed on my political freedom.

There was also the matter of my application to the University of Baltimore Law School. Pursuit of even more education in America would emphasize my desire to remain in the United States to learn skills rather than merely to stay out of Kenya. Nonetheless, Dave and Bernie could not bring themselves to advise me to forgo the opportunity to become a lawyer simply because it might marginally improve my chance of winning my asylum case. They left the decision to me, and I did file the University of Baltimore application. But fate solved the problem: I was rejected. That settled the issue for the moment, but I told the students that I planned to file some other law school applications. They decided not to discourage me from trying to further my education.

. . .

As they planned for the hearing, Dave and Bernie had to grapple with one more problem that worried them a lot. How could they persuade Judge Churchill that I was eligible for asylum even though I had gone back to Kenya during the summer of 1997 to rescue Njoka from prison?

They developed two approaches to dealing with this problem. Interestingly, the first was based on an example from a Justice Department manual, titled *Basic Law Manual: U.S. Law and INS Refugee/Asylum Adjudications*. This 1994 manual had been written by the Asylum Office of the Department of Justice (which provided training for the asylum officers who initially adjudicated asylum applications) and published by the attorney general to guide the asylum officers in their work. In many respects, the manual was weighted against asylum applicants, interpreting ambiguous phrases or doctrines in ways that suggested that asylum applications should be denied. But, amazingly, the manual specifically addressed, in a helpful way, the issue of what to do in the case of a refugee who had briefly returned home for a family emergency. In a particular case, the manual stated, "an alien may be able to show that he or she returned to the home country involuntarily or for compelling reasons that justify having assumed the risk of persecution."[5] Then it provided an illustration that was almost exactly like my case:

> Y has presented an asylum claim that tends to show that Y has a well-founded fear of persecution. Before arriving in the United States, however, Y returned to his home country. He did so because his wife and children had been arrested and subjected to torture in response to his having left. While back home, Y and some of his compatriots broke his family out of jail and were able to escape the country together.[6]

Dave and Bernie were thrilled to find this passage; lawyers rarely found authoritative illustrations so close to the facts of their own case, they told me. There were only two differences between this example and my case. First, Njoka had apparently been jailed because of Mugo's enmity, not because I had fled Kenya, as in the example. The students considered this difference inconsequential because it did not diminish the urgency of my return, which was the point addressed by the illustration. Second, I had used legal means (hiring a lawyer) rather than illegal methods (breaking a family member out of jail) to free my brother. If anything, this difference should count in my favor.

Dave and Bernie's second approach to my 1997 return was to rely on a previous case that the CALS clinic had won, the *Getaneh* decision. Years earlier, some CALS students had represented Getaneh M. Getanch, a native of Ethiopia, who was living in Virginia when he applied for asylum. When an asylum officer referred his case to the immigration court, it was assigned to Judge Churchill.

Getaneh was from a region of Ethiopia in which the majority of the population was Muslim. But at the age of thirteen, he became an evangelical Christian. As a young adult, he began trying to convert his Muslim neighbors to his faith. As a result, on four occasions, the local authorities arrested him, hung him upside down by his feet, burned him with cigarettes, flailed him with whips, and poured hot oil on the soles of his feet until he agreed to sign promises to stop preaching evangelical Christianity. During his fourth arrest, his family bribed his guards to let him escape, and he walked for five days through the desert to the border of neighboring Djibouti, narrowly escaping death by dehydration.

Getaneh lived in Djibouti for ten years. For part of that time, he was in a U.N. refugee camp. Later, he served as an assistant at the U.S. embassy in Djibouti. Several times, when relations warmed between Djibouti and Ethiopia, the government of Djibouti attempted to deport him back to Ethiopia. On one of those occasions, the Djibouti government put him on a train bound for Ethiopia, where he had been persecuted. The American ambassador and a local office of the United Nations intervened, and the train was stopped.

In 1991, the government of Ethiopia, then headed by dictator Mengistu Haile Mariam, was replaced by a regime that some thought would be more respectful of human rights. Getaneh went to the Ethiopian embassy in Djibouti and inquired whether it was safe for him to return to his country. When embassy officials told him that the new regime would respect his freedom of religion and his right to speak his mind, he flew to Addis Ababa, the Ethiopian capital, with the intention of returning home and proselytizing once more.

He was arrested at the airport, taken away by military officers, and put in a small room with barred windows and no furniture. He demanded that his guards take him to see the director of this facility. The director sympathized with him and spoke to him gently, saying that his own hands were tied by the Ethiopian government. Getaneh was wanted by the Muslim authorities in his home province—the very people who had tortured him in the past. The central Ethiopian government had to return Getaneh to these local authorities because it desired peace with the provincial government.

Through a friend, Getaneh bribed his new jailers to let him escape, disguised himself, and hid in Addis Ababa for a few weeks. Then he made his way back to Djibouti and immediately flew to the United States on a valid visa, which he had obtained in connection with his prior work for the U.S. embassy. Once in the United States, he applied for asylum. When his case was referred to Judge Churchill for a decision, religious organizations in the Washington area recommended that he get help from students at CALS.

During the hearing, Judge Churchill did not doubt Getaneh's account of the events that had befallen him. However, after hearing testimony for an entire day, she turned down his bid for asylum and ordered him deported to Ethiopia. Her decision was based on one of the four "cessation" clauses in the international Convention Relating to the Status of Refugees, which specify circumstances under which a person ceases to have refugee status. None of these four clauses appeared in the corresponding U.S. law. Nonetheless, Judge Churchill chose to rely on one of them, the clause which provides that a person ceases to be a refugee if "he has voluntarily re-availed himself of the protection of the country of his nationality."[7]

According to Judge Churchill, Getaneh's voluntary return was a "reavailment" through which he sought the protection of Ethiopia, making his four prior experiences of imprisonment and torture irrelevant to his case. He might still have won asylum if he had been directly threatened with persecution anew, after he got to the Addis Ababa airport. Judge Churchill noted that the jailer in Addis Ababa had said that the Ethiopian government planned to return Getaneh involuntarily to the provincial authorities in order to make peace with the Muslim leaders of that province. But, according to her, the jailer's statement did not prove that Getaneh would be persecuted by either the central or the provincial government. In fact, the judge suggested, the government might have been recruiting him to serve as an emissary of peace, the central government's go-between who would speak on its behalf to the provincial government.

In summary, Judge Churchill ordered Getaneh deported because he had returned to his country briefly to ascertain whether he could live safely there. Because of this return visit, Getaneh lost his right to be protected as a refugee.

The decision angered Phil. CALS was set up to teach its students about trial preparation and practice, not appellate work, so its students didn't work on appeals. Phil usually referred appeals to law firms that employed graduates of the clinic. But he was so mad that he decided to write Getaneh's appellate brief himself.

It took a year for the Board of Immigration Appeals to decide the case. Finally, it reversed the decision and granted asylum to Getaneh.

The board agreed with Phil's argument that Congress had not incorporated any of the international convention's cessation clauses into U.S. law. It wrote that Judge Churchill "gave inappropriate weight to the 1951 Convention. . . . Under United States asylum law, a victim of past persecution does not necessarily lose his 'refugee status' by attempting to 're-avail' himself of the protection of his country of nationality. Therefore, we find that the Immigration Judge incorrectly determined that [Getaneh] was no longer eligible for asylum due to Article 1(C)(1) of the 1951 Convention."[8]

Bernie and Dave informed me that this decision wasn't quite as helpful for me as it seemed, however. The board designates only a small fraction of its cases as "precedent decisions," which are binding on immigration judges in future cases. The board did not designate the *Getaneh* case as a precedent, so it would not necessarily affect my case. But the board had rebuked Judge Churchill for treating a refugee's brief return to the persecuting country as a disqualification, so perhaps she would be loath to make that particular mistake again.

I was outraged when Bernie and Dave told me Getaneh's story and explained how Judge Churchill had handled his case. I identified strongly with him. I could picture him in his cell in Addis Ababa, tormented by his misguided decision to return to Ethiopia. I knew how difficult it must have been to offer a bribe to the jailers, for even though bribing officials is very common in Africa, one can never be certain that offering a bribe won't result in even worse trouble. I felt angry that after all Getaneh had gone through, Judge Churchill had decided to force him to go back to face more torture in Ethiopia. And I feared that she would do the same thing to me.

· · ·

Dave and Bernie spent most of the next two months gathering corroborating evidence, while I returned again and again to Judy's office, where she helped me to face the horrible memories of my arrest, torture, and incarceration. Reliving these experiences was so painful that I again suffered from insomnia, and at times I simply wanted to drop my case. But Judy encouraged me to continue both the case and my work with her.

Dave and Bernie found and telephoned all my Peace Corps friends, several of whom were working abroad. With help from the students, all of them wrote corroborating affidavits. But obtaining similar affidavits from my friends and family members in Kenya was much more difficult. Dave and Bernie searched for people who were planning to go to Kenya and who might be willing to make a trip to Kangaita.

They also spent many hours trying to find academic expert witnesses who would supplement the published reports on Kenyan human rights violations. The published reports were useful, but the students wanted expert testimony on the human rights violations most relevant to my case, such as the government's restrictions on tea farmers and its use of torture, particularly water torture, against dissidents. Some of this work led to dead ends. The students contacted nearly a dozen experts on Africa, at universities and organizations all over the United States and Great Britain. But most either were too busy to help or worked for institutions that precluded them from testifying in asylum cases. Others lacked the particular expertise we needed. For example, the International Center for Prison Studies at Kings College School of Law in London did excellent reports on prison conditions in various countries, but it had never done a study on prison conditions in Kenya, because the Kenyan government had never requested such a report.

In the midst of this research, the students received my INS file, in response to the Freedom of Information request that Phil had filed in November. The notes of Patricia Craddock, the asylum officer, confirmed that I had made several incorrect statements to her. I had clearly stated that my arrest was in May 1992, not in July or August. I had also exaggerated certain facts. For instance, I had gotten carried away and told Craddock that "almost every tea farmer in Kenya supported our cause," although I had knowledge only of the activities in Central Province, the country's main tea-growing area. I had claimed that we had arranged a boycott and had stopped most of the country from working, not limiting my statement to tea farmers. Craddock followed up by asking, "You mean four people [the boycott leaders] caused the entire country to stop working?" But I had not accepted her invitation to qualify my remark. Instead, I had replied, "Yes, amazingly enough we did." I had also told her that an estimated one hundred thousand marchers had been at the stadium. Now, through my discussions with the students and with Judy, I had come to realize that even with the stadium full and surrounded by protesting farmers, the number of people in the march was probably closer to thirty thousand.

When we looked at Craddock's notes, the students and I understood why she had referred the case to Judge Churchill rather than granting asylum. If I really had brought the entire labor force of Kenya to a halt,

Craddock could have easily found evidence of such an event in newspaper stories from the period. If I had told her a more accurate version of what had happened, I might well have won asylum at the first stage of the process.

The students thought that the result might have been very different if I had been represented by a lawyer or law student before the interview. For example, Craddock had asked, referring to newspaper coverage of the protest, "Would you happen to have any articles?" I should have said that my protest had indeed been reported in the newspapers, but that I didn't currently have copies. Instead, I had told her, "No, but I use the Internet now and political opponents are being persecuted." If Dave and Bernie had been representing me, they would have found the corroborating articles from the *Daily Nation* before the interview or at least would have asked for more time to locate them.

Some of the students' work went nowhere, and some of their research, such as their study of Craddock's notes, revealed additional problems. But, as the deadline for filing the evidence neared, the pieces began to fall into place. In late March, Judy reported to Dave and Bernie that I had finally been able to reconstruct a much more accurate picture of my persecution. I could now definitely identify the date of my arrest as early August and the date of my release as just before Easter. Also, the antidepressant medication I had been taking was improving my ability to testify about my experiences.

• • •

By the beginning of April, Bernie and Dave had compiled 561 pages of evidence. At the top of this massive document submission was my 47-page affidavit, which the students had drafted for me on the basis of our weeks of work together. I was fascinated by how Bernie and Dave combined their different skills to produce this affidavit. Because Bernie was more sensitive to my emotional state, she was the one who was able to get me to explain my story. But once she had teased all the details out of me, Dave was the master at putting them into exactly the words I would have wanted to use if English had been my first language. Bernie was the intercultural bridge, but Dave drafted almost the entire affidavit.

Dave and I had grown much more comfortable with each other, and I learned a lot about American culture from him. Several weeks after he wrote my affidavit, he invited me to a party at his apartment, and I met his friends. At the end of the party, we walked to a bar together. Dave confided in me then that he had vastly underestimated the difficulty of obtaining detailed information from a person from another culture and that, without Bernie, he never would have been able to understand my experiences.

Most of my affidavit consisted of a very detailed narrative of my odyssey. In addition, six paragraphs explained why I had earlier provided incorrect dates for the boycott and other critical events.

In the package of evidence, my affidavit was followed by twelve other affidavits, amounting to 80 pages altogether. Six of them were from Kenyan witnesses. Wash had collected these affidavits, along with the peace bond and other key documentary evidence from my home. With his help, the students had even obtained an affidavit from the taxi driver who had driven me home from jail when I was finally released. Dave and Bernie received the final Federal Express package from Kenya just in time to file the papers in court. Most of the other corroborating affidavits were from the Peace Corps volunteers who had befriended me in Kenya and helped me come to the United States, including Phil Chinnici, Grant Ingram, and Jay Sugnet.

Judy Okawa's expert affidavit came next in the pile of written evidence. She planned to testify personally, but Dave and Bernie wanted Judge Churchill (who knew Judy from several previous cases) to know in advance what she would say. Judy related the extensive diagnostic work she had done with me and the psychological evaluation tests she had performed. She reported her conclusions and her basis for reaching them.

She described the difficult time I had experienced in several sessions with her, as I mentally relived the torture of the water cell. I had suffered from "profound visual, auditory, and tactile deprivation," Judy wrote, because I had been kept "in complete isolation, without clothes, without light, without any way to judge the passing of time, without any way to control [my] body temperature, and without nutrition." She explained that I "suffered many of the symptoms reported in the research literature about sensory deprivation."

She characterized my experience as "dissociation, which is a subjective sense of leaving one's body," noting that I had described my dissociative experiences "in the most eloquent detail." In fact, she considered my memories of kicking my own body in the water cell to see if it was alive "the most convincing descriptions of a dissociative episode that this clinician has ever heard." She concluded that I had "experienced a number of forms of torture in the following categories: psychological torture, physical torture, sensory deprivation, social deprivation, sleep deprivation, nutritional deprivation, hygiene deprivation and health deprivation."

In summary, Judy stated that I continued to suffer from complex posttraumatic stress disorder with severe memory disturbance and that, although her diagnosis was based on my reports to her, I was entirely credible. "Dissociative experiences are rarely, if ever, described convincingly by people who attempt to malinger, or falsify, symptoms. He did not over-report experiences of torture, rather stating that he was never beaten while in prison." She added her prognosis for my future: "This is a young man with great strength of character, a sharply honed sense of right and wrong, fine intelligence, and clear leadership qualities. I have no doubt that he will make significant contributions in his life."

Dave and Bernie followed Judy's affidavit with statements from two experts who could clarify aspects of my case about which Judge Churchill might have doubts. A professor whose expertise was cross-cultural communication helped to explain why I had originally gotten the dates wrong. He said that rural Kenyans ordered their lives by calendar seasons rather than by dates; that most of them do not know the day, month, or year of their birth; and that, for them, time is cyclical rather than linear. An expert on Kenyan native languages confirmed the plausibility of my statement that I understood the guards in the forest when they spoke

Swahili but that I could not understand them when they spoke Kalenjin. She reported that it is common for several languages to be spoken in the same conversation in Kenya and that native Kikuyu speakers could not understand Kalenjin without special training.

Dave and Bernie's next submissions were some powerful original documents to substantiate my story: large color photographs of my speech in the stadium in Kerugoya, the peace bond posted by the farmers for my release from prison, my restrictive tea license, the petition that we farmers had presented to District Commissioner Tiliitei, the draft constitution for the farmers' union that I had tried to start, the newspaper articles from the *Daily Nation,* and a letter from a Nairobi solicitor to Bernie. This solicitor confirmed that if records of my conviction for breach of the peace existed, they would be handwritten, and it would take at least three months for the court to produce them. Thus they would not be available in time for Judge Churchill's hearing.

Bernie and Dave also filed documents showing my achievements during my years in the United States, including my high school equivalency certificate, my college diploma, and the awards I had won while at school. To prove that my 1997 return to Kenya was a genuine family emergency, they introduced documents about Njoka's jailing and release: the short transcript of his guilty plea, the court's sentence of eight years in prison, my request to the courts for a copy of the case records, and the appeal written by the lawyer I had retained. These documents were followed by the last element of the proof package, the reports from the State Department, the U.N. Rapporteur, and many human rights organizations documenting Kenya's suppression of political rights and its mistreatment of prisoners, including those arrested for political offenses.

The Immigration and Naturalization Service had a right to offer evidence, too. But it filed none. The students told me that this was customary: in asylum hearings, INS lawyers usually tried to break the story of the applicant through cross-examination, not by presenting their own evidence.

When they filed the written evidence, the students also gave Judge Churchill a 48-page pretrial brief, complete with 288 footnotes, which summarized all the submitted evidence. It also laid out the facts of my case, which showed that I had been persecuted, and justifiably feared future persecution, on account of my political opinions. In addition, the brief presented the students with an opportunity to educate Judge Churchill on the other legal issue lurking in the background, the effect of my two-month return to Kenya in 1997.

Dave and Bernie worried about how much prominence to give that issue. On the one hand, if they dwelt on it extensively, they risked blowing it up into the main issue in the case, forcing Judge Churchill to focus on it. On the other hand, if they paid little attention to it, they would forgo their opportunity to argue that it should not be a basis for denying asylum.

They decided, in the end, to give this issue four pages of the brief, plus an appendix. They began by quoting the government's own *Basic Law Manual* and the example it gave of a man who returned to his home country to break his family out of jail. They then pointed out that my return had been entirely selfless: I had risked my own life to help free a brother who was actually more like a son, because I had been Njoka's surrogate parent after our father died. They added a footnote to try to forestall Judge Churchill from relying on the international convention on refugees, as she had in *Getaneh*, to disqualify me. They argued that the re-availment clauses of the convention did not apply to U.S. asylum cases, which should be evaluated according to the Refugee Act passed in the United States, not the international convention. As authority, Bernie and Dave cited the unpublished *Getaneh* decision, in which the Board of Immigration Appeals had reversed an immigration judge (they did not rub it in by mentioning her name) who had given what the board deemed "inappropriate weight" to the convention. And to make sure that she read the strong language from the board, they attached, as an appendix, a copy of the board's decision in *Getaneh*.

In preparation for the hearing, I participated in a four-hour mock trial, in which Phil played the judge, another clinic student played the INS lawyer, and Bernie, Dave, and I played ourselves. To get ready for this "moot court," the students prepared their direct examination questions for me and for Judy Okawa, and they tried to anticipate the cross-examination and any legal or procedural problems that might arise. In the moot court, we rehearsed various contingencies, including questions from the judge about my 1997 return.

Just before the hearing, the mail brought two good surprises. The first was a notice that I had been accepted by an American law school, the Southern New England School of Law. The second was a real shock, in the form of a notice from a branch of the U.S. government that dealt with immigration but had nothing to do with my asylum case. Months earlier, the clinic had filed an application for the annual diversity visa lottery on my behalf, as it did for all its clients. Under federal law, the U.S. State Department invites nationals of most countries—other than those already represented by very large U.S. immigrant populations—to enter a lottery to emigrate to the United States. About 10 million people apply each year. From these, the department selects one hundred thousand finalists, just 1 percent of the total. About half of those finalists end up not qualifying for visas—for example, if they have certain disqualifying diseases, or if they have not received sufficient education or training.[9] So in the end, the State Department gives out about fifty thousand visas each year, to half of 1 percent of the lottery entrants, such a small fraction that filing the application is almost not worth the effort. But CALS filed applications for its clients because its directors had figured that over a ten-year period, the clinic would have more than a hundred clients, and it was plausible to think that one of them might win the lottery.

I was the one! My notice said that I was a finalist for the fiscal year 2002 lottery; I had been "randomly selected and registered for further consideration." This meant that my name was one of the hundred thousand names drawn. That was great news. If I actually received a diversity lottery visa, I could become a legal permanent resident within months. In contrast, even if I won my asylum case, I would have to wait in line for several years before becoming a permanent resident.

Dave and Bernie cautioned me that becoming a finalist did not necessarily mean that I would actually be interviewed or considered for a visa. The State Department issued a serial number to each finalist. Between October 1, 2001, and September 30, 2002, it would work its way forward through the list, month by month. If the department reached my serial number by September 30, 2002, the end of the government's fiscal year, it would interview me to see whether I was eligible for a visa. But if it did not get to my number, my status as a finalist would expire at that time. Unfortunately, I had a high number, and at the monthly rate at which the department usually moved through the serial numbers, it would not get to me before September 30.

The letter from the State Department directed me to submit additional forms, a recent photograph, and certain biographical information. Dave and Bernie agreed to help me do so, warning me that because my number was so high, my chance of actually getting a diversity lottery visa was considerably lower than my chance of winning asylum. Furthermore, distribution of fiscal year 2002 diversity lottery visas wouldn't start for another six months; and because of my high number, if the State Department reached me at all, it would not do so for almost a year and a half. Obviously, I had to go ahead with the asylum hearing; and, despite being selected for further consideration, I could not rely on the hope of succeeding in the lottery.

· · ·

The hearing day arrived. When I entered the court's waiting room, I saw several small groups of people huddled together, whispering; in most of them, one person wore a suit and carried or wheeled massive files. I spotted Bernie and Dave. Bernie hugged me and then led me by the hand through a hallway into Judge Churchill's courtroom.

I had been in this room once before, for my scheduling hearing. But now I felt for the first time how much power this room contained, and how critically the future course of my life depended on what would happen here. Judge Churchill was not yet in the courtroom, so I had time to absorb the surroundings. To one side of the judge's raised desk were the flags of the United States and the Department of Justice. Above the desk hung the huge Justice Department seal, an eagle holding a bundle of arrows in its sharp claws. I began to sweat, but Bernie reassured me by explaining who would be in court and where each person would sit.

People began to file into the room. I sat with Bernie at one of the two counsel tables. The INS attorney sat at the other table, on the opposite side of the room. Bernie told me that his name was Michael Metzgar. Phil arrived, and he and Judy Okawa sat in the audience section. Dave kept walking in and out of the courtroom. At one point, he gestured for me to join him in the corridor. I followed him there. He was waiting for me, arms folded across his chest. When he saw me, he put his hands in his pants pockets, shook the pockets from the inside, and said, out of the blue, "That is a very nice suit. Do you have a hard time getting suits that fit you?"

"Not really," I told him. "I get my suits at Big and Tall." I couldn't figure out why he had called me out of the courtroom; surely it was not to talk about my suit. Bernie joined us and asked, "What's going on?"

"Nothing," Dave said. "I just wanted to check with my man and see whether he is okay." He gave her a glance indicating that he wanted to be alone with me. Bernie caught the signal and walked past us. Then Dave added, "I just wanted to know how you're dealing with all this. You know, this is it—this is the event we've all been preparing for."

I smiled at him, realizing that he was more nervous than I was and that he needed reassurance. "Dave, it's a trial. I have been tried before, and nothing here seems strange to me. At least I know that here in America the system works, and the judge will decide based on the law. In my country, someone pays the judges or gives them orders about what to do. So relax and do what you need to do, and I'll do my part."

"Damn!" he blurted out. "You're fine. Let's go do it!" We walked back into the courtroom.

I had seen trials on television, and I expected someone to yell, "Oyez, oyez, oyez, the court is in session, Honorable Joan Churchill presiding." Instead, Judge Churchill simply entered the room. For a while, she walked back and forth behind her desk, arranging papers. She turned on a tape recorder and started mumbling into a microphone, so faintly that she seemed to be purring only to herself. Then, more audibly, she announced, "This court is in session." She slumped as she sat in her chair. During the hearing, she often stood up and walked around, and I suspected that it was physically painful for her to remain seated for long periods. She also interrupted the hearing periodically when court clerks entered the room from a door behind her and handed her piles of papers to sign.

She began the hearing by returning to the issue of the erroneous summons. At the scheduling hearing, Metzgar's predecessor had promised to file an amended summons within a week, but despite repeated calls and reminders from Dave and Bernie, there had been no response until a few days before the hearing. Now Metzgar withdrew the allegation that I had failed to be at Hartnell College when the school was not in session, and Dave and Bernie admitted that after filing my asylum application, I had ceased to be a student.

During these preliminaries, and throughout the hearing that followed, I watched Judge Churchill, but she glanced at me only occasionally, avoiding mutual eye contact. She looked at me when she seemed certain that I was not looking at her, and then she looked away as soon as I turned in her direction. Our eyes met once, but she quickly frowned and then stared in the opposite direction before turning to the papers on her desk and writing something on them. She glanced at me again, and I thought I saw disgust or resentment in her face. I felt a chill down my spine. I feared that no matter what Dave and Bernie and I did, she had already decided to deport me to Kenya. During the hours that passed, she rarely acknowledged my presence, often directing questions to Dave and Bernie. Even when she did ask me a question, she looked at one of the students while she did so, as if I had no significant relationship to the subject under discussion. I felt demeaned and dehumanized because I was trying to tell the story of my life—which had cost me so much pain to reconstruct—to someone who treated me as if I were not in the room. I could not believe that she was going to judge my case fairly.

Rifling through the stack of documents the students had submitted, Judge Churchill asked Metzgar whether he objected to any of the documents being admitted into evidence. He did not, and I saw Dave breathe a sigh of relief. But then Judge Churchill did a surprising and troubling thing. Turning to the students, she asked, "You also turned in a brief?"[10]

"Yes, Your Honor."

"You [attached] copies of [an] unpublished decision . . . which I have to return to you because unpublished decisions cannot be cited and it is not proper to cite them now. . . . You can make the arguments but not cite any cases, so I will give those [pages] back to you." She physically unstapled the *Getaneh* decision from the students' brief and handed it back to them. At the time, I did not appreciate the significance of this maneuver, but I could see that Bernie seemed frustrated, and Phil looked stunned.

Phil later told me that judges sometimes refuse to consider arguments or precedents that they regard as irrelevant or invalid. But this was the first time he had ever seen a judge physically remove part of a brief and return it to an advocate. It worried him for many reasons. First, her removal of the *Getaneh* decision meant that she probably had not read it, even though this decision, reversing her erroneous reliance on the international convention, was the basis for one of our two arguments for why my return to Kenya in 1997 should not be a major strike against me. Second, if I lost the case and appealed, my lawyers would have to show that they had made their arguments to the trial judge and that the trial judge had rejected them. Her refusal to keep the *Getaneh* decision in the physical record of the case meant that it would not be transmitted to the Board of Immigration Appeals as part of that record.

In addition, her claim that "it's not proper to cite" unpublished board decisions seemed wrong to Phil. The immigration court had no rules either permitting or prohibiting a lawyer from trying to persuade a judge on the basis of a particularly apt unpublished decision of the board. But the board itself did have a rule on that subject, applicable to briefs filed with the board, which read: "Citation to unpublished decisions is discouraged because these decisions are not controlling on any other case.

When it is necessary to refer to an unpublished decision, the reference should include the alien's full name, alien registration number, the adjudicator, and the decision date. . . . A copy of the decision should be provided whenever possible."[11] Phil reasoned that if the board itself could consider its unpublished decisions under some circumstances, the lower immigration courts in which the cases were tried should be equally able to consider those decisions.

Dave gave a short opening statement, summarizing once again the facts and the law. Then Judge Churchill turned to Metzgar, asking, "What's your position on the case?"

"The [Immigration and Naturalization] Service opposes a grant of asylum, Your Honor."

Judge Churchill stared at him and seemed baffled, perhaps because Metzgar didn't state any reason for opposing asylum. "Did you want to make an opening statement?"

"No. The Service waives opening statement."

I surmised that Metzgar was so sure of an outcome in his favor that he believed he didn't need to do anything. But it was clear that Judge Churchill didn't like his response. She would have preferred to understand the government's objection. "It would help me, though, if you would let me know . . . why."

"The credibility is my main concern, Your Honor."

Judge Churchill seemed surprised, probably because she was familiar with the very extensive record the students had compiled, nailing down corroboration for all my testimony, even including expert statements that rural Kenyans don't pay much attention to calendar dates. "We have intensive materials," she said. "We have a lengthy statement."

"I would like to cross-examine him, Your Honor, on the founding of the organization . . . that allegedly brought the entire country to a standstill where the boycott involved 100,000 farmers. . . . An incident of this magnitude would have been more prominently displayed."

Bernie and Dave had been hoping that Metzgar would focus on credibility, not on why I left Kenya or on my 1997 return trip. They were not worried about my credibility because they had backup for every part of my story; even Judge Churchill seemed impressed by their "intensive" packet of evidence. In fact, in talking about bringing the country to a halt and the involvement of "100,000" farmers in the protest, Metzgar seemed to be relying on the short report that Patricia Craddock had written, based on the statement that I had later corrected. Metzgar seemed unfamiliar with my new lengthy affidavit or the other evidence in the file. The students had told me that the government lawyers were often so overburdened with cases that they did not read the files before going to court, choosing to rely primarily on their impromptu cross-examination of whatever oral testimony they heard.

Judge Churchill signaled that she was not likely to have doubts about the veracity of my story. She asked Metzgar, "Do you see any legal issues in the case?"

Metzgar could not see where she was trying to lead him. "No, Your Honor. I see this as just a credibility question. If the government did persecute the respondent because of his views regarding the tea cooperative . . . that could be a valid claim for political reasons."

This was going well, I thought. The INS was conceding that the only issue in the case was my credibility, and it didn't share Dave and Bernie's concern that engaging in an economic protest might not be considered political.

"What about the fact that he returned to his country and was there for a couple of months and had no problems after that happened?" the judge asked.

This looked like trouble. I might yet have a problem, not with the INS but with Judge Churchill herself, because of my two-month return. And she had just refused to consider the *Getaneh* decision in which the board had addressed that very issue in a way that favored my case.

Finally, Metzgar caught on and seemed to understand where she wanted him to go. "That could go to the respondent's claim that he would be persecuted if he were to be returned to Kenya at this stage."

Judge Churchill asked Bernie to address the point. Bernie noted that my return had been brief and had been undertaken under extraordinary circumstances. She said that I would testify that while I was there I had a "very low profile" and avoided any political activities and also that a police officer had warned me that I was being watched. "We also briefed this issue, and we have identified an unreported [unpublished] opinion—"

Judge Churchill cut her off. "There is to be no mention of any unreported opinions."

Bernie retreated to her other argument, the example in the government's own manual on asylum law. "Your Honor, then we would also like to point out that we did cite to the INS *Basic Law Manual*, pages 20 to 21."

Judge Churchill responded, "I am not familiar with the document. What's the INS *Basic Law Manual?*" I was very surprised that an immigration judge, who worked for the Department of Justice and decided asylum cases every week, had never heard of the asylum law manual that the attorney general had published during her years on the bench.

Before Bernie could say anything, Metzgar, who litigated asylum cases every week for the INS, interjected, "I am not familiar with that document either, Your Honor."

"That's curious," she said.

Ignoring the fact that the publisher of the manual, the attorney general, was also his own boss, Metzgar tried to minimize its significance and explain why he was unaware of it. "It may be an operation manual that the operational personnel use in their standard operating procedures but it is not one that the litigation staff is familiar [with]."

Bernie frowned and bit her lower lip, clearly thinking about how to respond. But before Bernie could react, Judge Churchill asked Dave to present the students' first witness, Dr. Okawa. She had interrupted Bernie's attempt to explain the significance of the manual and the similarity of its example to the facts of my return to help Njoka. Perhaps, I hoped, Judge Churchill had read the argument on that point in the students' brief.

Dave showed that Judy Okawa was qualified to be an expert witness and led her through her direct testimony. Judy stated that I had suffered through a terrifying ordeal. "I have never had a case that was quite so clear about sensory deprivation," she said. "Mr. Ngarurih was deprived of all stimuli that we use normally to have an awareness of life going on around us, like a passage of time. . . . He was deprived of everything except the feeling of the water, which is a constant threat of death." She also explained, in terms of my trauma, why my original asylum application and my interview with Craddock had included errors such as incorrect dates.

Addressing Metzgar's concern head on, Dave asked, "Do you have any doubt as to his credibility?"

"I do not," Judy asserted. "I don't have a single doubt about his story [and] the symptoms are consistent with the experiences he has claimed."

Metzgar tried just one cross-examination question before wisely refraining from asking Judy any others. He noted that, in her report, Judy had mentioned that I had also suffered traumatic events at the hands of my older brothers. Might these have contributed to my symptoms?

Judy turned this question into another positive statement on my behalf. "I have the sense that his childhood experience is what prepared him to have the strength to survive the extreme sensory deprivation in solitary confinement that he had."

When Judy left the witness stand, it was my turn to testify, and Bernie led me through my life's story. This time, when I discussed the farmers' protest, I correctly described it as occurring during the summer, not the spring, and I said that thirty thousand people, not one hundred thousand, attended the protest. I explained why the newspaper article about my speech referred only to "David Wachira" and not "David Wachira Ngarurih": "In Kenya, we don't address each other with your last name because your last name . . . represent[s] your father. . . . We address each other with your names. Like in Kenya, people would refer to me as David Wachira, they would see me as Wachira, they would not see me as Mr. Ngarurih."

Bernie's questions took me through the protest, my arrest, and my near-execution in the forest. Then she asked, "Mr. Ngarurih, what is the hardest part of the entire period that you spent in solitary confinement?"

"The part where I was in the water," I answered. She followed up with some objective questions about the depth of the water and my lack of food, drink, and toilet facilities. Then she asked, "Could you describe to the court how you feel right now talking about your experience in that flooded cell?"

"I don't like talking about it but if it's necessary for me to talk about it today in court—"

Judge Churchill interrupted, "Are you sure it is really necessary given his feelings?"

I thought that she was discouraging this line of Bernie's questioning because she didn't want to hear testimony that might move her to rule in my favor. But later Dave told me that her question was actually a very good sign for me. If she had any doubts about whether I was telling the truth, she would have wanted me to keep talking so that she or Metzgar could probe for inconsistencies. That she was willing to forgo even one area of testimony suggested that she had heard enough to judge me credible.

Bernie moved me quickly through the rest of my testimony, covering my solitary confinement, my release on the peace bond, and the farmers' pledges of their land to obtain my release. I concluded by pointing out that I would now be more at risk than I had been in 1992, because with an American college degree, "I can understand these [economic] problems more clearly and . . . rethink their solutions. That would be more of a threat."

Judge Churchill recessed the hearing, and we returned to her court the following week for Metzgar's cross-examination. It turned out he had only a few questions, primarily about my relationship to the committee that tried to form a tea farmers' union.

Bernie followed up with a few final questions. She wanted me to end by explaining why I would still be at risk in Kenya, so she asked, "If you were to go back to Kenya, what would you do?"

"I don't think that I would be safe . . . because of my big mouth," I said. "I'm not the kind of person who sees injustice [and just] stands there [without being] able to condemn what I believe is wrong. . . . I would continue to stand against injustice and I would stand against any corruption and I would stand against any government activity that suppresses people's minds."

Judge Churchill turned to Metzgar and asked again about his position on the case. This time, after hearing the testimony, Metzgar conceded that "the government finds the respondent to be convincing in his testimony and his demeanor to be convincing." Curiously, however, he added, "But the government isn't able to agree to asylum at this time because if . . . it was this large organization of . . . farmers [why] didn't it get any mention as an organization in the 1992 country report? . . . There is enough of a credibility question mark there that I can't agree to a grant of asylum because of that." He was referring to the State Department's annual *Country Reports on Human Rights Practices,* one of which focused on human rights abuses in Kenya.

Judge Churchill was on the ball. "What about the news articles? There are some news articles that mention it, from the Kenyan newspapers."

"Yes, that's true, Your Honor. . . . And that adds to the credibility of the respondent. But then . . . there is the fact that the boycott is over and the price [for tea] which was the primary reason that the boycott took place was increased [while the respondent was in jail]. [That] leads me to believe that the respondent would not be subject to further persecution if he was to return because the reason is no longer there for him to be protesting." I couldn't believe that he was implying that although I had been tortured and jailed, I should be deported because I had been somewhat successful in forcing the government to alter its policies. Apparently it was evident to Metzgar that the government's price hike was sufficient.

Dave's closing statement began with the Boston Tea Party analogy. "Your Honor," he said, "this is not the first time that tea has been the focus of a political protest against a powerful government tyrant. In 1773 the citizens of Boston were outraged because their government granted an official monopoly on tea marketing to a government-chartered corporation. They demanded an end to the government's tea monopoly and when their demands were not met, they expressed their political opinions by throwing chests of tea into Boston harbor."

My mind flashed back to Brother Nicholas's course in American history at St. Gregory's College. He had told us that Americans' fondness for morning coffee rather than tea began with this important political protest, and I remembered that he had shown us a painting of men dressed as American Indians who were throwing crates of tea from a ship into the water.

Dave continued, "This act of protest led to a resolution against a tyrannical head of state and to the establishment of the American Republic. In 1992, a group of frustrated farmers in the Central Province of Kenya grew outraged by President Moi's eagerness to grow rich at their expense. These farmers were led not by Ben Franklin and Thomas Paine but by David Wachira Ngarurih. His Boston harbor was the Kerugoya Moi Stadium and his message was the same: let the people dictate the course of their own lives."

As I listened to Dave, I realized, for the first time, how significant our farmers' boycott could have been if it had succeeded fully. Dave was right. When the American patriots had dumped those crates overboard, they probably felt much the same as we did when we forced the tea factory to close.

Continuing with his speech, Dave walked Judge Churchill systematically through all the testimony, pointing out how each of the documentary exhibits tied into and corroborated what I had said. Judge Churchill interrupted him several times. She asked, for example, "Do you agree that the [State Department] report does not mention the boycott?"

Dave had a response for each of her questions. He agreed that the boycott had not been mentioned in that report, but he pointed out that the farmers had not been allowed to register their organization, so "it had no official name. It would have been difficult to report on it in the State Department report."

He closed as eloquently as he had begun: "You can never give back his months in solitary, you can never give him back the week that he spent in the water cell, you can never give him back complete freedom from fear. But you can give him the same thing our own founders sought during their tea boycott in 1773. You can give him the opportunity to determine his destiny, free from domination by a tyrannical ruler. You can do this by granting him asylum."

I was very impressed by Dave's entire statement. My big chipmunk had come through for me when it counted.

"Very articulate," Judge Churchill commented. And she asked everyone to wait for five minutes while she thought about her decision.

· · ·

While she thought, the students and I whispered together at our table. Bernie and Dave had no idea what she would do. The hearing had proceeded as flawlessly as they could have hoped. But I had no doubt that she was going to deny my request for asylum. Phil had told me that the clinic's students had often been unpleasantly surprised by Judge Churchill, and he had warned me not to take anything for granted. As Judge Churchill pondered and wrote a few notes for herself, the three of us remained at the counsel table, watching her, sweating, and worrying about what the next few minutes would bring.

Then Judge Churchill began to dictate her decision. She spoke in a very low voice and never looked at me. I had to strain to hear what she was saying, and for a long time I could not tell where she was going.

"The respondent presents a case with very interesting facts such that they lead to an analogy with our own country's Boston Tea Party," she said. I was happy that she had accepted Dave's patriotic metaphor. She continued by describing the facts to which I had testified. Sometimes she hadn't seemed to be listening carefully, but in fact she had followed my fairly complicated story closely, and she described many details accurately. She also drew attention to the Kenyan newspaper article referring to me by name. Slowly, I was becoming convinced that she was planning to rule in my favor. I thought, "Why else would she bother to describe the corroborating evidence that supported my testimony?" I was further encouraged that when she referred to the water cell, she noted that it had been "described by a witness as a horrendous and extreme form of torture."

She did a very good job of describing the facts of the case. Then, without looking up or changing her tone of voice at all, she suddenly delivered the blow that doomed my chances.

"We do not agree that the respondent fits the definition of a 'refugee.' . . . The Refugee Act of 1980 . . . was enacted to bring United States law into compliance with our international obligations. . . . It is argued that the U.N. Convention [is] not binding on the United States as part of our law. However, because of our international obligations, the Refugee Act was enacted. . . . The 1951 Convention on Refugees contains cessation clauses. It specifically states that refugee status, if one has that status, ends upon voluntary re-availment of protection. Going back to his country in 1997 after he was in the United States was a voluntary re-availment of the protection of his country. Therefore it is deemed that the respondent had refugee status [at] the time he left in 1995 [but] he lost that status as a legal concept when he went back to Kenya during the summer of 1997."

I didn't understand the details of what she was saying about the international convention concerning refugees, but I could tell by her refusal to look up and by the grimace on Dave's face that she was ruling against me. I was sweating again, but I had to sit quietly at the table while she continued to dictate to her tape recorder.

"During those two months," she added, "he did not suffer persecution, he did not suffer torture. He testified that he did not engage in any political discussions but maintained a low profile. . . . [However, he was] active in being involved in a legal case on behalf of his brother [and was not] in hiding. [And] the authorities did raise the price of tea by [50 percent]."

I understood that she was condemning me just for having tried to help Njoka. Although I knew that Dave and Bernie had worried about this issue, I was stunned. The students and I had come so far, only to be stopped by the very theory that Judge Churchill had used—and had been reversed for using—in the *Getaneh* case. Of course, she may not have known that the Board of Immigration Appeals had rejected the idea that Congress had incorporated the convention's cessation clauses into the Refugee Act. She had torn those pages out of Dave and Bernie's brief. Or maybe she had read those pages. Maybe she had torn them out precisely because she didn't want to have to deal with the board's rejection of her theory, and she felt that she could take refuge in the idea that the board had not designated its *Getaneh* decision as a precedent.

She had returned, in the end, to the issue she had raised at the very beginning of the case, when she had tried to prompt Metzgar to object to asylum on this ground. She was probably planning all along to rule against me because of my 1997 trip. But during the several hours of my testimony, she had focused on the facts of the boycott and persecution and had not come back to the issue of my return or given any indication that this would be the basis for her decision.

Continuing with her decision, Judge Churchill said, "We found the respondent to be a basically credible person. He does appear to be a person who is the type [of] person that makes a good citizen of whatever country he's in, and he is the kind of person we admire. That is not a basis for a grant of asylum but [he has also asked for the right of voluntary departure]. There appears no reason to deny that." She acknowledged that voluntary departure "is the most minimal form of relief available."

She ordered me deported to Kenya if I did not leave within the time permitted by the grant of voluntary departure. That period would be sixty days, but the students had told me that if I lost but was granted voluntary departure, I wouldn't actually have to leave right away. Whenever a trial judge granted voluntary departure, the board itself would do so as well. If I appealed to the board and lost my appeal there, the board would at least grant me an additional thirty days after its decision.

As we left the courtroom, Bernie and Dave were upset, but they said that the judge's finding that I was telling the truth was very important and helpful. The clinic would file an appeal for me, and this finding would significantly simplify the appeal. It is very difficult to reverse an immigration judge's finding that an asylum seeker is lying, because on the issue of whether a witness is telling the truth, appellate bodies want to defer to the judgment of trial judges who have observed the demeanor of the witness. Judge Churchill had removed that issue from the case. In fact, she had explicitly stated that she found me ineligible for asylum "as a matter of law." Appellate judges usually think that they are as good as trial judges, or better, when it comes to interpreting the law.

The students were happy, too, about the grant of voluntary departure. I would have to post a $500 bond within five days, but I had the money. If I happened to lose the appeal, I could avoid leaving under an order of deportation, and I would not be saddled with an order that would prevent me from reentering the United States for ten years.

I posted the bond right away. I was neither angry nor surprised by Judge Churchill's denial of my request for asylum. Except for a few minutes while she dictated the first part of her decision, I had expected that denial throughout the trial. Her refusal to look me in the eye from the very beginning of the trial had convinced me that she was leaning against granting asylum or had already made that decision.

Because my case was so much like the example in the government's own manual, and because of the *Getaneh* case, I was hopeful about winning the appeal. The students advised me that the INS did not arrest asylum applicants who were appealing to the board, so I would be free to continue my normal life during the year or more that it would take the board to consider and decide my appeal.

Dave and Bernie's semester in the clinic was drawing to a close. They helped me file the additional papers to continue my application for a diversity lottery visa, which now took on additional importance. But they were unable to stay with the case during the appeal process. Phil decided that in this case, as in *Getaneh*, he would handle the appeal himself rather than trying to find a CALS alumnus or a law firm elsewhere to volunteer to work on it.

Phil filed a short "notice of appeal" stating the basis for the appeal. After that came a long period of waiting. Phil's next step would be to file an appellate brief, but he could not do so until the government's stenographers typed up the transcript of the hearing and gave him a copy. That process would take six to nine months because of their backlog.

. . .

With the hearing behind me, I was determined to get on with my life. More law school acceptances arrived, including one from the University of Tulsa. I attended the University of Tulsa's law school for a summer pre-law course, but while I was there, I was accepted by the Catholic University of America in Washington, D.C., where Phil's wife, Lisa Lerman, was a member of the law faculty. I decided to enroll at Catholic, both because it was in the community where I had already settled and because Lisa offered to admit me into the Law and Public Policy Program, which she directed, and to serve as my faculty advisor. I knew that going to law school was somewhat risky, because if I lost all my appeals, I might have to leave the country before I completed my studies. A law degree usually requires three years of study; given that my English language skills were still imperfect, I might need four or five years to get my degree. But I hoped that if I had to leave the United States before I finished law school, I might be able to find a haven in a country that would allow me to transfer my Catholic University credits.

I started at Catholic in September 2001. My first semester had just gotten under way when, on a gorgeous late summer morning, terrorists flew three hijacked airliners into the World Trade Center and the Pentagon, and a fourth hijacked plane crashed in Pennsylvania. The terrorists had come from countries in the Middle East, and although none of them had received asylum, Phil feared that all would-be immigrants would be affected by increased fear of foreigners and by new legal restrictions.

In December, Phil received the transcript of the hearing, and he wrote his brief to the Board of Immigration Appeals. He argued that Judge

Churchill had relied on a cessation clause in the international convention that had never been incorporated into American law. He also contended that even if the four cessation clauses of the convention had any bearing on the case, Judge Churchill had used the wrong clause.

She had invoked the first of the convention's four cessation clauses, clause 1(C)(1), which provides that refugees lose their status if they have "voluntarily re-availed themselves of national protection." Although the convention itself does not define "voluntary re-availment," a handbook issued by the U.N. High Commissioner for Refugees, which offered a definitive interpretation of the convention, said that this paragraph "refers to a refugee . . . who remains outside the county of his nationality. (The situation of a refugee who has actually returned to the country of his nationality is governed by the fourth cessation clause, which speaks of a person having 're-established' himself in that country.)"[12] Because I had actually returned to Kenya in 1997, Judge Churchill should have invoked the fourth cessation clause, clause 1(C)(4), if she relied on the convention at all. But according to the handbook, clause 1(C)(4) causes cessation of refugee status only if the refugee returns "with a view to permanently residing there."[13] I had returned between college semesters only to free my brother, not to live in Kenya again.

To shore up his argument, Phil asked the Office of the U.N. High Commissioner for an advisory opinion on the cessation clauses that he could submit to the board with his brief. This clause of the convention, the High Commissioner's Office told the board, "requires freely chosen re-establishment, *not mere return*, before cessation ensues. . . . The adjudicator should determine whether the person's decision to return was voluntary and whether, at the time of return, he or she had the *intention of remaining there permanently*. Voluntariness and intention to remain would be absent, for example, if the individual returned under duress or had other compelling reasons to return."[14] Applying this standard, Phil argued, the board should at least direct Judge Churchill to reconsider her decision in the light of clause 1(C)(4). Under that clause, my trip was not disqualifying because I had no intention of remaining in Kenya permanently. Alternatively, the board should itself grant me asylum because none of the cessation clauses were part of U.S. law.

The INS did not file a brief. That was no surprise; during the hearing, that agency's lawyer had not vigorously opposed granting me asylum. Judge Churchill, not the INS, had been my problem.

After Phil filed the brief, we began another period of waiting. Phil anticipated, based on past experience, that it would take the board at least six months, and perhaps more than a year, to get around to deciding this case. Meanwhile, he kept me abreast of larger political developments as the American reaction to the September 11 attacks unfolded. Congress passed the USA Patriot Act, providing the government with new powers of surveillance over suspected terrorists. The government began a program called "special registration," requiring legal permanent residents from specified countries—notably several Middle Eastern countries—to appear in person to register their addresses (and, in some cases, to be arrested if immigration officials found something wrong with their documentation). The rate at which asylum officers ruled favorably on applications quickly dropped from 50 percent in fiscal year 2001 (which ended on September 30 of that year) to 42 percent in FY 2002, and then to 32 percent in FY 2003.

The overseas refugee program also suffered. Under this program, the United States had annually awarded immigrant visas to as many as eighty-five thousand people, many of them living in refugee camps, whom the United Nations had identified as needing resettlement because of continuing persecution in their own countries. This number fell from sixty-six thousand in FY 2001 to nineteen thousand in FY 2002 as, across the globe, American consular officials became much more cautious about approving visas of any kind. The number of visas approved for would-be university students also declined.

None of these developments impinged on my case directly. Kenya was not one of the countries selected for special registration, and I had already gone through most of the stages of processing that were affected by the reaction to September 11. But Phil called me one afternoon in the spring of 2002 to report that Attorney General John Ashcroft had taken

several actions that would diminish the quality of appellate review by the Board of Immigration Appeals, where my case was now lodged.

The board is an unusual federal agency in that it was not established by a statute. The U.S. attorney general has the authority to decide appeals in immigration cases. Deluged by such appeals, the attorney general in 1940 had established the board and delegated to it his power to decide these cases. Because Congress neither created the board nor imposed rules for appointment and retention, the board "members" are for all practical purposes appellate judges, although they have no tenure in office and can be hired or fired at will by the attorney general. In principle, at least, the insecurity of their employment reduced the independence of their judgments; but in practice, attorneys general had rarely paid attention to the board, except to select new members.

By 2002, the board was one of the busiest appellate courts in the country, deciding about thirty thousand appeals annually. Under President Bill Clinton, Attorney General Janet Reno had increased the size of the board, from seven to eighteen members, to help it keep up with an increased number of appeals, but even so the board had to rely heavily on hundreds of staff lawyers to do most of its work. The board worked through panels of three members, each of which had many staff lawyers. Those lawyers reviewed the appeals and prepared recommendations for the panel members, who then voted on each appeal and wrote a four- or five-page opinion, such as the one in *Getaneh* holding that the cessation clauses had not entered into American law. In high-visibility cases or those in which the board believed that it was providing an important new interpretation of law, all the board members considered the case together and wrote longer opinions. Those were the cases that resulted in precedents binding all immigration judges.

Even with the addition of several Reno appointees, the board was very conservative. Despite this tilt, when he had filed my appeal, Phil had thought that it was a reasonable court. Based on the confidence that he and other lawyers had in the fairness of the board, he had been somewhat optimistic about my appeal. The CALS clinic had won some cases before the board and had lost some cases there, but, on the whole, the CALS staff had had no complaints.

Ashcroft's "reforms," which he put into place ostensibly to make the board more efficient and to help it reduce its pending backlog of fifty-five thousand appeals, changed the board's operation in fundamental ways. First, the attorney general announced that he would reduce the size of the board from eighteen members to eleven, a curious response to the problem of increased caseload. The downsizing would occur by the fall of 2002, and Attorney General Ashcroft would decide which members would be fired; neither seniority nor any objective measure of performance would determine who remained. In fact, Ashcroft fired only Clinton administration appointees, particularly those who had written decisions that favored immigrants and those who had once represented immigrants or taught immigration law in universities.[15] Those remaining on the board had come primarily from the ranks of the INS, other Department of Justice law enforcement agencies, or the staffs of Republican members of Congress. This purge left the board a far more conservative body than it had been before.

Second, Ashcroft directed the board to stop writing opinions in most cases. Attorney General Reno had earlier authorized the board to speed up its work by deciding limited categories of cases—not including asylum cases—through a "summary affirmance" procedure. If a case was in a category for which summary affirmance was allowed, if any errors made by the immigration judge were "harmless or nonmaterial," and if the case did not involve a novel issue of law or a novel fact situation, a single board member (rather than a panel of three) could uphold an immigration judge's ruling without writing even a short opinion. Ashcroft and Lori L. Scialabba, whom he appointed as board chair, expanded this procedure to virtually all cases, specifically including asylum cases.

Henceforth, a single member of the board would consider each appeal initially. If the member found the decision of the immigration judge to be correct and uncontroversial, he or she could affirm it without writing a word. If the judge's decision seemed to need minor correction, the board

member could write a few words or sentences modifying the opinion, while still upholding the decision. But if the decision of the immigration judge was found to be inconsistent with the law, it would have to be referred to a three-judge panel for further consideration and the writing of an opinion. Therefore, in cases like mine, in which an immigration judge had denied asylum, the board, which was under huge pressure to decide cases quickly, would have to do a lot more work to reverse than to affirm the denial.

When he made these changes in board procedure, Ashcroft also directed the board to dispose of its fifty-five thousand pending cases within 180 days. Human Rights First, one of the leading organizations advocating on behalf of asylum applicants, calculated that to clear the backlog on time, each board member would have to decide one case every fifteen minutes. This order, combined with the abandonment of three-member panels in most cases and the vastly expanded use of summary affirmances without opinions, made it very likely that the cases in the backlog, including mine, would receive much less scrutiny from the board than cases the board had decided before February 2002, such as *Getaneh.*

Despite these procedural changes, Phil remained hopeful that my case would receive serious review. Even if most cases received rubber-stamp affirmances from the board, he thought that several factors would flag my case as worthy of scrutiny by a three-member panel: it involved only an issue of law, not a complex sifting of facts; the issue was relatively novel, in that the board had never addressed the consequence of a brief return in a precedent opinion; Judge Churchill's decision seemed inconsistent with the three-member decision in *Getaneh;* and the U.N. High Commissioner for Refugees had demonstrated an interest in the case.

While Phil kept an eye on the deterioration of the board as an appellate body, he also periodically visited the State Department web site, which each month lists the most recent serial number reached in the diversity visa lottery. The new fiscal year had started shortly after the September 11 attacks, and diversity visa processing was very slow. At first, Phil concluded that there was no chance that my number would be reached by September 2002; but as winter turned into spring, the department's advance through its serial numbers accelerated. As my chances with the board declined, the importance of winning a visa through the lottery increased.

In June, Phil recalculated the pace of progress through the serial numbers and alerted me that my number might be reached sometime during July or August. The State Department published its list of numbers monthly, not daily, so if my number came up, I would have only a few weeks to act on it, racing the clock to complete what could be a lengthy process before the September 30 deadline on the issuance of all lottery visas.

On July 13, I received my notice in the mail. My number would come up in September, and I could apply for an immigrant visa. But there was a hitch. In addition to various forms to be filed and fees to be paid, the application process included a personal interview. The State Department had scheduled such an interview for me. I was to show up at 8:00 A.M. on the morning of September 3—at the American embassy in Nairobi, Kenya.

SIX

Winning the Lottery

Once in a while, it pays to check the mail. The State Department's notice alerted me that I was just one step away from receiving a visa that would allow me to remain permanently in the United States. Overjoyed, I called Phil to tell him the good news. He was not as encouraging as I expected him to be.

"The situation is not so simple," he cautioned. "You are not a typical diversity lottery winner. Come to my office tomorrow, and I'll explain the complications and your options."

There were two problems, he told me the next day. I was in the United States, and I was still in the midst of a deportation case. "Typical diversity lottery winners," he informed me, "are people who apply by mail and win the lottery while living in their own countries, not in the United States. The system is really set up for them. State Department officials can easily interview them at the nearest U.S. embassy or consulate in their own countries."

"But some of them, like people with student visas, win the lottery while they are here," I argued.

"Yes, some lottery winners are already in the United States when they win. But, unlike you, those who win while they're in the country usually have valid visas at that time. The U.S. government is willing to hold an interview in the United States for someone with a tourist visa or a student visa rather than making them return home for an interview. But someone like you, who has no currently valid status, has to be interviewed outside the United States."[1]

"To make matters worse," he added, "you've been told to go to Kenya, where you were tortured, the place you fled. Apparently, neither the American Congress nor the INS ever contemplated that an asylum seeker would win the lottery and be summoned to a consulate in the country where he fears persecution. Nobody ever made any rules to cover asylum applicants who are also lottery winners. There are only a very small number of people in that category."

Even though I had avoided arrest during my 1997 trip to help my brother, I was fearful about returning in 2002 because the political situation had become even more volatile. Although President Moi still held office, he had scheduled presidential elections in December. He claimed to be retiring, but he was using the machinery of state to keep his KANU party in power. The opposition groups in Kenya were beginning to mobilize the public to vote against the KANU candidate. The atmosphere, already charged, could be more tense by September. I was afraid that if I returned then, Moi and his followers might still see me as a troublemaker who should be incarcerated, or possibly terminated. I might never get out of the Nairobi airport. If I did, I might disappear before long.

Even if I bought an airline ticket, paid the $345 processing fee, risked the trip, and avoided arrest, Phil explained, there was no guarantee that the U.S. consulate in Nairobi would grant me a diversity visa. I would need a medical examination by a Kenyan doctor who had been approved by the consulate. I didn't think that I had any disqualifying diseases, but the doctor might find something I didn't know about. If I passed the medical test, I would also have to prove to the consulate's satisfaction that I had enough income or assets to ensure that I would not end up on American welfare. Would the consulate find me wealthy enough? I had been going to law school rather than working in the United States, and my stock market investments had fizzled when the market declined in the wake of the September 11 attacks.

If for some reason I didn't get the visa, I wanted to be able to continue my case before the Board of Immigration Appeals. With that in mind, Phil outlined five problems he saw with risking the trip to Kenya and relying on the pending appeal as a backup.

First, an asylum applicant who leaves the United States with an appeal pending before the board is deemed by law to have abandoned the appeal.[2] If I went to Kenya and did not receive a diversity lottery visa, I would be trapped there, with no chance of winning asylum. I could not even reapply for asylum, because in 1996 Congress had passed a law barring a person who loses an asylum case from applying again.[3]

The second problem would arise even if the appeal could somehow be continued. If I returned from Kenya empty-handed, the Board of Immigration Appeals might remand my case to Judge Churchill and ask her to reconsider it. She would look at me and say, "What? You went to Kenya *again?* I denied you asylum because you returned there one time, and now you want me to grant you asylum after you went to Kenya *twice?*" The INS could even report to the board itself that I seemed to be commuting between the United States and Kenya.

The third problem with going to Kenya was that if my lottery visa was denied, I might never be able to get back into the United States to continue my law school studies. I had entered the United States in 1995 and 1997 on a student visa, but my student status had ended in 2000. As an asylum applicant with a pending appeal, I was not a typical "undocumented alien," but I no longer had a valid visa. Immigration officials might stop me at Dulles Airport and refuse to let me return to my apartment in Virginia. The problem of returning was further complicated because Judge Churchill had ordered me deported. That decision was on appeal, so it wasn't final. But an airport inspector might not understand the legal significance of that detail.

Fourth, the order of deportation could hurt my chances of being given the diversity lottery visa in Kenya. People who had been ordered deported were barred by law from reentering the United States for ten years.[4] According to Phil, that law shouldn't prevent me from getting the visa, because the deportation order was being appealed. But a consular official in Nairobi might not understand the distinction between a final and a nonfinal deportation order and might deny my visa because of the ten-year ban.

Finally, going to Kenya for the visa would cost both money and time. With my stocks virtually wiped out, I would have to ask my industrialist friend for airfare. I would also have to suspend all my normal activities for at least a week, and possibly longer.

Phil suggested four options, none of them perfect. The first two were relatively simple, while the last two were quite complicated.

The most straightforward option was to stick with my asylum appeal and forget about the lottery. I would not need to leave the United States, face possible arrest in Kenya, risk not being allowed to return, or incur the time and expense of an international trip. But this meant that I would have to bank everything on the appeal and forfeit my chance to get an immediate "green card" (a certification of having been given an immigrant visa, which in prior years was colored green). Getting this card would be a lot better than winning asylum because it would give me immediate permanent status in the United States.

The second option was to go to Kenya in September for my medical examination and visa interview. With luck, I would become a permanent U.S. resident right away. But this strategy meant that I risked arrest in Kenya, and if something went wrong, I would be marooned, as Phil had already explained, unable even to recover my belongings from Virginia.

The two more complicated options had their own risks. One was to try to get a diversity visa from an American immigration court. The law provides that certain people who become eligible for green cards (for example, by winning the lottery) can "adjust" their status in an immigration court in the United States. This was the method used by students who won the lottery while their visas were still valid. If I could adjust in an immigration court, I would not have to leave the United States at all.

But this plan would require me to overcome many hurdles and uncertainties, as Phil described.

Because I had an immigration case and an accompanying deportation case file already pending with the Board of Immigration Appeals, I could not go before an immigration court unless the board sent my file to that court. I would have to make a motion requesting that the board do so. Michael Metzgar, the INS lawyer who had cross-examined me in Judge Churchill's court, would need to agree to it. Even if he agreed, however, the board might be slow to consider the motion: the board itself was in turmoil because the attorney general had recently ordered it to decide fifty-five thousand cases in six months, to clear its voluminous backlog. If the board did not resolve my motion very quickly—it was already July—I could not get into an immigration court before September 30, when my winning lottery ticket would expire.

There was also a chance that the board would deny the motion because I was still in deportation proceedings. The board might choose to first resolve my appeal, which might take a long time; or it might send the file back to Judge Churchill, whose calendar was full for the next several months. And while Phil tried to get my file back from the board and my adjustment application onto Judge Churchill's calendar, the clock in this uncertain schedule would be running toward and beyond the September 3 interview date in Nairobi (which I would miss) and the September 30 drop-dead date for a visa, after which neither the State Department nor Judge Churchill could award me a green card. Finally, Judge Churchill had already come up with a reason to deny asylum; I wondered whether she wouldn't find some other reason to deny the lottery visa.

The final option Phil presented was to request a visa interview at a U.S. consulate in a foreign country other than Kenya. The United States had consulates all over the world. If Phil could find one that was willing and able to complete "third-country processing" for me before September 30, I could go there instead of to Nairobi. This procedure would avoid the risk of being arrested in Kenya or being perceived as a commuter, and it could be less expensive than flying to Africa. However, if something went wrong with the processing, my appeal might be considered abandoned and I might not be able to reenter the United States.

The first and second options, which involved completely relinquishing one of my claims, seemed too stark; and the third option seemed too risky. I chose the fourth. Phil immediately started making calls to consulates and to immigration lawyers who might have helped other clients with third-country processing. He discovered that some U.S. consulates in Canada had provided this service until recently but had stopped doing so within the past several months, possibly as part of the general constriction of immigration after September 11. Then he learned that the U.S. consular officials in Juarez, Mexico, might be sympathetic to compelling cases like mine, although they had not handled a third-country case in the last seven months. On July 25, twelve days after I'd received the notice about the appointment in Kenya, Phil emailed information about me to a vice consul in Juarez.

The vice consul was noncommittal, saying that he wanted to discuss the case with the consulate's visa manager. However, the visa manager, Santiago Burciaga, was out of the office until the following week; and the vice consul would be away when the visa manager returned. So we couldn't expect an answer from the Juarez consulate for nearly two weeks.

On August 6, Burciaga emailed Phil. He had decided that my case did present "compelling reasons," and he was willing to request a transfer of the case from Nairobi and conduct third-country processing. I was elated. But Phil was still worried. The consulate in Mexico, like the consulate in Kenya, could grant the visa only if it did so by September 30. But it could not act on my case without my lottery file. When the State Department's National Visa Center in Kentucky had reached my lottery number early in the summer, it had sent my paperwork to the consulate in the U.S. embassy in Nairobi.

The State Department sends files from one post to another only through diplomatic pouches, not through Federal Express or other commercial delivery services. Various signatures are needed before a file can be sent to another post. An immigration lawyer had warned Phil that the consulate in Kenya wouldn't even send the file directly to Mexico—it would be sent back to Kentucky for retransmittal to Mexico. Just getting my file from Nairobi to Juarez could take six months, and by that time, the consulate in Juarez could no longer issue a visa. So Phil asked Burciaga whether he could be sure that he would receive the file in time to act on it.

Burciaga's email reply was immediate but crushing: "There is a huge possibility that we will not get the case here by that time [September 30]. However, we can try and hopefully everything will work out."

Phil followed up, asking whether Burciaga could telephone his Nairobi counterparts and have the file sent directly to his office by air. He replied that he was "sorry but we cannot push to try and get the case here any faster. The most we can do is request it and hope that we receive it on time. Taking into consideration the short time frame we have . . . to work with, it would probably be a much better decision for him to continue with his appointment in Nairobi. Please let us know what you decide as every minute is critical if your final decision is to seek consular processing here in Ciudad Juarez."

This answer presented me with a terrible choice. I could risk a confrontation with the security forces in Nairobi for the certainty of a September 3 appointment there. Or I could go to Mexico, where I would face no personal risk but where there was a "huge possibility" that my file would not arrive in time. My industrialist friend was willing to give me an airplane ticket to Africa, so my choice depended on balancing the relative risks, not on money.

In the end, I couldn't face the possibility of the deadline running out while my file was making its way around the world on a months-long journey. I therefore chose to return to Africa.

It was true that traveling to Kenya might cause the government to consider my asylum appeal abandoned, and it might also leave me stranded in Africa. Phil suggested that we try to prevent these consequences. He had me apply to the Immigration and Naturalization Service for a procedure called "advance parole," through which foreign nationals who are in the United States can receive written advance assurances that after a brief trip abroad for compelling reasons, they will be allowed to return within a specified number of days.[5] We weren't sure that this procedure would prevent the abandonment of the appeal, but perhaps it would at least get me back home.

Phil submitted an application form for advance parole, along with copies of my letter from the State Department, proof of the pending appeal, more photographs, and proof that I was not destitute and would not go on welfare after I returned. I also had to pay a $110 filing fee. Phil personally went to INS headquarters in Washington and handed a letter to a senior official explaining why I needed permission to come back in case something went wrong during the consular processing in Kenya. We hoped that the INS would allow at least forty-five days of advance parole so that I could remain in Kenya through the September 30 deadline. The agency did grant me advance parole, but only for thirty days. Phil contacted the Kenyan doctor who had been approved by the State Department and asked him to see me by August 26 in order to have lab tests available for my September 3 interview. To see the doctor on time, I would have to leave the United States by August 23 at the latest, and I would not be able to stay in Kenya through September 30. Still, the thirty days of advance parole seemed sufficient, as I hoped to have a visa in my hands by September 4.

· · ·

On August 18, I flew to Nairobi. I didn't know whether my name was on a detention list at the airport, but since I had been allowed to enter the country without any significant incident in 1997, I hoped to do it again, despite the upcoming election. Perhaps Moi's officials would be so busy ensuring the election of their cronies that they would have no resources left to bother with me. I also hoped that the American consulate would help me if I did have a problem with the Kenyan government, because I was coming for an appointment that it had scheduled.

As in 1997, I did not alert anyone explicitly about my arrival. However, by this time an Internet café had come to Kerugoya, and my sister

Lucy was working there. I emailed her, advising her to be at the Nairobi airport to meet a friend of mine who would be changing planes there en route to South Africa. "She will give you an important package, which you are not to open until you get back to Kangaita. I suggest that you bring Wash with you to help you get the package to Kangaita safely."

On the day I was to arrive, Lucy woke before dawn. She took care of the animals and then knocked on Wash's door at 4:30. "Why are you knocking at this hour?" he asked.

"I need you to come to Nairobi with me this morning. Don't ask me why. Get ready, and I will explain it to you on the way."

"You sound like Jeff," Wash complained. "This better be worth it."

Three hours later, they were standing at the Nairobi airport with very little idea of why they were there or whom they were to meet. "How are we going to recognize the passenger?" Wash asked.

"I guess the passenger is supposed to recognize us," Lucy replied.

"The last time I was here was when Jeff took off. Could he be coming back?"

"If he's on that plane, I will kill him for making me get up so early."

"He's bigger than Arnold Schwarzenegger," Wash said. "You'll need something bigger than your handbag to kill that guy."

I was among the last passengers to leave the plane. After getting my baggage, I saw two familiar people scanning the crowd, hoping to be recognized by a passenger. "It's Jeff. . . . I told you!" Wash shouted. They both jumped over the metal barrier separating the baggage area from the arrival lounge. A gesturing police constable tried to stop them, but Wash ran past him. I ran toward him, too, and we slammed into each other like two mountain goats fighting over territory. I am much larger than Wash. He lost his balance and stumbled onto the luggage conveyor belt.

I felt someone touch my back, and when I turned, I saw a tall woman smiling with her arms extended. For a moment, I didn't recognize Lucy. Then she screamed at me, "Is it really you? Why didn't you tell me that you were coming?" She punched me in the stomach, jumped on my chest, and kissed me on my cheeks. Wash and I both fell on the floor under the force of her body. The other arriving passengers stared at us, curious about the disruption we were causing.

"Give me a hand, you wacko," I told her. She pulled me to my feet. I had been trying to enter the country inconspicuously, but I could hardly have called more attention to myself. Still, none of us could contain the joy of seeing each other for the first time in five years.

I stared at my sister. When I had last seen her, she was a teenage girl who, with tears in her eyes, was holding the hand of her frail twin brother, then just released on bail. Now she was a beautiful and evidently self-confident woman, six feet tall, with a sharply chiseled jaw.

I picked a bag off the conveyer belt. "I think this is yours," I said. "It has your name on it." She was puzzled but looked at the luggage tag and saw her name. "How did my name—you did it!" she exclaimed, hugging me again as she realized that I had brought her a bag full of gifts from America. Then I gave Wash a second bag of gifts, this one with his name on the tag.

"You are the same mischievous Jeff," he said.

I wanted to see my mother, Njoka, and all my friends in Kangaita. But my mother's health had deteriorated dramatically. She had been in and out of the hospital, and she could not travel to Nairobi to meet me. Njoka was still dealing with the complications of his legal case, primarily because of my older half-brothers' continuing vindictiveness and the corruption of the Kenyan legal system. He had again been incarcerated, and there seemed to be little I could do to help him during my short stay. Also, I wanted to avoid places where I would be very visible and might be arrested. I rented a car, and we drove to a Nairobi hotel. I was happy that at least I would be able to spend some time with Lucy and Wash.

Later that evening, I experienced an unpleasant reminder that racism, which I had experienced in Italy when black and white passengers were separated in the airport lounge on my first trip, and in America when I was threatened by a black man for riding in a car with white people, was also practiced in my native country, though its existence was not as openly acknowledged as it was in the United States. We all went to dinner at the

Carnivore, a Nairobi restaurant popular with Western tourists and famous for serving African game. When we arrived at the restaurant, two American families on safari were waiting for tables. I struck up a conversation with them. Soon they were seated, and we were the only people waiting. But then another group of white tourists arrived, and the Kenyan head waiter passed us by and seated them immediately.

"Excuse me," I interjected. "We were next in line."

"I know," he said. "But we don't have a table for you. Can't you see that we have visitors?"

"But we are visitors too, and we have been waiting for more than thirty minutes. This other group just arrived."

He looked at me strangely and took the white group to its table.

Lucy was astonished. "Are they not serving us because we are black?" she asked.

Wash said, "They will serve us, but they don't pay as much attention to local blacks."

"We shouldn't be treated like this," Lucy glowered. She walked past the receptionist, heading for a waiter at a podium who had a tag on his chest identifying him as a supervisor. The receptionist tried to stop her.

"Don't you dare touch me, or I will break you into pieces!" Lucy roared, towering over the receptionist. "My brother just arrived from abroad, and I brought him here for dinner. Your waiters are seating every white person ahead of us." She got the attention of the supervisor and repeated her complaint. "Is this how you treat your own citizens?" She bent over him with clenched fists on her hips. I saw in her my mother, beating up anyone who defied her. "You will seat us now, or you will call the manager."

The supervisor walked over to where Wash and I were standing. "I am sorry," he said. "I would like to seat you now."

A couple of days later, I went to the medical exam, where I gave blood and had a chest X-ray. The doctor found no problems. I had cleared an important hurdle.

Early on the morning of September 3, I went to the consulate, which was in the U.S. embassy building. Before it was bombed by terrorists in 1998, the U.S. embassy had been located at a busy intersection in the heart of Nairobi. By 2002, it had been moved to a strongly guarded compound a few miles from the city center, near the main airport. As I arrived at the main entrance gate, I saw armed Kenyan security guards patrolling the outer perimeter. A long line of people, most of whom looked like Somalis, waited in line to be cleared for entrance.

I had brought my application for a visa and the supporting documents, including my birth certificate, my financial records, and a detailed letter that Phil had written to the consulate, describing my personal history and the procedural status of my asylum case. Phil had been worried that my pending asylum case might make the consular officer wonder whether, for some reason, he or she should not give me a diversity visa. For example, the consular officer might wrongly suspect that the immigration judge had denied asylum because I had made up a false story. Phil's letter explained that Judge Churchill had found me credible and had even granted me voluntary departure, which required that I have good moral character. Phil wrote that Judge Churchill had denied asylum for a purely legal reason, on the basis that, in her opinion, my return trip in 1997 disqualified me. The letter pointed out that because my case was on appeal, there was no final order of deportation against me. Phil provided his office and home phone numbers in the letter, in case the consulate had questions.

After I was allowed to enter the embassy, a cashier took my $435 fee, and a secretary directed me to a consular officer, who sat in a cubicle on the other side of a window. The officer was a young woman, perhaps in her mid-twenties, with short brown hair and a rounded face. She was wearing loose, light blue cotton pants and a white blouse that exposed her upper shoulders. She had a long-sleeved shirt tied on her hips, in the style of an American college student. There was no name plate on her window, nor was she wearing a badge with her name.

"Hi," I greeted her. "My name is Jeff. I'm here for my interview. What is your name?"

She did not respond to my question; in fact, she didn't even look at me. She simply gestured for me to hand over my application and the required documents.

Phil's cover letter was not physically attached to the application form. I didn't know whether I should insist that she read it first. She held my future in her hands, and I didn't want to challenge her way of proceeding. Since she asked only for the application form and its required attachments, I gave them to her. She started going through the papers. Almost immediately, she started finding fault with the documents. The printed visa application instructions specified that I must bring with me "a certificate from the police authorities of your country of nationality and of the country where you now live if residence in either was more than six months." I had brought with me both a clean police certificate from Virginia and the Kenyan police certificate of good conduct that I had obtained before I left Kenya in 1995. My records were clean. The certificate from Kenya stated that "nothing to his detriment has been traced."

Although I had complied with the instructions, the officer stated that my 1994 police certificate was too old. She told me to get a new police certificate from my district police headquarters in Kerugoya. I explained that because I had been living in the United States since 1995, the Kenyan police files would contain no more recent information on me. I added that it would not be safe for me to visit the police in Kerugoya, where the security police had arrested me on political charges in 1992. She paid no attention to my comments, so I told her that I had a letter from my American lawyer explaining my situation. I tried to hand it to her. She refused to accept or read it. She told me to come back in four days with an up-to-date Kenyan police certificate. She said that she didn't care how I got it, but she could not process my visa without it.

I was frustrated by the delay and had no choice but to go to Kerugoya and risk arrest. I spent the next three days paying police officials about

10,000 shillings for what they should have given me on request, without bribery. At the end of that time, I had a new, clean police certificate, issued by an office in Nairobi that showed I had no police record in any district in the country. This was just what the consular officer had asked me to obtain.

Then I returned to see her. This time, I was able to get her name—Margaret Hartley—from someone else at the consulate. When I gave her the police certificate, she asked, "Have you ever been arrested?"

"Yes," I said. "I told you a few days ago that I was a political prisoner in 1992 and 1993."

"Then this police certificate is false," she asserted. "If you were arrested, you can't have a clean police certificate."

"But there, you see, I do have it," I insisted. "I have a clean record with the police because I was not arrested on a criminal charge or by the regular police. I was jailed in secret, by the security forces, and probably the security forces don't keep records. Even if they do, it would be impossible for me to get them in the few days remaining before your authority to grant my visa expires."

"That's not my problem," she snapped. "You say you have been in jail. But if you were in jail, there should be a record of it on your police certificate. And if you are an asylum applicant, you must be afraid of the police, but you went to the police to get this certificate. Why weren't you arrested if you are in danger?"

"Because they have no reason to arrest me at present," I explained. "And there is no record of my arrest because I was not arrested for a criminal offense. The Kenyan police keep records only if you are accused of a crime. They don't keep records of people who are arrested and tortured for political purposes. There were never any criminal charges against me."

"If you were not charged, you shouldn't have claimed asylum," she stated. "I am going to forward your case to the INS for a fraud investigation."

I wanted her to read Phil's letter, explaining the history of my case. After a trial that lasted more than a day, Judge Churchill had found me to be truthful. I couldn't believe that this officer was judging my case all over again, suspecting me of fraud because my police record was clean!

I realized, then, that perhaps I had been too truthful. If I had just brought Hartley the clean police record and had said nothing about being an asylum applicant, she might have treated me as a routine visa applicant, and I might already have my visa.

"Come back in another week," she ordered. "And when you return, bring me some proof that you were arrested. And bring me some court records showing what happened after that. I want proof of exactly when you were arrested, when you were released, and what jail or jails you were in."

"I can't do that," I said. "I have a plane ticket to return to the United States on that day, and also my advance parole will expire and I won't be able to go home."

She looked at my advance parole letter. "Your advance parole is good for nearly two more weeks. So you don't have to leave Kenya in one week. If you don't want to change your plane ticket and get the records, you can just forget about your application for the visa."

"But last week, you asked only for a police certificate, not for any court records," I pointed out. "I have lost several days in which I could have been trying to get them, if I had known you wanted them. Also, I probably can't get any court records, because the proceedings in my case were secret. And it would be dangerous for me to go from office to office trying to get them. I don't even know where to go, because I don't know what prison I was in."

"If it is so dangerous, you should have been arrested yesterday at the police station," she said. "Now leave and get those records."

I had no choice but to try to get more records. I had been in the jail in Kerugoya for the last few months of my imprisonment, so I returned to Kerugoya and paid another police officer to ask the jail officials for my incarceration records. He reported that he could not find any record of my having been in the Kerugoya jail. He was not surprised by that, however, because records were not always kept on prisoners who had been transferred there by Nairobi security officials.

I felt desperate. I paid a man I knew to try to get records of my detention from the national intelligence office in Nairobi. He took my money but did not produce any records for me, claiming that he could not find them.

So I returned to Margaret Hartley empty-handed. She still could not seem to understand that in the early 1990s, Kenya had two different sets of detention systems, one run by the ordinary police and one run by President Moi's security forces. She still seemed to think that I was lying, either about being arrested or about having a clean record.

Finally, she asked one of the Kenyans who worked in the consulate to interview me. Perhaps she figured that a Kenyan could more easily tell whether another Kenyan was lying. He and I had a very weird meeting. He was laughing at me the whole time. Instead of inquiring about the facts of my case, he kept asking me where I was staying in Kenya and with whom I had been talking. I got worried that he might be connected with the Kenyan security forces. I thought that I should be talking to American officials concerning an American visa, not to a Kenyan national. So I refused to continue the interview with him and asked to speak with the INS official who worked in the embassy. The Kenyan man advised me to wait in the lobby while he called the INS officer.

An hour later, an American official met me in the lobby. He introduced himself to me as the deputy security attaché. "I have been informed about your refusal to leave the embassy grounds," he frowned.

"Refusal?" I asked. I didn't know what he meant.

"Our Kenyan man who interviewed you said that you refused to leave the embassy."

"I am not sure that you are talking to the right person. I asked to speak to the INS officer, and the Kenyan gentleman told me to wait here for him. Nobody has asked me to leave."

The security official left through a door and returned almost immediately with the Kenyan man who had interviewed me. "Is this the gentleman who refused to leave?" he inquired.

"Yes," said the Kenyan man.

"Can you repeat what you just told me?" the American asked.

I said, "Why don't you ask him to repeat what he told me an hour ago, and what I asked him to do?"

The Kenyan man bowed his head and wiggled his feet nervously as if he were writing on the carpet with his toes. "I don't remember what he asked me for," he replied.

The American asked me to explain what I wanted. I related how Hartley had sent me to be interviewed by the Kenyan gentleman, who instead had laughed at me, ignored the facts of my case, and insisted that I tell him with whom I was staying in Kenya. As a former detainee and torture victim of the Kenyan security forces, I had become anxious about talking to him and had asked to see the representative of the INS. The Kenyan man had told me to wait and had never requested that I leave the embassy.

The American asked the Kenyan to leave the room. He conceded that the procedure being employed seemed odd and took me to the INS officer. When I explained my situation to him, the INS officer said that he would look into my case but advised me to return at once to the United States because I might be in danger in Kenya and because my advance parole would soon expire.

I had no choice but to return. On September 18, the last day on which I could safely depart, I got on a plane for home. I was dejected because I was not returning with the visa that had seemed so close at hand. On the plane, I started to feel ill. By the time it landed, I was feverish and light-headed. When I landed, I called Phil and reported briefly what had happened. Then I collapsed onto my bed. For the next ten days, I lay in bed with a flu that was more terrible than any illness I had ever experienced.

. . .

Phil told me later what happened while I lay ill. The consulate still had eleven days in which it could issue the visa if it was satisfied that I deserved it. Phil learned that if the visa was actually issued by September

30, I could return to Kenya after September 30 to pick it up. He tried to call Margaret Hartley, but she would not accept his calls or respond to the many messages he left for her. When he could not get through by phone, he faxed her a copy of his letter, the one she had refused to take from me. He also faxed the peace bond I had received when I left the jail and the two newspaper articles, one about my role in the protest and the other containing President Moi's threats against me. He offered to fax the many affidavits that Dave and Bernie had collected from people who knew that I had been in jail. His fax was eighteen pages long. But since the telephone system in Kenya, on which the U.S. embassy relied, was far from state of the art, only the first seven pages were received at first. He kept resending the fax until all the pages went through. Hartley never responded. Four more days passed.

Finally, Phil received a fax from the "Immigrant Visa Chief" in Nairobi. The letter bore a scrawl above that title, but no printed name. The chief said that he (or she) had reviewed the faxes and "the information gathered in the investigation conducted by our anti-fraud unit" and had referred the case to the Department of State for an advisory opinion. If State's response was positive, the visa would be issued by September 30.

Now Phil raced to locate the unit in the State Department that issued advisory opinions to consular officers, hoping to influence the decision that would be made in Washington. The department's Kenya desk officer said that the request had probably gone to the advisory unit in the Visa Office, but he warned that this unit received only email and would not accept telephone calls from the public. Frustrated by his inability to contact Hartley, Phil wanted to speak to a human being. Through colleagues in the world of immigration law, he finally located Kevin Aiston, in the proper unit, who explained that even though the consulate in Nairobi did not think I was lying, their operating manuals required them to obtain documentation of prison records in the case of any substantial detention.

Phil protested that the printed instructions I had received from the State Department stated that prison records were required only "if you

or an accompanying family member has been convicted of a crime." My police certificate showed no arrests for any crimes, much less convictions.

Aiston advised that his office merely gave legal opinions to the consulate and that the consular officer was responsible for making the final decision. Phil faxed a copy of the peace bond to Aiston, emphasizing that it was the only record we had been able to obtain. He also sent both Aiston and the consulate a copy of the letter Dave and Bernie had received from the law firm in Kenya, reporting that it took at least three months to retrieve records from Kenyan courts because they were written by hand. Phil offered to send the consulate volumes of additional information, if the officials would tell him what they wanted, including affidavits from witnesses and the pages from Judge Churchill's decision in which both she and the INS lawyer found me credible. "I will try to send them," he told me, "even if I have to spend all day at the fax machine, sending pieces at a time" because of the poor telephone service to the embassy.

Phil received no response from the consulate, and the next day he faxed again:

> Can't we talk? I've tried to call Ms. Hartley several times, and neither she nor anyone else from your office has ever taken or returned my calls. All I want is to be able to know what information might help you reach a positive decision, and to provide any documentation or information that might meet your needs. But it is very difficult to work with your office at such an arm's length. Couldn't we have a simple telephone conversation?

Again, he got no reply. He recontacted Aiston, who now told him that despite the operating manuals, the consulate had authority, under volume 22, section 42.65 of the Code of Federal Regulations, to waive receipt of required documents if they were unobtainable. In that case, the consular officer could accept "other satisfactory evidence" instead of the required document. With five days to go, Phil faxed the immigrant visa chief again, calling his attention to the letter from the Kenyan law firm and arguing that court records were not obtainable. Phil also tried to send copies of the affidavits attesting to my imprisonment on political charges as "other satisfactory evidence."

Although he pruned the affidavits, selecting only the most relevant, there were still twenty-eight pages. As before, the embassy's fax machine kept shutting off after only a few pages went through. Phil scanned the documents, created .pdf files, and tried to attach them to an email. The embassy's server rejected them because they took up too much space. He tried to break them into several smaller emails, but these too were rejected by the server. He faxed the embassy, offering to break the alternative evidence into even smaller pieces, if only embassy officials would give him some guidance on how to communicate with them.

Three days before the deadline was to expire, Aiston notified Phil:

> The consular officer has concluded that the requested documents are not unobtainable. . . . Therefore, unless the applicant can present the requested documents . . . he would not meet the documentary requirements and cannot be issued the visa. This is a determination within the exclusive purview of the consular officer, and is not amenable to review by this office, which only has authority over issuing opinions on pure questions of law.

Phil called Aiston once again, on the Friday before Monday, September 30. Apparently, the basis for the conclusion that prison records were "not unobtainable" was that the State Department's thick *Foreign Affairs Manual* declared that in Kenya, prison records were obtainable. The manual made no mention of secret political detentions during the 1990s, even though a bureau of the State Department itself had reported extensively on Moi's human rights violations. Aiston said that it was up to the consulate, not up to him, to decide whether the *Foreign Affairs Manual* was incorrect in this instance.

Phil asked whether the consulate could issue the visa conditionally and put it in a safe. Then I might return to Africa and spend six months trying to track down my prison record. If I found it, I could bring it to the consulate and pick up the visa.

According to Aiston, however, such a procedure would not be lawful. "Every year," he told Phil, "hundreds of lottery winners are stranded because they were called for their interview at the end of the fiscal year, and they just don't have their birth certificate or something with them. It's too bad, but if it's any consolation to your client, there are hundreds of other people all around the world whose rights will expire on Monday because they are missing a necessary document. If Mr. Ngarurih were the only one, it still wouldn't be legal, but the argument for an exception would be stronger. However, there are many like him all over the world."

The inevitable denouement came three days later: a fax for me from an unnamed "American Consular Officer." It read: "We have done extensive research on this and have concluded that if you were indeed in prison for nine months, prison records *are* obtainable. Your case is therefore documentarily incomplete and you can not be issued a Diversity Visa." This note was followed by a letter from the immigrant visa chief, who wrote: "Since Mr. Ngarurih did not present prison records, but instead chose to claim that they [*sic*] were unable to obtain them, his visa is being refused."

This was a crushing ending for Phil and me. But Phil pointed out that in the letter's last line the immigrant visa chief had made an important statement: "This refusal . . . does not have any impact on any applications he may make for any other kind of visa in the future." If I had been found guilty of fraud, it could have prevented me from winning my asylum appeal or being eligible to win the lottery again. Small comfort though it was, I was being denied my visa only because of the technicality that I had been unable to come up with a desired document before time ran out.

. . .

By October, I had recovered from my illness, but I was unable to kick the frustration and disappointment of having gone all the way to Africa without getting the visa. This was a very difficult time for me. I had taken a semester off from my legal studies at Catholic University's law school. Now I wasn't going to school, and because I didn't have a valid immigration status, I wasn't allowed to work. I became depressed and didn't leave my house for weeks.

Every year, my faculty advisor and former contracts law teacher, Lisa Lerman, who was also Phil's wife, organizes a Halloween costume party for her friends and students. The year 2002 was no different, and she emailed me an invitation.

I didn't feel in a partying mood, so I didn't reply to her email. I had always responded to notices that she sent me, so when she did not hear from me, she became worried and called to ask whether I was all right. I told her that I didn't feel like being around people, and I asked whether I could pass on her invitation.

"No," she said emphatically. "You cannot pass. You need to get out of the house. This is your professor speaking."

"I don't have a costume."

"You don't need one," she told me. "You are one of the few people I know who doesn't need a costume. Really, I don't care about the costume. You need to get some fresh air."

I said that I would try, but I didn't plan to go.

In the following weeks, Lisa called me three times to remind me about the party. She realized that I had become a recluse and that I rarely answered the phone. On the night of the party, she called me again at 6:00 P.M. and insisted that I attend.

I got out of bed slowly and looked into the bathroom mirror. My own reflection frightened me. I had grown a large beard, and my hair had started to develop tiny dreadlocks. "I can't go to the party looking like this," I thought. I shaved, but then I realized that since the party called for a costume, I could go dressed as a Rastafarian. From my closet I retrieved a Rastafarian hat I had bought on a trip to Atlanta. It fit perfectly, covering my messy hair. It made me feel and look like Bob Marley. A seven-foot-tall Bob Marley.

"Bob Marley"

After about half an hour at the party, I was chatting with some students in the kitchen. Lisa came over and pulled me by the arm. "Jeff, I want you to meet one of my students who served in the Peace Corps in Latvia." She pointed out a short girl who was dressed as a witch. Her wig was thick and black, and her face was painted green with shades of bright red makeup around her mouth. She held her hands together in front of her thighs and swayed like a ghost on a desert wind. She wore a long, pointy black hat, and her long black gown draped over her legs. Bags of Starbucks coffee hung from her waist. Her hazel green eyes seemed lit by distant golden lights. Her smile suggested a kind heart and an adventurous spirit. She seemed familiar, as if I had known her before, though I didn't even know her name.

I wanted to start a conversation that would give me a clue of where I might have met her. Before I could do so, she blurted out, "There you are. I've been looking all over for you."

That seemed like a strange remark. I replied, "It's been a long time." I kept thinking that I would recognize her if she washed the green paint from her face.

"What's the deal with your costume?" she asked.

"I am Bob Marley!"

She burst out laughing. "That's funny. I can't believe you pulled that off. A black guy dressed like a white guy attempting to be Bob Marley. I've never seen that on the East Coast."

"What about you?" I inquired.

"Not that controversial. The Wicked Witch of the Northwest. Here's my wand." She held up a black and yellow lollipop. Just then, a scarecrow approached and kissed her. "By the way, meet my husband," she added. I shook hands with him, but before I could even introduce myself, he pulled her away, and she disappeared into the crowd.

Lisa approached me and told me that I looked dazed. "What's going on?"

I pointed to the witch across the room. "I am going to marry that girl," I declared.

"How many glasses of wine have you had?" she asked.

"Just this one."

"Let me acquaint you with some reality, Jeff. In case you did not get it, that was her husband. That means that she is already married. In our country, women can't have more than one husband." We both laughed.

"Still," I said, "I am going to marry her. I don't know why I feel that way, but I do."

"Do you know her name?" Lisa asked.

"No, but I wish I had asked her that."

Lisa laughed, more at me than with me, and she joined another group of students. I poured myself another glass of wine.

I didn't see the Wicked Witch for the rest of that evening, and I figured that she must have left shortly after we met. But while I was driving home, I kept trying to figure out whether I had really met her before. I was so drawn to this girl, even though she was married.

"The Wicked Witch"

The spring semester started in January, and I returned to law school. More than two months had passed since I'd met the Wicked Witch, and I still did not know her name. I reconciled myself to never seeing her again and tried to put her out of my mind because she was married.

I had performed poorly in my property class the previous year, and I had to retake it with some of the first-year law students. I arrived ten minutes before the first class and waited for it to begin. Students drifted in, and finally the professor arrived. Just as she was about to start the class, a blonde girl walked in. Her law school book bag was hanging loosely over her left shoulder. She was wearing a red skirt with flat red shoes, but she walked on her toes as if she wore heels. Her shoulder-length hair bounced over her shoulders with every step she took. She strode confidently across the front of the classroom. I looked at her face, and our eyes met. I saw a distant but familiar speck of light in her eyes, and she smiled. She stopped and looked for a place to sit, standing still as if she couldn't make up her mind. A moment passed. I felt as though we were frozen in time. We realized that the whole class was staring at us. We didn't care.

"Melissa, we are about to begin the class, if you could please find yourself a seat," the professor said.

She was the Wicked Witch of the Northwest! "Melissa," I thought. "Her name is Melissa."

At that moment, Melissa shook her head as if waking from a dream. "I'm going to sit there," she gestured. She walked past me and took the seat right behind mine.

Our first class assignment that day was to form study groups for the rest of the semester. At the end of class, I turned around and introduced myself. "I'm Jeff," I said, offering to shake her hand.

She shook my hand. "We met at Professor Lerman's Halloween party. My name is Melissa."

I asked, "Would you like to be in my study group?"

"I would love to," she responded. We exchanged email addresses, and she walked out of class, on her toes.

We began to study together. During the second week, she missed class for two days. When she returned, I asked whether she had been sick.

"Yes, I have," she told me.

"Do you want a copy of my class notes? I would be happy to share my notes whenever you have a problem getting to class."

"I'm going to miss class next week," she said. "I have to have some minor surgery."

"What do you mean?"

"They found a lump on my breast. If they don't take it out, it could become cancerous."

I felt very touched that she had confided this very personal problem to me. "I'm glad that you told me," I responded. "But I am sure that you and your husband will get through it. I've never had surgery, but I do know that the best thing you can do is to get the support of your family."

She looked away. "That man is not my husband. He is only my boyfriend. I live with him, and we tell everyone that we're married because some of our Virginia neighbors might raise their eyebrows if they thought we weren't married. In fact, our relationship is not very good. He doesn't care that I have to have surgery. He decided not to come with me to the hospital, and the rest of my family is in Oregon."

I was relieved to hear that she was not married and was so happy that she had confided so much in me. I also felt a need to do something about her health problem. "I will go to the hospital with you," I offered.

"What?"

"I mean, I'll go to the surgery with you, if you don't mind."

"But you have school. You can't miss class because of me."

"Yes, I can. I can miss class for someone I care about. My family is in Africa, and there are times when I wish they could be with me. So I understand the importance of knowing that someone who cares will be with you."

A week later, Melissa and I went to the hospital, where the lump was removed. After the surgery, we went for ice cream. Later, I took her home and made soup for her. I really liked this girl. Life was good again. But just as my romance with Melissa was beginning to take off, my asylum case took a serious turn for the worse.

SEVEN

The Fourth Circuit

Early in January 2003, Phil called with the awful news. The Board of Immigration Appeals had affirmed Judge Churchill's order deporting me to Kenya.

The decision was written by only one board member, Frederick Hess, but it was not quite a summary affirmance. Hess agreed with Judge Churchill that I should be deported because I had returned to help Njoka in 1997. Hess did not accept Judge Churchill's view that a cessation clause of the Convention Relating to the Status of Refugees disqualified me from receiving asylum. But he reached the same result by relying on the U.S. Refugee Act's definition of a refugee as a person who is "unwilling or unable" to return home because of persecution or a well-founded fear of persecution. In a one-paragraph order, Hess dismissed my appeal: "The respondent's return constitutes a fundamental change in circumstances and diminishes his claim to have a well-founded fear of future persecution. See [the statute] (defining 'refugee' to include people 'unable or unwilling to return' to a country on account of a protected ground)."[1]

I was devastated by the decision, and Phil was just as upset. Instead of responding to Phil's main argument, Hess simply ignored the statement in the *Basic Law Manual* explaining that a person could remain a refugee if he or she returned home temporarily because of a compelling family emergency. Also, Hess substituted a new theory for Judge Churchill's flawed reasoning without giving us a chance to address it. Most of the argument in Phil's brief had attacked Judge Churchill's theory, and to that extent it apparently had been successful. But instead of asking the parties to file additional briefs on the interpretation of the phrase "unwilling to return" in the Refugee Act, Hess had decided what it meant without hearing from anyone. As far as Phil or I could tell from his brief explanation, he might have been saying that if a refugee returned home for *any* reason, such an action proved that the person was not "unwilling to return."

Although Hess did not refer to the *Basic Law Manual,* which Phil had quoted, he did at least mention Phil's other argument, which emphasized consistency with the board's prior *Getaneh* decision. Hess did not wave away the *Getaneh* case, as Judge Churchill had, on the grounds that it was unpublished. However, he purported to distinguish the *Getaneh* case from mine in that it "involved an alien who secured a passport from his country, as opposed to an alien who returned to his country." This was simply wrong: the most important fact about Getaneh's case was that he had been rearrested at the airport as soon as he actually returned to Ethiopia.

Hess added a footnote to his opinion that may have explained why he released his decision during the first week of January rather than months earlier. One week before Hess reached his decision, Moi left office. Mwai Kibaki, with whom I had once met during the farmers' protest, had recently been elected president of Kenya. "In light of our conclusion," Hess noted, "we find no reason to address the recent election in Kenya, but note that the respondent stated that he shared goals with Mwai Kibaki, who recently defeated Daniel arap Moi."

This footnote was both factually incorrect and legally irrelevant. It was incorrect because Moi had not been a candidate in the election; Kibaki had defeated Moi's preferred candidate, but not Moi himself. The footnote was irrelevant because an appellate decision should be based only on the evidentiary record. The board could have remanded the case to Judge Churchill to consider the impact of the election, requiring me to show that I continued to risk persecution if I went back to Kenya now. If Hess had done this, the government and I would have had the opportunity to argue about whether I still had reason to fear returning to Kenya.

In fact, I was more afraid than ever because Kibaki, who led a coalition of many contending factions, quickly appointed Francis Tiliitei as deputy secretary of defense, second in command of the security forces.[2] Tiliitei was the district commissioner who had tried to bribe me to stop the boycott, and he had probably approved or ordered my arrest and detention. But since Hess chose not to send the case back to Judge Churchill, and there would be no hearing on the risks of my return to Kenya, Phil thought that Hess had written the footnote with only one purpose in mind: to poison the atmosphere in the event I took the case further, to the federal court of appeals.

Although Hess upheld the denial of asylum, he did extend my permission to depart voluntarily for an additional thirty days, until February 6, 2003. This extension was not the result of any special generosity on his part; it was the board's standard practice to extend voluntary departure, if granted by an immigration judge, until thirty days after the board's denial of asylum.

I asked Phil about Hess's background. He told me that Hess had served for nearly twenty years as director of the Office of Enforcement Operations of the Criminal Division of the Justice Department, where he had been responsible for a dramatic increase in the number of domestic wiretaps approved by the government.[3] Attorney General Ashcroft had appointed Hess to the Board of Immigration Appeals in September 2001.[4] Just two days before he decided my case, the *Los Angeles Times* identified Hess as the Energizer Bunny of the Ashcroft speed-up. According to the *Times*, the board had begun its accelerated disposition process in February 2002 rather than waiting for the new rules to go into effect in September of that year, and its members had issued 16,275 decisions without explanation between March 1 and September 24. During that period, the board rejected 86 percent of the appeals. Hess in particular "dispens[ed] justice at a brisk pace. On October 31 [Hess] signed more than 50 cases—a decision every 10 minutes if he worked a nine-hour day without a break."[5]

The next day, Phil called me to say that I needed to make an important decision very quickly. My period for voluntary departure was only thirty days long, and the time in which I could file with the federal court of appeals would also expire within one month. I could leave the United States now and appeal from abroad, or I could remain in the United States while I appealed.

I had just started another term of law school at Catholic University, so leaving the country would have ended my legal education. I was still afraid to return to Kenya, not certain that I would be safe under the new Kibaki administration. I had no connections with or any right to enter any other country.

I was also deeply in love with Melissa, the Catholic University law student I had met at the Halloween party. The evening after learning the news about Hess's decision, I told Melissa about my arrest in Kenya and my immigration problems in America. I could barely speak because I felt so afraid of how she would react to hearing about my detention, the gruesome details of my torture, my therapy, and the possibility that I would be deported. Finally, I simply gave her my case file to read. Only then did my voice return. I warned her that continuing a relationship with me could lead to terrible disappointment.

Melissa read the file quietly for several hours. Shutting the file, she turned toward me, wrapped her arms around me, and kissed me deeply. "I knew you were a great guy, but I had no idea how really wonderful you have always been."

"You have no idea what you are getting yourself into, do you?" I asked. Before I could babble further, she put her forefinger on my lips to hush me.

"Shhh. . . . I wish I had known you before you came to America. You are an amazingly courageous man. Thank you for sharing that with me. I love you."

Astonished and overwhelmed, I simply held her tight as she burrowed her head into my chest. I wished the circumstances were different. "You know, our relationship could easily be construed as a sham to resolve my immigration issues. You may not want to be involved with someone in my position."

"Is this one of your strategies to get rid of women you don't like? Because if that's the case, you are pretty sick," she grinned.

"It's one of my strategies to let someone I love know what to expect before getting herself too involved with me," I explained.

She gently cradled her small hands around my cheekbones and smiled. "We Oregon women are stronger than you think. We don't let anything stop us from following our hearts. Even if it means I have to leave the United States, I will be with you."

"You really have no idea what you are getting yourself into," I warned her again.

"Oh, yeah?" She climbed onto my lap. "Want to know about Oregon women?"

"Sure," I said, becoming convinced that Melissa either did not comprehend the gravity of my case or was completely crazy.

"Three guys met in a bar," she began, "an Ohioan, a Texan, and an Oregonian. After knocking back a few, they started chatting about their wives. The Ohio guy said, 'After our honeymoon, I told my little woman what I expected to see from her: I expected to see my house clean. The first day when I came home, I didn't see anything. The second day, I didn't see anything. But, boy, by the third day, . . .'—the Ohio guy punched his fist into his hand—'I saw the house clean!'

"The Texan sat up and bragged: 'You think that's good? After our honeymoon, I told my wife what I expected to see: the house spotless *and* dinner on the table. The first day, I didn't see anything. The second day, I didn't see anything. But on the third day, I saw my house spotless and dinner was on the table!'

"The Oregonian finished his beer. 'Oh, yeah? When I married my wife, I told her I expected to see dinner on the table, the house spotless, and my laundry done. The first day, I didn't see anything. The second day, I didn't see anything. But on the third day, I could see a little bit out of my left eye.'"

Melissa stared into my eyes. "I think it is you, my friend, who has no idea what you are getting yourself into." She clambered off my lap. "When I was in second grade, my father's Christmas present to me was a .22 Winchester hunting rifle. I used to beat up the neighborhood boys when they tried to pick on my little brothers. I played chicken on my bike and always won. I can change oil, tires, and brake pads on most cars. If my car is stranded in a frozen wilderness, I can hike out with a pocketknife, matches, some twine, and some fabric from the vehicle. I am the first female in my immediate family to go to college or graduate school, and I did it with little help from my family."

I stared at her. She continued, "I loved you the moment I saw you. I've spent my whole life looking for you, and now that I've found you, there is no way I'm going to let some immigration bullshit interfere with us."

I stopped trying to warn her off, but I suspected that my immigration ordeal would yet test her determination.

. . .

Most decisions made by the Board of Immigration Appeals are never appealed, in part because clients can't afford the lawyers' fees. In my case, cost was only a minor consideration. Just as CALS charged no fees for asylum hearings, it also handled appeals for free. If I appealed, my out-of-pocket cost would be only the court's $250 filing fee.

But, finances aside, Phil explained that remaining in the United States during the appeal carried a real risk. To begin with, the chance of winning an appeal was very slim. The federal appeals courts are divided into twelve regional circuits. An appeal of a deportation order must be filed in the circuit in which the immigration judge rendered the decision.[6] Because I had applied for asylum after moving from California to Virginia, my application had been considered in the Asylum Office in Arlington, Virginia. That office had summoned me to a deportation hearing in Judge Churchill's court, also in Arlington. Therefore, my appeal could be heard only by the U.S. Court of Appeals for the Fourth Circuit, in Richmond.

The Fourth Circuit was well known as the most conservative federal court of appeals in the nation.[7] For example, in 1999, the Fourth Circuit ruled that federal agents did not need to warn suspects of the right to remain silent and obtain legal advice, undercutting the Supreme Court's own 1966 *Miranda* decision. The Supreme Court overturned the Fourth Circuit's ruling in that case,[8] but the Fourth Circuit has continued to decide against citizens' rights in other areas—for example, making it harder for citizens to sue polluters, ruling that the Food and Drug Administration could not regulate tobacco, and striking down a law allowing domestic violence victims to file federal lawsuits against their attackers. One press account noted that the Fourth Circuit often writes decisions that "lead the way [to the right], issuing groundbreaking rulings in the hope that the Supreme Court will ratify them as the law of the land."[9]

The Fourth Circuit's record in asylum cases was just as harsh as the rest of its jurisprudence. In asylum cases, it rarely even allowed lawyers to argue orally, and it often issued summary affirmances of deportation decisions, just as the board had done in my case. It routinely sustained the board's asylum denials with short, dry statements, such as "we dispense with oral argument because the facts and legal contentions are adequately presented in the materials before the court and argument would not aid the decisional process."[10]

Only very rarely, probably once or twice a year, did the Fourth Circuit issue an order remanding the denial of an asylum case to the board for further consideration. Those few orders were almost always unpublished and not regarded as precedents; only twice in its history had the Fourth Circuit written a published opinion criticizing the board for denying asylum. So my appeal was highly likely to be an exercise in futility, resulting in deportation. My best chance on appeal had been with the board itself, and that avenue had proved fruitless.

By remaining in the United States during what might be a hopeless appeal, I would risk being jailed or forcibly deported while my appeal was pending. The government almost never jailed affirmative asylum applicants while immigration judges or the Board of Immigration Appeals considered their cases. But it could arrest me while my further court appeal was pending, once the thirty days of my voluntary departure period elapsed. If I was arrested, the government would deport me to Kenya, where, news reports suggested, little had changed. Even incarceration in an American jail would rekindle all the horrors of my detention in Kenya.

I could avoid incarceration and deportation if, during my appeal, I requested and received a "stay of removal" from the Fourth Circuit. However, courts did not grant such stays automatically. Phil would have to make a motion requesting a stay, deliver a copy of the motion to the government's lawyers, and give them a chance to oppose it. Whether or not they opposed a stay, the Fourth Circuit might deny the request. Then the very fact that Phil had brought the case to the attention of the government might draw special attention to my situation and cause my arrest as soon as the motion was denied, or even while it was pending.

Phil called a Washington lawyer who had represented several asylum applicants in the Fourth Circuit to ask whether the government actually arrested and deported people whose cases were pending. She informed him that, in our region of the country, the government was so busy deporting undocumented immigrants with criminal records that it made little effort to arrest affirmative asylum applicants with pending court appeals. Therefore, she never asked the court for stays, and her clients usually had not been singled out for deportation during appeals. The government sent one of her clients a letter asking him to report for deportation while his appeal was pending, but she believed that the letter might have been a clerical error. She had been able to cancel the deportation until the appeal was over, just by phoning the government's local deportation director. She agreed with Phil's guess that applying for a stay of removal was more risky than not applying for one.

Phil reminded me, however, that if I got arrested for some other reason, or if I received so much as a speeding ticket, the local police might discover that I had been listed in a federal computer as a person who should be deported. In that case, I might very quickly be turned over to federal authorities, jailed, and deported.

A second problem with remaining in the United States while appealing was that I might also lose my right to depart voluntarily. Under the extension ordered by the board, that right would expire in thirty days, just when any appeal had to be filed. The appeal would take at least several months. If the court of appeals also denied asylum, would it again extend the deadline for voluntary departure? Phil found a 1994 case, *Ramsay v. INS*, in which the court noted that the several federal circuits had different rules about reinstating voluntary departure when they affirmed deportation orders.[11] Some of them always reinstated voluntary departure; others never did so. And the First Circuit, based in Boston, took a middle ground, reinstating voluntary departure unless the government asserted some special reason to oppose the reinstatement. Somewhat uncharacteristically, the Fourth Circuit in *Ramsay* had not taken the most conservative path of never reinstating the privilege. Instead, it announced that it would follow the First Circuit by routinely granting an additional thirty days of voluntary departure after it affirmed a deportation order, in the absence of a special objection from the government.

In 1996, in the same law that had imposed a one-year deadline on asylum applications, Congress tinkered with the statute governing review of deportation orders by the court of appeals, so Phil had to determine whether the Fourth Circuit was still following the practice it had announced in *Ramsay*. Apparently, it had not issued any precedent-setting decisions citing or discussing the procedure set in *Ramsay* since 1994. However, in an unpublished 1999 case posted on its web site, the Fourth Circuit sustained a deportation order against an asylum applicant and reinstated her voluntary departure in accordance with *Ramsay*, citing that case by name.[12] Although this case did not establish a precedent, Phil was confident that even if I lost the asylum appeal, I would at least hold on to my voluntary departure option.

The biggest risk seemed to be the possibility that if I had any minor encounter with the police while my appeal was pending, I could be jailed immediately. This risk had to be balanced against the pain of giving up both my legal education and my relationship with Melissa and trying, within thirty days, to find a country other than Kenya that would accept me as an immigrant or at least allow me to remain for an extended time.

After Phil and I discussed my options, I decided to appeal and to remain in the United States. I would be exceedingly careful to obey all laws, including traffic laws; and I promised Phil that I would call him night or day if I experienced any trouble that might result in arrest or deportation.

While appealing, Phil found that Catholic University was willing to issue me a new I-20 form proving to the immigration authorities that I was a student in good standing. Perhaps, then, I could get a new student visa or, more accurately, a reinstatement of the student visa under which I had completed my undergraduate education. That visa had been valid for the duration of my studies and my year of practical training, but I had interrupted my schooling after receiving my bachelor's degree and had not had a valid visa since shortly after I filed my application for asylum in 2000.

In 2003, the immigration regulations stated that the government "may consider" reinstating a student visa for someone who resumes studies after violating student status if the violation of status resulted from circumstances beyond the student's control or if nonreinstatement "would result in extreme hardship." In addition, the applicant must be someone who has not engaged in unauthorized employment (which I had not) and who is not deportable. I had become "deportable," but the regulations made a specific exception for persons who were deportable because they had been admitted as students and had failed to remain students.[13] My main problem would be showing the INS that I would suffer extreme hardship if I couldn't stay in school in the United States. Phil would also have to persuade government officials that my pending appeal to the court did not bar them from reinstating the visa.

Applications for reinstatement of student visas are filed with still another part of the bureaucracy, the office of the district director of the Immigration and Naturalization Service, also located in Virginia. Actually, it was somewhat unclear what office the district director directed, because, on January 24, 2003, just as Phil was filing the application, the Immigration and Naturalization Service ceased to exist. Congress terminated the agency and transferred its functions to the new Department of Homeland Security. DHS was still in the process of getting itself organized into bureaus and offices.

Whatever its name, the district director's new office had inherited from its predecessor a form for submitting the application, which imposed yet another filing fee, this time $102. Because the form asked whether I was the subject of deportation proceedings, I explained that I was currently appealing Judge Churchill's decision; that her decision was based on her determination that I was not legally eligible for asylum rather than any suspicion of fraud; and that, in any event, I had been granted a period of voluntary departure that had not yet expired. Phil wrote a lengthy cover letter, arguing that denial of the application would cause me extreme hardship by disrupting my education and by causing me to face possible imprisonment if I had to return to Kenya. He submitted and cross-referenced about a hundred pages of backup documents to explain the entire history of my case.

About three weeks after my thirty-day voluntary departure deadline expired, Phil and I were disappointed—but not really surprised—when the district director denied the application. What did surprise us was the sloppiness of the government's short decision. It claimed, for example, that I had filed the application on February 27, after my period of voluntary departure had expired, when in fact I had filed on February 5, before the expiration. It also cited an incorrect date for the voluntary departure deadline. Then, with no further explanation and no discussion of the hundred pages we had filed, the decision asserted that "the applicant has not shown that . . . failure to receive reinstatement to lawful F-1 status would result in extreme hardship," and it quoted a regulation stating that "if the Service does not reinstate the student, the student may not appeal that decision." Now only a successful appeal of the asylum denial could prevent my deportation.

· · ·

As federal agencies kept ruling against me, I had to start planning for the possibility that I would be forced to leave the United States. Was returning to Kenya safe for me now that Kibaki was president? When I was in jail, my interrogators wanted me to accuse Kibaki of leading the boycott, and I had not done so. Would his new government protect me if I returned? Current Kenyan politics were quite complicated. Kibaki's loose coalition incorporated many former Moi officials, including my former nemesis Francis Tiliitei. Kibaki had ended some of the human rights abuses of his predecessor and had exposed Moi's water torture cells for public inspection.[14] But he had little control over most government officials. Bribery remained rampant, and news reports from Kenya indicated that Kibaki was unable to deal with the massive corruption in his administration and in the judiciary. I feared that the former Moi officials who were now in the Kibaki government might be threatened by my presence in Kenya and might use the government's administrative resources to punish former and current enemies.

Nevertheless, I decided to investigate moving to Kibaki's Kenya. Perhaps the new Kenyan government would welcome the entrepreneurial efforts of a Kenyan expatriate who had an American college degree in international business management. Melissa and I devised an investment plan for the area around my home village in Kangaita. Located in the foothills of Mount Kenya, this region is one of the most beautiful places in the world. An area of publicly owned land between the village and the forest appeared to be a prime site for a hotel and safari base. Melissa and I formed a small company, the Ngarurih Investment Group, which became a member of the Corporate Council on Africa, the principal trade association of American entrepreneurs interested in African economic development. By email, I renewed contact with numerous people I had known in the early 1990s who had now taken minor roles in Kibaki's government. They would alert me when economic development officials from the new government were scheduled to visit the United States.

Lucy, Melissa, and I decided to demonstrate the development potential of the region by building a community center on my property and, with Njoka's permission, on his adjacent land. We hired Wash to manage the project. The center would include a pediatric clinic, a library, and a computer training center. Relying on my advice, which I conveyed through email and frequent transatlantic telephone calls, Wash and Lucy started to work. They cleared my property and fenced it. They dug the foundation for the community center, put down timbers and posts, and built a shed for the contractors.

We immediately ran into a snag. Although my older sister, Wangithi, had a house of her own, she decided to occupy an old shed on my land and moved her son into an unfinished house on Njoka's land. Wash needed to use that building as his residence and as a storage facility during the construction of the community center, after which we would tear it down to make room for part of the community center. At the beginning of March 2003, we wrote a letter to Wangithi advising her and her son to vacate the property to allow the contractors to begin their work. Wangithi ignored our notice. We offered to help her move, but she refused to leave and threatened to burn down the construction site if we tried to force her out.

Melissa and I asked Wash to report her threats to the local police. I also wrote a letter to the local district police officer describing the threats. Then I advised Wash to have the contractors demolish the shed. Wangithi and her son finally left the property, and Wash moved into the unfinished house.

On April 28, 2003, in broad daylight, Wangithi's son, my brother Njogu's son, and two others from the village who had been connected with Moi's KANU party arrived on the property and forcibly evicted Wash. The removal created a commotion and attracted a big crowd of people from the village. As the crowd watched, the invaders burned the house, tore up the fencing, and destroyed the foundations for the community center. Wash had to run from the property, fearing for his life.

Wash promptly reported the arson to the local police, but they refused to investigate the crime unless he paid them. When he refused, the police stated that they would not get involved. They threatened to arrest Wash and charge him with making a false police report. Wash later called us to say that he could not press the matter further, because it was obvious that either the police were out for themselves or they saw the matter as a family dispute rather than a criminal offense.

In June 2003, President Kibaki sent a delegation of cabinet ministers to Washington, D.C., to meet Kenyans living in the United States. The delegation, which sought to generate American investment interest, included, among others, the trade minister, Dr. Mukhisa Kituyi, and the minister of national security, Chris Murungaru. Melissa and I contacted the Kenyan embassy in Washington and arranged to attend a reception at the Kenyan ambassador's residence to meet with the ministers.

The ambassador's residence is located in an upscale Washington suburb, near the Maryland border. We arrived at the reception just before 7:30 P.M. The event seemed disorganized, with no food, no microphones, and no clear agenda. We pushed our way through the crowd inside the residence, moving out to the back courtyard, where another crowd had congregated in the hot, humid summer evening. I left Melissa in the courtyard and went to stand in line at the bar. A tall, gangly man with dark tinted glasses approached me. He shook my hand and gestured to me to stay at the bar.

"Wait, I need to bring my girlfriend her drink," I told him.

"Do you know who I am?" he asked.

"No, I don't—please refresh my memory," I responded.

"You should, because I am the one who made all this happen," he smiled.

"What did you make happen?" I asked. His smile faded. I tried to remember where I had seen him before, but nothing about him seemed familiar. "You look like you could use a drink," I offered. "What would you like?"

"A Coca-Cola," he requested. I had expected him to ask for a beer or something else with alcohol. "Would you like something in it?" I asked.

"No. Why would you want to put anything in a Coca-Cola?"

I asked for a Coke for him, and he drained the whole can immediately.

"You must be thirsty and quite tired," I noted. "Where did you come from?"

"The Pentagon. The U.S. government is upgrading our airport security."

"I presume you are a member of the official delegation?"

"I am not a member of the delegation. I *am* the delegation," he stated.

"I am honored," I told him.

He replied that he was the national security minister.

"That's great," I exclaimed, "because you are one of the reasons why I am here."

"Everyone is here because of me," he added.

"I would like to discuss a local security issue that has frustrated our efforts to establish an investment project in Kenya," I said to him and then proceeded to explain the arson on my farm. I offered to give him the letter I had written earlier, describing the refusal of the local police to investigate the incident.

Murungaru waved off the letter and refused to accept it. "If you want to stop these things, then you should return to Kenya," he said curtly and then walked away.

I was shocked. I had expected him to at least express some concern about one of the obstacles to American investment.

Impulsively, I pushed through the crowd and got in front of him. "Doesn't police inaction concern you?" I questioned. "Maybe you can help us understand the kind of security challenges that Kenya is being faced with at the moment and what the new government is doing to enforce the law."

I had raised my voice above the din, and suddenly the noisy crowd quieted. Everyone turned to look at us. Murungaru looked at me coldly and said, "Crimes are committed and people die every day. Who do you think you are to be asking me these kinds of questions?"

"I am a concerned citizen of Kenya, sir, and just like most of us here, we would like to know what your office is doing to address the security situation."

"That is not what ministers do," Murungaru retorted. "Someone tell this drunkard that I am the internal security minister, not a police officer."

"What kind of a security minister responds to reports of police negligence by advising the person reporting the problem to take care of it himself? Is that the kind of security minister you are?" I continued. (Two years later, I found out that Chris Murungaru had been fired from Kibaki's cabinet amid allegations of corruption. Both Britain and the United States announced that they would deny him entry.)[15]

I must have challenged Murungaru more loudly than I intended. A small section of the crowd applauded, and several young men in the crowd yelled out, "These are legitimate questions, and they deserve your response."

A hand reached out from the crowd and pulled me aside. I looked down at a short, balding man with glasses. Dr. Kituyi released my hand and said softly, "Wachira, you haven't changed."

I had met Dr. Kituyi once, when I was mobilizing the tea boycott. The clarity of his memory shocked me. I had not expected anyone at this reception, let alone someone like Dr. Kituyi, to remember me and address me by name, especially after having met me only once, ten years earlier.

He registered my surprise. "Yes, I remember you," Dr. Kituyi continued, "and I must warn you that even though the government has changed, not much has changed in Kenya since you left. You are still a threat," he concluded, turning away to greet others in the crowd.

His warning reinforced my desire to win my appeal for asylum and remain in the United States.

.   .   .

For Phil, taking my case to federal court was a much bigger project than taking it to the Board of Immigration Appeals. The federal court has a 128-page manual with detailed procedural rules for lawyers handling appeals. For example, before Phil could file the appeal, he had to make a motion and pay a fee to be admitted to the bar of the Fourth Circuit. Along with the appeal, he had to file a "docketing statement" with various attachments. His brief could not exceed fourteen thousand words. The rules specified that "either a proportionally spaced or a mono-spaced face may be used. . . . A proportionally spaced face must include serifs, but sans-serif type may be used in headings and captions. A proportionally spaced face must be 14-point or larger [and] a mono-spaced face may not contain more than 10½ characters per inch."[16] Eight copies had to be filed, bound in one of several specified ways, with a blue cover.

Phil learned the hard way that each of the court's many rules had to be followed to the letter, even when they were a bit ambiguous. For example, the rules said nothing about the font for footnotes. Phil wrote the brief in a 14-point font, as specified, and used a 12-point font for the footnotes to distinguish them visually from the text. The clerk of the court rejected his brief and ordered him to retype and reprint it, at considerable expense, with both the text and the footnotes in a 14-point font.

The task of preparing the appeal was complicated by the cascading results of the Ashcroft "reforms" at the Board of Immigration Appeals. The board's new practice of summarily affirming deportations without opinions, or with very short statements such as Hess's, had apparently led to an explosion of cases in the courts of appeals, probably because lawyers felt that they would have a chance of obtaining a fair appellate review only at a higher level. In January 2002, the board issued summary decisions in 10 percent of its cases; by April of that year, more than 50 percent of the cases received similar treatment. Also, before the spring of 2002, the board had reversed the deportation orders of immigration judges in 25 percent of its cases; but as soon as the Ashcroft reforms kicked in, reversals fell to 10 percent. During the same period, the number of board decisions appealed to federal courts each month increased from about two hundred to seven hundred; by January 2003, nine hundred decisions were being appealed monthly. Before the Ashcroft reforms began, the federal courts had no backlog of immigration cases; but by January 2003, they had a backlog of nearly five thousand. A study conducted for the American Bar Association concluded that "the [Ashcroft] 'Procedural Reforms' are not resolving, but only shifting, a backlog from the [board] to the federal courts."[17]

The federal courts were not the only institutions burdened by the Ashcroft reforms. The Justice Department lawyers representing the government in the federal courts of appeals also had much more work on

their hands—so much so that the department had to request additional appropriations to handle the increased burden. And at the board itself, the clerks were completely overwhelmed because they had to prepare and certify the case records that were being sent to the appellate courts.

Their inability to do their jobs resulted in more work for all the lawyers who represented appellants like myself. According to the court rules, the board was supposed to file the official record of my case, including the transcript of the hearing before Judge Churchill and all the exhibits, within forty days after Phil filed the appeal. It was also mandated to send copies to the opposing lawyers. Phil's brief had to cite page numbers in that record. But when the brief was nearly due, the board was so backlogged that it was months away from preparing the record in my case. As a result, Phil had to do the board's work for it, compiling a 321-page appendix with copies of all the exhibits on which he wanted to rely and copying and binding this document for the court. This requirement added hundred of dollars in costs to the already expensive work of preparing the brief.

When Phil finished compiling the relevant documents and sat down to do the actual writing, he tried to figure out how to get the court's attention so that the judges would take my case seriously. He knew that the court rarely granted oral argument in asylum cases and that it almost never ruled against the board. He surmised that it was not very interested in asylum cases and that it processed them rather mechanically, perhaps delegating most of the work to clerks. He wanted to get the judges interested enough in my case, and particularly in the issue of my return to rescue Njoka, that they would want to hear more from him in person. Once Phil was face-to-face with the judges, he thought, it might be more difficult for them to reject the appeal without giving it real thought. Also, he wanted to present an oral argument so that he could seat me in the front row and make the judges know that if they turned down my appeal, they would be deporting a human being, not merely an African name.

Phil's brief started with a relatively long statement of facts. He used seventeen pages to relate what he thought was the compelling tale of the protest I had led on behalf of the tea farmers. He described in detail how

I risked my life by returning to Kenya to try to save Njoka from the kind of harsh treatment that I myself had experienced in jail.

Then he proceeded to the legal argument. The basis for Hess's very brief decision denying asylum was unclear, making Phil's job difficult. If Hess had said clearly that any return was disqualifying, Phil would have made one type of argument to rebut him. But if Hess had stated that some returns were not disqualifying but that I had returned for an insufficiently compelling emergency, a different argument would have been appropriate. But because Hess's decision was so ambiguous, Phil's brief had to deal with both possibilities.

First, he considered the possibility that Hess meant to disqualify all returning refugees by treating any return as proof that the individual was "not unwilling" to return. To appeal to those conservatives who believe that words in statutes usually have clear meanings that judges can discern, Phil started with the dictionary definitions of "unwilling," citing several that equated this word with "hesitant or loath," or "done reluctantly." Phil argued that people often do things with reluctance, such as running into burning houses to save their children. That was exactly what I had done to save my brother.

Phil turned to Shakespeare to show that in the English language, "unwilling" has long been a relative term, not an absolute bar to action. For example, in *Richard II*, the king stopped a duel between Mowbray and Bolingbroke. After consulting his council, including Bolingbroke's father, John of Gaunt, the king banished both fighters. John of Gaunt, who now might never see his son again, reveals that he gave the king advice that he had actually been unwilling to provide:

> You urged me as a judge; but I had rather
> You would have bid me argue like a father. . . .
> But you gave leave to my unwilling tongue
> Against my will to do myself this wrong.[18]

Still working on the assumption that Hess intended to deny asylum to all applicants who had revisited their countries, Phil turned to the second

prong of his challenge, in which he asked the court to consider how the Justice Department itself had construed the term "unwilling." He argued that Hess had ignored the attorney general's own *Basic Law Manual*, which noted that in a particular case, an asylum seeker could justify a return for compelling reasons despite a continuing risk. In fact, as recently as 2001, the Department of Justice had issued a new training manual for asylum officers stating that a temporary visit may be justified if one of the applicant's immediate family members dies or is in "a grave situation that compelled return." The manual added that the asylum officer "should not conclude that return due to compelling factors establishes that the applicant is able and willing to return."

The third prong of Phil's argument was the one that he thought might most interest the judges of the Fourth Circuit, because it injected new legal research and international human rights law into the case. Judge Churchill had cited a bit of international law against me, one of the cessation clauses of the Convention Relating to the Status of Refugees. Phil had argued to the board that she had used the wrong cessation clause. Now he turned her argument around, pressing the point that the correct cessation clause, the one that applied to people who actually returned home, excluded refugee status only for those who returned home intending to reestablish residence there. Through weeks of research, Phil had found extensive support for this view in the handbook issued by the U.N. High Commissioner for Refugees, the writings of international law scholars, and the subtle changes that diplomats had made in successive drafts of the convention while they negotiated its terms in 1950. He also found that although no U.S. court had ever decided whether short returns for compelling reasons negated the possibility of asylum, two cases in Canada and France had been decided in favor of asylum applicants who returned to their home countries for family emergencies, one to care for his mother, the other because his mother had died.

Phil and I talked about the other possible interpretation of Hess's opinion. "What if Hess had not meant to exclude *all* asylum applicants who visited their countries? What if he meant to say that for reasons he did not explain, my trip to rescue Njoka did not qualify as 'compelling'?" I asked Phil.

To address the possibility that the court would interpret Hess's opinion that way, Phil argued that although the board could legitimately distinguish among different reasons for return, it should be required to make an individualized analysis and to state its reasoning, not a bare conclusion. He cited the famous *Chenery* case from the late 1940s, when the Supreme Court held that an administrative agency's decision "must be set forth with such clarity as to be understandable."[19] Several other circuit courts of appeals had applied the *Chenery* doctrine to the Board of Immigration Appeals, requiring it to explain its reasons for concluding that an individual did not qualify for asylum or other relief from deportation.[20] Typically, these cases held that "the Board must articulate its reasons for denying relief sufficiently for us, as the reviewing court, to be able to see that the Board considered all the relevant factors."[21] Unfortunately, the Fourth Circuit had never explicitly held the board to this standard of clarity.

To help the court see that return visits to one's homeland could be caused by a wide spectrum of considerations, Phil arrayed several hypothetical cases along that spectrum. At one extreme was a refugee's comfortable return for a period of years. At the other was a refugee's temporary return because his wife had been captured and was being tortured. If the board considered my return more like the first situation than the last, it should have to explain why. In fact, Phil argued, I had returned under very extreme circumstances, because although Njoka was technically my brother, he was for all practical and psychological purposes my son: I had raised him and my sister Lucy when they were toddlers, after my father died; I had been tortured in jail, so I knew what Njoka faced; no other relative could protect him; I avoided political activity while I helped Njoka; and I left Kenya as soon as he was freed on bail. The board had not said why these facts did not make my return compelling.

Even though Phil did not want to distract attention from the asylum issue, he had to protect my voluntary departure in case the court was not persuaded to reverse Hess's decision. So in the very last sentence of his brief, he asked the court to at least reinstate my voluntary departure pursuant to its *Ramsay* precedent.

As Phil later explained, "Litigation is often a process of hurry up and wait." After docketing the appeal in February 2003, Phil filed his brief on time in May. The government's brief was due thirty days later. But the government's lawyers were swamped by the thousands of other appeals from the board's summary affirmances. The court twice excused the Department of Justice from its deadline and gave it more time to answer Phil's arguments.

.   .   .

While Phil worked on the brief, Melissa and I decided to test how committed we were to each other by taking a trip of more than a month to drive across the United States. I could meet her family in Oregon, and she could meet my friends. We would also discover the similarities and differences in our cultures. We thought that by the end of such a long trip, we would know whether we wanted to spend our lives together.

Phil wasn't blind to my romance with Melissa. He cautioned that, for several reasons, marrying Melissa would not solve my immigration problems, even though spouses of American citizens are usually entitled to become lawful permanent residents.

First, if the Department of Homeland Security believed that I was marrying Melissa only so that I could immigrate, it would refuse to grant me permanent resident status. Second, Congress prohibited the immigration courts from allowing a person who is appealing a deportation order to become a permanent resident simply by marrying an American citizen.[22] "If you marry Melissa but lose the appeal," Phil warned me, "you will have to leave the United States, return home to Kenya, and try to obtain an immigrant visa abroad."

The third problem might prevent me from getting that visa, if the court affirmed my deportation order and did not reinstate my voluntary departure. People who are deported from the United States, or who leave on their own after a deportation order, are barred for ten years from returning to United States unless the Department of Homeland Security waives that bar. "If you lose the appeal and leave the country," Phil continued, "there is no way of knowing in advance whether the Department of Homeland Security will grant you a waiver to return to your wife. On the other hand," he emphasized, "if you two decide to marry anyway and the court reinstates your voluntary departure order as it did in *Ramsay* and other cases, you could leave during the period of reinstated voluntary departure, avoid a formal order of deportation, and not be affected by the ten-year bar."

All I wanted was to be with Melissa. I was crazy about her. To me, Phil's advice was "blah, blah, blah," as I daydreamed about summer, Melissa, and our upcoming road trip. For the first time, my immigration woes no longer put me in constant fear.

During our visit with Dave and Irena Straus in Sharon, Massachusetts, I thought about the possible perceptions of Americans who met us. When Melissa and I first dated, I was worried about holding hands with her in public, concerned that she would be ostracized for being with a black man. But in Massachusetts, people kept smiling at us. As Melissa put it, "If a seven-foot-tall black man and a barely five-foot-tall white woman are holding hands with big smiles on their faces, how could anyone not find them funny?"

My enormous height seemed to make it easier for white Americans to talk to me. Everyone felt free to approach me and ask how tall I was, and when they heard my accent, they asked where I came from. Their third question was always whether I was a basketball player. Melissa had never asked about my height.

We drove into Indiana. A small forest of billboards advertised the local attractions, including the Yogi Bear Campground. "Do you know who Yogi Bear is?" Melissa asked me.

"Oh, yeah," I confidently responded. "He was a baseball player for the Yankees."

After she stopped laughing and could breathe again, Melissa described the difference between Yogi Berra and the cartoon Yogi Bear.

"And Americans let their kids watch a bear steal picnic baskets?" I asked as I tried not to laugh. "You know, American humor is deeply hidden inside American cartoon characters. When I first saw the Simpsons, I wondered why anyone would want to watch a bunch of badly drawn cartoons. But I realized that each character represents what I have found in almost every American community: a black, overweight, balding doctor; a Lisa who is too smart and cultured; a Pakistani working in a convenience store; a sour-mouthed and bitter local bartender; a school bully; a cool dude who drives the school bus and introduces all the kids to heavy metal."

"American humor simplifies very complex relationships and makes its point by finding the commonalities," Melissa commented.

"You're right. Even after 9/11, Americans were making Osama jokes."

"That's different. That is a reaction to pain," Melissa clarified.

We approached a town that featured itself as the Sleeping Capital of the World. I realized how proud Americans are of everything they do. Every town is a capital of something: the Capital of Roses, the Fireworks Capital, the Home of the Biggest Pancake in the World. I marveled at the moment, riding down the highway with an extremely beautiful woman, watching farms, cornfields, and cows pass by, framed by a fiery sunset. We smiled at each other.

"Why do you think we don't see any blacks in the passing cars?" I asked Melissa. Before she could answer, I said, "Maybe it's because American blacks identify road trips with white culture. But they have these highways. This is absolutely beautiful."

"Well, haven't you seen the motorcycle groups that tour Virginia and Maryland?" Melissa asked. "There are a lot of all-black bike clubs there."

"Hmm," I murmured. We drove on. The sunset faded ahead. "You know, if I were a white guy discovering this beautiful land for the first time, I would have stolen this land from the Indians, too."

"My turn to drive," Melissa giggled.

"My turn to sleep."

Rain woke me in Minnesota, and I discovered Melissa driving through a terrible storm at twenty miles per hour. "Adrenaline's great at first, but not for more than two hours straight," Melissa quipped as lightning bolts appeared every few seconds, on both sides of the road. The rain fell so heavily that our headlights could penetrate only ten feet ahead of us, but the lightning lit up the sky so frequently that we could still see the road. Strangely, we could hear no thunder.

Several times, we observed lightning emerge from the ground next to our car and hover in a ball in the air for a moment before shooting up to the clouds. Twice, the air all around us flashed the world entirely white, and my muscles tensed as if I'd had a full morning workout in thirty seconds. Melissa's hair stood on end. A huge spark exploded immediately to the right of our vehicle.

"The storm came too quickly for me to find a hotel," Melissa explained, "and I didn't want to wake you until I needed you to drive. But it's too dangerous for me to stop driving now, and we'd die if we left the car, even to run into a hotel. We'd get hit by the lightning. At least the tires will insulate us from the electricity."

Melissa had never seen a midwestern storm before, and now she was driving us through the worst storm I had ever seen, more powerful than some of the very strong ones I'd experienced in my two years in Oklahoma. I sat quietly and prepared for our death.

From 8:30 P.M. to 3:30 A.M., Melissa drove doggedly ahead until, miraculously, the storm clouds parted and we could see stars. She pulled into a truck stop and set her watch alarm for two hours of sleep. Early the next morning, we got back on the road, crossing the Mississippi. The land became softly rolling grasslands, with the road winding like a river between low bumps. On top of one of the bumps sat a roadside gas station and restaurant. Melissa drove us in for breakfast and gas.

"We gained an hour," she said, glancing at the clock above the counter. Our watch said 8:30 A.M., but the clock read 7:30 A.M. "Dorothy, eat your heart out. You might have ridden a storm to another land, but we traveled through time." She noticed my puzzled look. "I'm sorry, it's a *Wizard of Oz* reference. I'll explain it later."

As we were seated, all conversation among the middle-aged white men stopped, and their John Deere caps turned in our direction. I looked at Melissa, and she looked nervous. The men's faces and hands looked wrinkled by hard work, and their weathered faces peered at us.

I spoke first. "Hi, everyone!" I said out loud as Melissa and I slid into our booth. She leaned forward toward me and whispered, "Everyone is staring at us . . . and they all look grumpy."

"I didn't even notice," I responded. But I saw that a man with Scandinavian features was looking at us from the next booth.

"Hi," Melissa piped up. "We just drove through a huge storm. Where in South Dakota are we?" she asked.

The man looked a little puzzled. "Sath Da-koo-ta? Yur not 'n South Da-koo-ta, yur in Minn-na-soo-ta."

"Oh, damn. I can't believe we are still in Minnesota," Melissa mumbled. Because she had driven for so long in the storm, she found it hard to believe that we hadn't yet crossed the state.

Tunnel-eyed, Melissa sipped her coffee, but I struck up a conversation with our neighbor. We learned that almost all the men in the restaurant were farmers and that this particular gentleman had a master's degree in biochemistry and had recently retired after working for many years as a testing engineer in the local Hormel plant where Spam is made. I immediately told the waitress, who was the only female besides Melissa in the restaurant, that I wanted Spam for breakfast. "Um, I'm sorry, we're out," she said.

Everyone in the restaurant began laughing. I ordered an omelet. My neighbor told me that there are more than forty types of Spam and that Hawaiians buy more Spam than people in any other state.

By now, everyone in the restaurant had joined in our conversation. They were surprised that we had survived the drive through the storm. "That was the worst storm we've had in years," one of the John Deere caps said. "This fellow over here lost his whole crop last night." The unlucky farmer just shook his head and sipped his coffee.

"What about crop circles? Do they happen here too?" I asked.

"Crop circles are just a bunch of superstitious crap!" retorted the oldest farmer.

"Speak for yourself. We might have advanced degrees," another farmer chimed in, "but we're still superstitious."

Another man interjected, "Crop circles are caused by dust devils."

"What are dust devils?" I asked.

"Small tornado-shaped funnels that create what look like crop circles," the oldest farmer explained.

"Allegedly," chimed in another farmer.

As a onetime farmer, I found it easy to connect with these men, and they made an effort to fit me into their conversation, particularly when Melissa revealed that one of her maternal grandfathers had emigrated from Norway to Minnesota, where he had worked for the railroad.

"He lost his arm in a coupling accident and was put into managing warehouse stock," she said. "He later became a senior vice president in charge of shipping."

By this time, all the men were nodding.

"Even now, the railroad takes care of its own people. They provide great benefits, and the pay is very good," one of the farmers told us. Our booth neighbor turned to Melissa and said, "You know, you do have very Norwegian features. I can tell by your nose and face. Also your personality—you are like the Norwegians here. You look like you could come from here."

"I'm in love with this woman," I blurted out. "She is the one who suggested that we stop here, and I love her for it. And I think you guys can help me understand a characteristic about her that I haven't quite figured out. When she sets her mind onto something, it's going to get done, no matter what—like driving through that storm last night. You're all Norwegians, so what advice do you guys have for me?"

"You're in trouble," one offered. We all laughed.

A week later, we arrived at the home of Melissa's parents, Bob and Edna Kenney, in the small coastal town of Netarts, Oregon. Melissa had earlier told Bob that she was very serious about me. Unbeknownst to me, she had asked Bob to tell her his honest opinion of me, no matter how harsh. Melissa had also described me as "kind of on the short side." She had asked him not to comment on my stature because I was very sensitive about being so short.

After we pulled into the driveway, Melissa asked me to sit in the car for a moment and not stand up until her parents arrived. After Edna's grandkids and dogs gave us the welcome wagon, Melissa stepped forward. "Dad, Edna, I'd like you to meet Jeff." I stood up. Her dad stared up at me, paused, looked back down at Melissa, and quietly asked, "Pup?" Edna and the grandkids, all in on the joke, giggled with Melissa.

I guessed Pup was her dad's nickname for her.

They lived in the biggest house in the neighborhood. I sensed that it was the local community center. "It's never empty," Edna agreed.

"Your husband should be the mayor of Netarts," I said to her.

"Even if I paid him a million dollars, Bob wouldn't want to be a mayor. Not even of the couch he's sitting on."

Bob had no misgivings about my race. Eight generations earlier, one of his ancestors, the Irish co-owner of a Virginia plantation, had become an abolitionist. According to family legend, he had vanished from the plantation and emerged later in Grants Pass, Oregon, with a curly-haired "Indian" woman, whom he married.

During our first evening, Bob and Edna put out an impressively beautiful spread for dinner. One of Edna's grandchildren announced out loud at the table that she had never seen such a big table of food before, so I must be someone important. After dinner, Bob motioned me to come with him and took me through a door that appeared to lead into a closet. I walked into a huge gun room. Even though by this time I had lived in the United States for eight years and had become used to Americans' fascination with guns, seeing so many guns in one collection astonished me. Bob picked up a Winchester hunting rifle and then pulled out an Enfield rifle, the gun that British troops had used to conquer Africa. He cocked it and gave me a funny look and then asked me, "What are you doing with my daughter?"

I would be lying to say I was not intimidated. In an effort to duck the question, I blurted out, "You have more guns than the entire police department in my district in Kenya. Is this legal?"

"Oh, yes. This is America. They can't take our guns away," he explained. "If a government wants to take away its people's freedom, the first thing they take away is the people's guns."

"But why do you have so many guns?"

"Here on the West Coast, ever since World War II, the idea of an invasion has never left our minds. If anything happens out here, we want to be able to take care of our families in case the government can't get out here fast enough. Our guns are the reason why the Japanese never invaded this country."

"I don't think the Japanese are still intending to invade the United States again after what Americans did to them in 1945, do you?"

"That's true, but these guns also represent the history of our family. You see this rifle? Melissa's grandfather spent time in South Africa, where the settlers fought the Zulu with these guns. This was his weapon."

"Can I hold Melissa's first rifle?" I asked. He handed it to me. "You know," I said, "I am very much in love with your daughter, and I would like to marry her."

He smiled wryly. "That all depends on how she feels about you. I have never been able to tell her what to do. She has always done what she wants. But here is something you should always keep in mind: I love my family, and I would never let anyone hurt them. I will shoot anyone who hurts my family," he grimly stated and proceeded to close the closet.

"The law allows that too," I said, and we left the gun room to join the rest of Melissa's family at the dining table.

The next day, Bob and I shared our views on politics and rural economies. Bob believes that people can't trust politicians to represent the interests of average Americans. Like me, he could never stand injustice. As a union leader in the 1980s, he had stood up against the federal government managers in the Bonneville Power Administration, and Melissa's family had suffered for it. Bob was now happily retired with a good severance check, and he helped his community by volunteering to drive school buses, particularly for athletic teams and children with special needs.

Guns appeared to be Bob's way of symbolically protecting himself from the harm the government can cause in people's lives. I thought of my own situation. Maybe studying the law was my way of protecting myself from the government.

On the third and final day of our visit, after I had gotten to know all the members of Melissa's family, her father sat down with me. "You know, I was raised in this area. We didn't have many blacks living here when I was a kid, and I never grew up knowing any," he started cautiously. "I don't know much about what it is like for you here, but I hope we won't seem too strange to you."

I had passed the test. I asked Melissa's father again if I could marry her. He smiled and stated knowingly, "I think you'd better ask her."

The next day, Melissa and I drove to California to visit some of my Peace Corps friends. We then drove through Las Vegas, where we spent the night walking the Strip and watching the Blue Man group. On the way to Monument Valley, Utah, I got food poisoning from some dried jerky and was terribly sick. Melissa nursed me back to health by forcing liquids down my throat and dosing me with Immodium AD from her ever-present first aid kit.

That evening, we entered Monument Valley. "Oh, my God," Melissa exclaimed as we passed each monolith. She stopped the car every fifty yards to capture photos of the red soil, the green sages, and the light from the setting sun on the rocks. At the peak of the sunset, we pulled up to Cathedral Rock. As we stepped out of the car, the rays of the sun split over the valley. Melissa had never looked more beautiful. Her eyes glowed like jewels, and her hair flowed and reflected the shadows from the valley. She spun around, trying to experience the whole scene at once, stone walls that enclosed the wide valley, drumbeats from a distant powwow, coyotes barking, the jackrabbits jumping past us.

As the sun set in this incredible landscape, I felt my past disappearing with it. The night emerged like a new life. I told myself, "You have to propose to this woman now, for there will never be another moment like this." Instinctively, I put a knee on the ground and said, "Mel, I want you to marry me." I kept praying, "Please, just say yes."

"Yes, I'll marry you," she responded. Her joyful tears washed away all my fears.

I remembered that I was supposed to have a ring, and I hadn't thought to buy one. I looked around and saw the poptop from a soda can on the ground, and I gave it to her as my ring. We held each other and kissed, and I knew from that moment that I never wanted to kiss anyone else for the rest of my life.

. . .

When we returned to Washington, Melissa was wearing a real ring that we had purchased in Santa Fe. We thought about a wedding, and about what we would do if the government deported me. Dr. Kituyi's warning in June had both surprised and worried me, but I still hoped that I might be welcome in Kenya if I could foster American investment. Just before leaving on our trip west, Melissa and I had traveled to a conference in New Jersey, where we talked to Karisa Maitha, the Kenyan minister of local government. Maitha stated that he was interested in developing an effective solid waste management system for Kenya's major cities. Because of his interest, Melissa and I met with some waste management experts during the return leg of our summer trip, and we talked to some potential investors.

After we returned, we learned that President Kibaki himself was scheduled to visit Washington. He would meet with President George Bush and would be the guest of honor at a Corporate Council on Africa luncheon. As members of the council, both Melissa and I were invited. We attended the luncheon, where I met President Kibaki and gave him a copy of my proposal to develop the region near my village. Dr. Kituyi was at Kibaki's side, and Kibaki passed the proposal to him. Later,

Dr. Kituyi promised to get in touch with me after he returned to Nairobi. I never heard from him.

After the luncheon, Melissa and I attended a dinner with senior Kenyan officials in Kibaki's entourage. A man introduced himself to me as Steve Wachira. He said that he was a close associate of Minister Murungaru, who had asked him to talk to me, and that he lived in the Washington area. Later that fall, I met with him privately. During that meeting, Wachira told me that my project would obviously require the cooperation of the Kenyan government. If I wanted to work with the government, he advised, I would have to change my approach. Wachira knew specific details of our development proposal, so I knew that he had received it from the president's delegation. He told me, "You will have to salt the water to encourage the cows to drink it." I knew from having lived in Kenya that this phrase referred to bribery.

The combination of Dr. Kituyi's warning and the prospect that I would have to pay bribes to organize development in Kenya was more than I could manage. Despite the election of Kibaki, I had no future in Kenya. If I tried to work there, I would not be able to stop myself from speaking out against the climate of corruption, and I would risk arrest. I called off the investment project and began to look for other countries in Africa where I could live and work if I had to leave the United States.

Meanwhile, Phil filled me in on the battle of the briefs that had been taking place while I was traveling. He had waited two months for the government's response to his opening brief. Finally, in July, the Department of Justice sent him its brief, written by Deborah N. Misir, the lawyer it assigned to my case.

As Phil expected, Misir began by reminding the Fourth Circuit of its long tradition of deferring to the "greater immigration-related expertise of the Executive Branch."[23] This was a particularly powerful argument in the Fourth Circuit. The eleven circuits that hear asylum cases seem to have different cultural attitudes toward their reviewing function—and thus they remand cases to the board for reconsideration at markedly different rates.[24] The import of this variation for my case was that I happened to be stuck in the circuit that least frequently overturned the board's decisions.

In his brief, Phil had tried to encourage the court to overturn the board's decision by characterizing what the board did as a purely legal error—a misinterpretation of the statutory phrase "unwilling to return," rather than a misapplication of the law to particular facts or, even worse, a finding of fact in which the court should defer to the board. Misir, by contrast, tried to characterize Hess's action as fact-finding, in order to minimize the scope of the court's review. "A court that supplants the Board's findings by making alternative findings engages in impermissible fact-finding," she wrote.[25]

What were the "facts" that the court should not second-guess? Misir started with an undisputed, noncontroversial fact. When I returned to Kenya in 1997, a police officer told me, "We'll be watching you." I took this to be a warning of possible arrest. But Misir noted that despite the warning, no harm actually befell me during the two months while I was helping to obtain Njoka's release from jail.

Then Misir's brief took what Phil thought was a plunge into the deep end. She acknowledged that the government's own training manual included an example of an asylum applicant who was considered a bona fide refugee despite returning home to rescue family members. But, she argued, the court records from Kenya that Dave and Bernie had introduced to show that I had obtained Njoka's release also showed that Njoka had actually raped Mugo's daughter and her friend. After his arrest, she noted, Njoka had initially pled guilty to the crime and had been convicted "on the basis of physical evidence. . . . Ngarurih does not explain how the physical evidence was fabricated, nor why the other little girl would be motivated to press charges against his brother." In the example from the manual, the family members had been "unlawfully imprisoned and persecuted," whereas I had helped Njoka to appeal "a criminal conviction for multiple rapes." In other words, I was properly denied asylum because I had returned to Kenya for an ignoble reason—because Njoka really was a rapist. Similarly, Misir dealt with the French and Canadian cases that supported my case not only by pointing out that they were not precedents for American courts but also by claiming that my "reasons for returning home were neither involuntary, nor as compelling as the death of a parent."

At the end of her brief, Misir attacked Phil's alternative request for reinstatement of voluntary departure if the court affirmed the denial of asylum. She devoted only two sentences to this point, little more than Phil had. She called the court's attention to the March 2003 *Zazueta-Carillo* decision of the Ninth Circuit Court of Appeals, in California, holding that a 1996 amendment to the immigration law had eliminated judicial authority to reinstate a board grant of voluntary departure.[26] Phil, too, was aware of *Zazueta-Carillo*, but he hadn't been too worried about it, for three reasons. First, the Fourth Circuit had reinstated voluntary departure in a 1999 decision, although it had not issued a formal decision analyzing its authority to do so and establishing precedent. Second, Zazueta-Carillo had not been seeking asylum and did not have as great a need for reinstatement of voluntary departure.[27] Third, the *Zazueta-Carillo* case had been decided *after* my board-granted thirty days for voluntary departure had expired, and after I had appealed to the Fourth Circuit, so it would have been grossly unfair to apply this decision to me retroactively. When I decided to remain in the United States during my appeal to the Fourth Circuit, neither Phil nor I could have imagined that the court might later decide that it did not have authority to continue its practice, under its *Ramsay* precedent, of reinstating a short period of voluntary departure.[28]

Phil was unhappy that Misir was contesting even a thirty-day extension of my voluntary departure. If the court agreed with her, I would lose the one tiny benefit that Judge Churchill had granted me. But Phil was pleased that the essence of her argument rested on the claim that Njoka was a rapist, because he thought that he could knock that argument down with ease. And he believed that, while the court might ultimately rule against me because it almost never remanded an asylum case, at least Misir had not helped it to find a way to uphold the decision.

Phil began his short reply brief by pointing out that the Kenyan government's failure to arrest or harm me during my 1997 return was irrelevant to whether my return proved that I was not "unwilling to return." Unwillingness to return is a subjective psychological state of mind. The appropriate time to assess whether I feared returning to Kenya was the moment before I departed, not when I actually escaped further harm.

The bulk of his reply brief ripped into what he called Misir's "Njoka-was-guilty theory." He noted that the board had not relied on this theory; and, under settled principles of law, it was improper for the court to uphold a board decision based on a theory that the agency had never considered. Phil also argued that the court should give no weight to Njoka's confession or to anything in the record of Kenyan criminal court proceedings other than Njoka's conviction and my efforts to get the conviction set aside. Phil could not introduce new evidence in the appellate court. But fortunately, in Judge Churchill's hearing, Dave and Bernie had introduced volumes of reports on human rights in Kenya, so everything he needed was already buried in the record of the case.

Official reports, including those of the U.S. government, showed that persons accused of crimes could not get fair trials in Moi's Kenya and that the police often tortured prisoners to obtain false confessions. The State Department had written that "the judiciary is often corrupt." It had cited approvingly the report of a commission appointed by the chief justice of Kenya, which concluded that "corruption, incompetence, neglect of duty, theft, drunkenness, lateness, sexual harassment and racketeering" were "common problems in the judiciary."[29] A report issued by the U.N. Commission on Human Rights found that physically rough treatment of suspects was a "tradition" in Kenya and that it "routinely" included "sustained beatings on all parts of the body with sticks, metal bars and lengths of rubber . . . [and that the] purpose of such beatings, which can only cause intense pain and suffering, is generally to obtain information or confessions."[30] Furthermore, the police frequently threatened doctors to get them to falsify medical reports, a practice that could explain the "physical evidence" of Njoka's guilt.[31] Nor did the suffering end after a defendant entered a guilty plea. In Kenya, "prisoners are subjected to

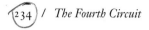

severe overcrowding, inadequate water, poor diet, substandard bedding, and deficient health care. Police and prison guards subject prisoners to torture and inhuman treatment. Rape . . . is a serious problem, as is the increasing incidence of HIV/AIDS. Disease is widespread in prisons, and the death rate is high."[32]

I knew about some of these practices and conditions from my own personal experiences as well as from word of mouth and published sources. Therefore, in 1997, I had every reason to believe that my brother was being tortured, as my family reported; that a false confession had been extracted by torture; and that Njoka faced years of dreadful imprisonment based on Mugo's false accusation. Under these conditions, my case was just like the one described in the government's own manual, the case of a man who returned for "compelling" reasons, to rescue a close relative who was unjustifiably detained.[33]

Phil wanted to focus the court on asylum, so he devoted only a paragraph to Misir's claim that the court could no longer reinstate brief grants of voluntary departure to unsuccessful asylum applicants. He pointed out that three years after the 1996 immigration law was enacted, the Fourth Circuit had extended the voluntary departure of a man named Ayalew. The *Ayalew* decision was available on the court's own web site and from other web-based services.[34] Unfortunately, however, the board had not designated it as a published case that would set precedent. Nevertheless, it was entitled to some weight because a court that treated identical cases in dissimilar ways would be acting arbitrarily, something no federal court likes to do.[35]

. . .

On Halloween 2003, shortly after Phil filed his reply brief, Melissa and I were married. We chose the day that would mark exactly a year since we had met at the party at Phil and Lisa's house. In fact, our meeting at that party held such magical associations for us that we chose to marry in the clerk of the court's chambers in Rastafarian and witch costumes similar to those we had worn a year earlier.

The wedding

The ceremony was special and lots of fun. We were the only costumed couple getting married in the courthouse that day, and the friends and family who witnessed our marriage also dressed in costume. The best man was a huge, inflated skeleton balloon. Melissa became Melissa Kenney Ngaruri, and I became David Ngaruri Kenney, finally shedding the "h" that the registrar at Hartnell College had attached to my name. Molly Ruhl, the clerk of the court, took our Halloween marriage in great humor, administered the vows, and wished us a great life together, unaware that the cloud of deportation hung over our heads.

EIGHT

A Cold Day in Richmond

Phil phoned me a week after the wedding. "The court has scheduled your appeal for oral argument in January," he said.

"That's a good thing, right?"

"It's a great thing," he responded. "The Fourth Circuit is notorious for affirming denials of asylum without listening to oral argument. The fact that they've scheduled an argument means that there are contentious issues of law that they want to consider. That's why this is a very good sign."

A few hours later, Phil called me again. I heard despair in his voice. He had checked the court's web site to see what other cases would be heard on the same day and to read the court's short description of the issue in my appeal. That posting stated that my case concerned "whether this Court retains authority under [the 1996 amendment to the Immigration and Nationality Act] to reinstate voluntary departure."

When Phil finished reading, I slid down and sat on the floor, stunned. Phil remained silent on the phone. "There's no mention of the asylum issue? Has the court already decided to affirm the board's decision?" I asked.

Phil hesitated. "It looks like the court is getting ready to overrule its decision in the *Ramsay* case."

If that was the court's intention, there was no doubt that I would be deported.

Furthermore, without voluntary departure, I wouldn't be able to come back to the United States for ten years. I wouldn't be able to live with Melissa.

I couldn't think of how to give Melissa this bad news without upsetting her. I remained silent, listening as Phil breathed heavily on the other end.

"Maybe the court's web site listing doesn't actually reflect the judges' view of the case," Phil finally suggested. "Perhaps they haven't even read the briefs yet. Maybe some court clerk looked at the case and took a special interest in the material at the very end of the briefs, where Misir and I debated whether *Ramsay* was still a valid precedent."

"I hope you're right," I said.

That evening, Phil found a statement on the court's web site confirming that the clerk's office had prepared the description of the case.[1] It did not necessarily reflect the judges' view of the issues in the case, and it did not limit the issues that the attorneys could argue. This discovery wasn't entirely satisfying. Phil thought that the judges themselves had read the description and might be predisposed to think that voluntary departure, not asylum, was the important issue in my case.

A few weeks later, Phil received much worse news. The court issued a notice directing each party to write a supplemental brief on the voluntary departure issue specified in the clerk's description. This notice probably meant that at least one of the judges wanted to focus on voluntary departure. Despite Phil's desire to have the court give all its attention to the asylum problem, he now had to write a full brief on the voluntary departure issue. After both sides submitted briefs on voluntary departure, the court would likely zero in on that problem, perhaps to the exclusion of the asylum question.

Phil's research over the next few days eased my fears somewhat. Although the issue of whether federal courts could still reinstate voluntary departure had emerged only in mid-March, when the Ninth Circuit decided the *Zazueta-Carillo* case, a great deal of action had occurred in the courts during the six months after that decision. Four circuits had already considered the voluntary departure question. Fortunately, all four decided that appeals courts retained the power to allow an unsuccessful asylum applicant who had been granted voluntary departure to continue to use that privilege for at least a few days or weeks after losing in the court of appeals. Two of these federal circuits had decided that they retained the power to reinstate voluntary departure.[2] The other two had concluded that, although they could no longer reinstate this status, they could temporarily halt, or stay, the expiration of the board's thirty-day grant of voluntary departure from the time that a foreign national files a court appeal until the court issues a final decision.[3] (Court of appeals decisions become final when the court issues a "mandate," about three weeks after it renders an opinion.)

If the Fourth Circuit adopted either of those approaches, I could still receive the limited benefit of voluntary departure. But the courts that had concluded they could still reinstate voluntary departure had not stated a sound rationale for disregarding the language in the 1996 amendment that had given pause to the Ninth Circuit in *Zazueta-Carillo*. Also, in one of the two cases in which courts had decided that they could stay the expiration of voluntary departure, the foreign national's lawyer had made a motion before the voluntary departure expired asking the court to stay the removal from taking place during the appeal. The court deemed the motion to stay removal to include a request to stop the expiration of voluntary departure. Phil hadn't made a motion to stay removal because in Virginia, the government rarely if ever even attempted to deport asylum applicants whose appeals were pending. Even if the Fourth Circuit thought that it could stay the expiration of the thirty-day period, it might distinguish my case from those in the other circuits on the ground that Phil hadn't made a motion, before my voluntary departure expired, to stay removal. So, to protect me, Phil included in his brief a motion for such a stay "nunc pro tunc" (now for then).

Some courts, such as the Ninth Circuit, routinely granted nunc pro tunc motions to stay the expiration of voluntary departure when justice required.[4] Phil argued that my case was exactly the situation in which the Fourth Circuit should use its "equitable power"—the power of a court to be fair to the parties—because we'd been blindsided by the *Zazueta-Carillo* decision, which, after Phil's opportunity to make a timely motion for a stay had already passed, heralded a more restrictive doctrine on voluntary departure. But Phil feared that a very conservative court such as the Fourth Circuit might decline to allow even this small mercy.

. . .

Tuesday, January 20, 2004, was a frigid day in Richmond, Virginia. At 8:30 that morning, Melissa and I met Phil at the imposing nineteenth-century federal court building. I later learned that this grand edifice had once housed the treasury of the Confederacy.[5]

Phil entered the clerk's office to register his attendance and to see which judges had been assigned to my case. Though many judges work in each federal appeals court, judges are randomly assigned to sit on cases in panels of three for each day of appellate arguments. The Fourth Circuit has the unusual practice of assigning the three judges weeks before the argument but not disclosing their identities until the argument day dawns. Then the court clerks post the judges' names in the clerk's office. Phil brought with him biographical information about each of the fourteen judges. He wasn't hoping for a liberal judge, since not one of the Fourth Circuit judges had that reputation. But four or five of them were thought to be more moderate than the others. If, through some fluke, at least two of the judges on my case were from the moderate end of the court, I would stand a much better chance of winning. And even one moderate judge would be better than three very conservative ones.

When Phil returned from the clerk's office, he sat next to Melissa and me on a hallway bench. His expression was blank. "The news isn't particularly good or particularly bad," he announced. "The three judges assigned to your case are a cross-section of the court." He hunched over, his arms on his knees, his fingers knotted.

Judge J. Harvie Wilkinson III

His teenage son, Sam, stood in front of him. "Dad, you look scared," Sam commented. "What the hell did they tell you in there?" We all laughed, as Sam surely intended. Phil placed his arm on my shoulder and said, "Two of the judges are strong conservatives, but the third might be more of a moderate." Phil pulled his biographical research from his briefcase.

"The most senior judge on the panel is J. Harvie Wilkinson III," he reported. "He'll sit in the center and preside over your case. He's fifty-nine and the press calls him 'one of the judicial heavyweights on this conservative-dominated court.'[6] When he was a law student, he ran unsuccessfully as a Republican candidate for Congress. After clerking for Supreme Court Justice Lewis F. Powell, Wilkinson taught law and then joined the Reagan Justice Department, where he helped select federal judges. Reagan appointed him to the Fourth Circuit in 1984.[7] Supposedly he is on George Bush's short list of possible candidates for eventual appointment to the Supreme Court.[8] I'm sure it will thrill you to know that *Judicature* magazine recently studied the decisions of the most likely Bush nominees for the Supreme Court, and it concluded that of all of the possible candidates, Wilkinson is the most conservative.[9]

"Dennis W. Shedd will also be on the panel. He's fifty. He graduated from the University of South Carolina law school in 1978 and spent ten years working as a U.S. Senate staffer. He was chief counsel to Strom Thurmond, South Carolina's senior senator and one of the Senate's most conservative Republicans. The first President Bush appointed Shedd as a federal district judge. In 2001, when Thurmond was ninety-eight and nearing retirement, his 'last hurrah' was to persuade George W. Bush to nominate Shedd to serve on the Fourth Circuit.[10]

"Civil rights and women's organizations were outraged by Shedd's appointment," Phil continued, consulting some of his clippings and research. "Ralph Neas, president of People for the American Way, called Shedd 'consistently hostile, insensitive to the rights of minorities, women, and people with disabilities.' During his confirmation hearing, Shedd was asked whether any of the 'dozens and dozens of civil rights plaintiffs' who had come before his court had been ultimately successful. Shedd 'couldn't come up with one example where a civil rights plaintiff won.'[11] The National Organization of Women complained that Shedd 'dismissed one woman's lawsuit despite evidence that a supervisor sexually harassed her on a daily basis, making dirty jokes, asking her whether she had been up all night "getting some," and commenting about her breasts and buttocks as well about the anatomy of the women the supervisor dated. Shedd reasoned that the plaintiff had resigned because she "quit enjoying her job." '[12]

"Leading Senate Democrats opposed Shedd's nomination, but they chose not to mount a filibuster to defeat him when the nomination went to the floor in November 2002. They probably declined to filibuster in part because they were about to lose control of the Senate as a result of the election earlier that month and in part because Shedd's confirmation was, according to one report, 'the only thing [that Thurmond] asked . . . as a last request in return for his [nearly fifty years of Senate] service.'[13] Shedd was confirmed by a vote of 55 to 44."

"So you're telling me I'm going to lose."

Phil lowered his papers. "If there's a shred of hope in the lineup of judges on your panel, it's with Judge Roger L. Gregory, who's also fifty years old. In June 2000, Clinton nominated Gregory to become the first African American to serve on the Fourth Circuit. Gregory is a graduate of the University of Michigan law school and spent two decades as a partner in the law firm of Douglas Wilder, the first African American governor of Virginia. The Republican-controlled Senate let Gregory's nomination languish without a hearing or a vote. Three weeks before leaving office, Clinton gave Gregory a temporary recess appointment to the circuit.

"The recess appointment presented George W. Bush with a dilemma. If he didn't renominate Gregory or nominate another African American to the seat, he could be seen as opposing racial integration of the court. In May 2001, on the same day that Bush nominated Shedd, he also nominated Gregory to serve on the court. Gregory was confirmed four months before Shedd was approved.

"Gregory is fairly new on the court," Phil said. "He hasn't served on a lower court, so I don't have much insight about his outlook. Perhaps his life experience as a member of a racial minority in Virginia might make him more sympathetic than the other judges to the plight of an African man who fled from persecution. I don't like to stereotype anyone, and I could be wrong. Still, I would hope that he won't be as deferential to the government's view of your case as the two other judges are likely to be."

We entered the huge, green-carpeted courtroom, where, as one observer put it, "beneath the pendulous chandeliers and the oil portraits of former jurists, a hush prevails [and] whether or not the judges are on the bench, people whisper."[14] Phil asked Melissa and me to sit in the front row, hoping that at some point in his argument he could draw the court's attention to us and indicate that we were a married couple. Some colleagues had cautioned Phil that the sight of an interracial couple might still trouble conservative judges in Virginia; interracial marriage had been a crime in Virginia, punishable by up to five years in prison, until the Supreme Court declared the ban unconstitutional in 1967.[15] But Phil felt confident that even very conservative judges would long ago have shed their racist attitudes and that it was more important to demonstrate to the judges that by sustaining the deportation order, they risked breaking up a marriage.

· · ·

Mine was the second case heard that morning. By some stroke of good luck or, more likely, sensible scheduling by the clerk's office, the first case that Wilkinson, Shedd, and Gregory heard was another asylum case, that of Maria Isabel Blanco De Belbruno. That case challenged the constitutionality of Ashcroft's one-member summary affirmance procedure. Similar challenges had already failed in other, much more liberal circuits.[16] Phil felt certain that the Fourth Circuit would sustain the legality of the summary affirmance procedure used by the Board of Immigration Appeals (BIA).[17] Although we had decided to limit my appeal to the board's reasoning, not its procedure, Phil and I hoped that through the argument in Blanco De Belbruno's case, the judges would learn more about the cursory nature of the board's review since 2002 and might realize that, as a result, the justification for judicial deference to board decisions was diminished. Predictably, the judges gave Blanco De Belbruno's lawyer a hard time. We hoped that they would at least balance their decision against his client with a decision in my favor.

The atmosphere in the courtroom was somber when my case was called. Given the judges' backgrounds, I didn't think Phil stood a chance. Phil still hoped that he could win over at least two judges, but I couldn't see much hope after hearing those biographies.

The argument started badly. Phil had provided a phonetic spelling of my name at the beginning of his brief, but Judge Wilkinson introduced the case by saying, "We are happy to hear Na-ga-ree versus Ashcroft." Phil didn't want to hear my name mangled every two minutes, so, as politely as he could, he began by correcting Wilkinson's pronunciation.

Phil had been allotted twenty minutes. He first attacked the essential ambiguity of Hess's opinion: Hess had not said that all returns to a refugee's country were disqualifying. But if some returns did not disqualify a candidate for asylum, Hess did not explain why my return disqualified me. Phil reminded the court that the Justice Department had published a policy under which returns for compelling reasons were justified, a policy that the asylum officers were required to apply when adjudicating asylum applications.

Judge Wilkinson broke in with the first question: "I understand that the two months [that Ngarurih spent in Kenya] were uneventful."[18]

Phil pointed out that a police officer had delivered a warning to me, cautioning that "we have our eye on you."

"So it was *largely* uneventful," Wilkinson insisted.

Yes, Phil conceded, but the board did not base its decision on the fact that I had escaped unscathed in 1997.

"But it was among the total mix of factors," Wilkinson pressed.

"We can't know from the board's opinion whether that was the reason that the board affirmed; or whether [it was because] he reentered Kenya, period; or whether the board thought he intended to live there permanently; or because the board thought his brother was guilty of raping his niece. There are perhaps ten different grounds on which the board could have reached its decision." If the board had specified its reasons, the court could review its validity. But the board had affirmed Judge Churchill's decision without explaining its rationale.

Judge Wilkinson shifted ground, asking about the standard the court should use to review the board's decision. Shouldn't the court sustain the deportation order unless no reasonable fact-finder could make the decision that the board had reached?

That was not the proper standard, Phil argued, because the job of the court in this case was to decide the meaning of the phrase "unwilling to return," a decision the court was as competent as the board to make. The Fourth Circuit had itself once said, "We subject [not only pure questions of law but also] mixed questions of law and fact to 'de novo' review"— that is, to review without deferring to the opinion of the board.[19] Besides, Phil continued, the board's brief opinion may have reflected a view that anyone who returned was not "unwilling to return," which would have been an erroneous interpretation of that phrase.

Phil smiled a little and pointed to his son, Sam, who was now sitting behind me in the audience. "My son, who is sitting in the back of the courtroom, is sometimes 'unwilling' to do his homework, but he does his homework anyway because he knows he needs to do it." He noted that I had returned to Kenya only under great duress. I had raised Njoka as my son, and I feared that he would be subjected to torture—perhaps even water torture—as I had been. Departing from the usual etiquette, in which the judges ask all the questions, Phil asked Judge Wilkinson, "What would you do under those circumstances, Your Honor? Would you stay in the United States in safety and let your brother or son be tortured? Or would you go back and try to rescue him?"

Judge Wilkinson refused to accept Phil's terms of debate. He said that he wouldn't criticize why someone returned, but he asked why the board couldn't conclude that I lacked a well-founded fear of persecution when I returned to Kenya for several months, hired an attorney, assisted a family member, and, during that time, encountered no new human rights abuses?

This question convinced me that Judge Wilkinson had already decided that I should be deported because, to him, I wasn't in danger in Kenya, even in 1997. I closed my eyes and began to sweat, and I held Melissa's hands tightly. I felt her tiny hands warmly disappear into my arms, and I heard her sniff back tears as she sensed my fear.

This question, Phil later told me, made him believe that, although Judge Wilkinson understood the facts of my case very well, he had an incorrect understanding of the law. The disagreement between Phil and Wilkinson centered on which moment in time was relevant to judging whether I was "unwilling to return." It seemed obvious to Phil that the relevant time was the day in June 1997 when I left the United States to rescue Njoka. On that day, I returned to Kenya despite being "unwilling to return" because of a well-founded fear of persecution. I could not possibly know before I boarded a plane to rescue my brother that I would return unscathed. But for Wilkinson, the fact that the police did not arrest me during my two months in Kenya somehow justified the board's conclusion that I didn't qualify for asylum.

Phil pointed out to Wilkinson that the board didn't even mention in its decision that I had not been persecuted in Kenya in 1997. The court, he said, "was doing a great job guessing what the board might have thought, but under *Chenery*, the board is required to say what its reasoning is."

At that point, Judge Wilkinson excused Phil, promising that he would have some time for rebuttal after Misir argued.

Phil whispered his relief that Wilkinson hadn't asked a single question about voluntary departure. He hoped that the court was satisfied by his brief on that subject and that the only issue in the case would be whether the court would remand the case to the board for further consideration of asylum.

As soon as Misir stood up, Wilkinson asked her whether there was "a *Chenery* problem here."

She asserted that there was not, and she echoed Wilkinson's argument that the Kenyan government had not persecuted me during the summer of 1997. "No harm befell him," she stated.

Judge Gregory broke in. "That has nothing to do with the question of whether it was a willing return."

I glanced at Phil, who seemed elated. Gregory, at least, got the point that the relevant time for assessing my willingness to return and my fear of persecution was when I faced an unknown fate in Kenya.

"Doesn't that decision have to be made before he hits his home soil?" Gregory addressed Misir, but he was clearly speaking to Wilkinson. "You're bootstrapping it to say we're going to judge based on what happened after he got there. Your willingness or unwillingness to go has to be determined before you get there."

"It goes to his fear," Misir responded.

"But it's not resolved simply by what happened to him when he was there."

"What happens when he's there would bear on whether he has an objective fear," Misir argued.

"Isn't that illogical? It's undisputed that he was subjected to torture, right?" Gregory asked.

"Yes," Misir agreed.

"He returned because of his brother, didn't he?"

"But his return . . . coincided with his summer vacation, and he returned to the United States for a new school term. . . . He didn't [just] go back for a week to find his brother an attorney. . . . Who knows what his motivations were? He returned for two months and nothing happened to him. . . . That weighs heavily against any claim of future persecution in that country," Misir contended.

Judge Shedd entered the discussion. "The fact that [he] went back and [was] not tortured, of course that could be considered on the objective standard of whether [his] previous fear was well-founded."

This was the moment at which asylum seemed to slip away. Shedd, like Wilkinson, considered the fact that I hadn't been arrested when I returned to be key. In these judges' minds, the case was not about the meaning of "unwilling to return," not about whether my reasons for returning were compelling, and not even about whether the board had sufficiently articulated its reasoning; rather it was about whether anyone had tried to arrest me and whether I had actually been in danger when I returned in 1997. At best, I thought, I would get only Judge Gregory's vote.

Gregory continued to challenge Misir. "When do you judge whether he meets the standard for an exception to unwillingness to return? What temporal framework are you looking at?" he inquired.

Misir shifted ground and claimed that the training manual for asylum officers, which contained the exception for a return for compelling reasons, had never been "published."

Wilkinson seemed to be aware that Misir's argument didn't answer Gregory's question. He shifted the debate back, asking whether Misir agreed that what happened in Kenya during the summer of 1997 could be taken into account in this case. Of course, she agreed that it could, claiming that "in the light of common sense," the fact that no harm befell me was important.

"That's about the most relevant evidence you could find to whether there is a well-founded fear of persecution," Judge Wilkinson interjected.

"Then you read the exception out completely," Judge Gregory objected. "They didn't harm you, so we don't have to look at whether you met the exception for going." He asked Misir, "Would there be an exception for a refugee who returned because the government threatened to shoot his mother, but who was not harmed upon his return?"

Misir conceded that returning home was not necessarily a bar to asylum but reiterated that I had not been harmed.

"But the BIA didn't say that," Judge Gregory pointed out. Clearly, he understood the *Chenery* rule, prohibiting a court from supplying a new rationale for an administrative agency's decision, as well as the issue of which point in time mattered. Still, Gregory had only one vote. I could only hope that perhaps, when the three judges discussed the case, he would persuade Judge Shedd that the case should be remanded. "They said that there was 'not an unwillingness to return,'" Gregory noted.

"I agree the BIA decision could be written more clearly," Wilkinson responded. "However I disagree with you. . . . They said his return undermined his claim to having a well-founded fear of persecution."

Judge Shedd broke in again, saying that what the board meant was that "under the facts of your return, your objective view of the well-founded basis doesn't really pass muster."

"That's exactly right, Your Honor," Misir agreed, obviously pleased that two of the judges seemed to feel that the board should be sustained. Then she told the court that she wanted to argue that I should be denied voluntary departure as well as asylum.

Wilkinson pointed out that since 1996 an alien could pursue an appeal in the court of appeals even after having been deported. Therefore, he said, it was no longer so important for a person who lost a board decision to stay in the United States for more than the thirty days of permitted voluntary departure. It was reasonable to think that Congress had intended to remove the courts' ability to reinstate voluntary departure.

Judge Shedd appeared to agree that the courts could no longer reinstate voluntary departure. But, turning to Phil's stronger, alternate argument, he asked Misir, "Why would we not use equitable powers to stay in this circumstance?"

He seemed to have accepted our argument that the court could temporarily suspend the expiration of my voluntary departure. But an instant later, he took it back, answering his own question for Misir. The court couldn't grant a stay "because the statute gives the sole authority to make that determination to the executive branch."

Judge Wilkinson asked to hear from Phil in rebuttal. He probably expected Phil to continue the discussion of voluntary departure.

During Misir's argument, however, Phil had sat simmering, distressed by how the court was treating the asylum issue. He wanted to shore up Judge Gregory's point that what actually happened to me in Kenya in 1997 was irrelevant to whether or not I'd been unwilling to return. Judge Wilkinson seemed to suggest that if I'd been arrested and killed when I returned to Kenya, I would only then have been eligible for asylum—and it would have been just too bad that I was no longer alive to pursue my application. As it stood, the Kenyan government's failure to apprehend me had apparently doomed my case.

"In feudal Europe," Phil began, gesturing emphatically with arms outspread, "when a woman was accused of being a witch, they threw her into the water. If she survived, it proved that she was guilty of being a witch, and she was put to death. If she drowned, she was innocent."[20] To judge my willingness to return by whether I was later arrested in Kenya was like putting a woman into that no-win situation, he reasoned. As my father had done when he was frustrated by farmers who could not understand him, Phil had resorted to a simple analogy to make his point.

Whether those judges understood Phil's analogy or not, they chose not to discuss it. Judge Shedd instead wanted to know whether my avoiding arrest in 1997 was relevant to the broader issue of my having a well-founded fear of being deported to Kenya.

Phil apparently realized that Shedd was going to follow Wilkinson's lead, so he pulled out a fallback argument that he had preserved in his brief. Because the board had disqualified me for my willingness to return, it had dismissed not only my claim of having a well-founded fear but also my claim that because I'd been tortured so severely I was eligible, under the government's own precedents and regulations, for "humanitarian asylum." Humanitarian asylum is provided when torture is so emotionally crippling that even after the danger has passed, the victims should not be forced to return to a country that had so abused them. As the government's regulation put it, a person may be granted asylum "in the absence of well-founded fear . . . if the applicant has demonstrated compelling reasons for being unwilling or unable to return to the country arising out of the severity of the past persecution."[21] This regulation, like the general test of who qualifies as a refugee, also excludes people who are "willing to return"; but Phil hoped that Judge Shedd might agree with Judge Gregory that I was not willing to return, either now or in 1997. Perhaps he would want to tell the board that it should at least consider whether my torture was severe enough to provide a compelling justification for my desire to stay out of Kenya in the future.

Wilkinson didn't want anyone distracted by this additional argument. "The overall question has got to be, as it is for all asylum cases, whether at the end of the day was there a well-founded fear of persecution?"

Phil pointed out that the regulation he had just cited dispensed with the well-founded fear requirement in cases of severe persecution, including torture.

"You've made your argument on that," Judge Shedd interjected. "I think you've made a good argument. Let's move to the next question,

about the stay of voluntary departure." Did the court have general equitable power to issue a stay?

Phil pointed out that the court had explicit statutory authority as well
as general equitable power to do so. He reminded the judges that all the
other circuits that had recently considered this question had reinstated
voluntary departure through one theory or another.

Judge Wilkinson asked whether Congress hadn't "prohibited the court
from exercising any equitable power to grant a stay." Phil had already told
the court his view of that matter. Sensing that this was his last chance to
explain what was really at stake in the case, he said that if the court neither remanded my asylum claim nor continued my voluntary departure,
I would be removed and prevented from reentering the United States for
ten years. Pointing to where Melissa and I sat huddled in the front row of
the audience, Phil stated, "In fact, while this appeal was pending, [the ap-
pellant] he married an American citizen, and for him to be barred from
reentering the United States for ten years would be very unjust."

Judge Gregory remained silent. Judges Wilkinson and Shedd seemed
to disagree about whether the 1996 law prohibited the court from entering a stay. According to Shedd, the law said that "no court shall have
jurisdiction to review any judgment regarding" a grant of voluntary departure. He then added, turning to Phil, "You would say that you could
handle a case in a way that 'affected' voluntary departure without actually 'reviewing a judgment' regarding it." Phil told me later that he was
unsure whether Shedd was putting words in his mouth in order to argue
with Wilkinson or was trying to associate Phil with a fairly weak argument that Shedd could later rip up.

The Fourth Circuit, known as much for its courtly manner as for its
conservatism, follows an unusual practice. At the end of each oral argument, the three judges descend from their high bench, walk the length
of the courtroom to the counsel tables, and shake hands with each
lawyer, almost like a receiving line. After they completed that ritual and
left the courtroom, Melissa and I hugged each other, and she started to
cry. Melissa rarely cries.

"They will kick you out. They're not going to let you stay in the United States," she said despairingly amid sobs.

"I think it's too early to say that," I consoled her. But, deep inside, I agreed with her. I began wishing that nothing would happen to us.

"I saw it in Shedd's eyes," she declared. "I've seen those eyes before, and I know what they mean. They're not going to let you stay." She took a deep breath to interrupt her sobs, shook her head, wiped her tears off, turned to face me, and smiled. "But, you know, I've always wanted to live abroad, so if it comes to that, I will just get a job abroad, and we'll go and live somewhere else." She grinned. I grinned back, and we kissed.

Phil was no more confident than we were. Judge Gregory's questions to Misir suggested he might agree that the board had analyzed the asylum issue badly. Judge Shedd had acknowledged that Phil had made a good argument about humanitarian asylum, so there was an outside chance of a two-to-one decision in favor of a remand. If not, perhaps I might get a two-to-one decision providing a few more days of voluntary departure, since Shedd seemed at least somewhat interested in exploring the court's power to provide that type of relief. But Gregory had said nothing on the voluntary departure issue, so it was possible that even he was not supportive.

· · ·

Blanco De Belbruno lost her case about two months later, but I waited for more than five months for my decision, checking the Fourth Circuit's web site daily because decisions are posted there as soon as they are released. Phil, Melissa, and I each finished another semester at our law schools. Winter eased into a warm spring.

In mid-June, the day before Melissa and I were to attend a friend's wedding, the phone rang. "I'm so sorry," Phil whispered.

I pulled up the court's web site and scrolled down the display, looking for the result before paying any attention to the reasoning.

The first word I saw was "Shedd," the author of the opinion.

The second word that struck me: "Denied."

The decision was devastating.

The court unanimously affirmed the board's denial of asylum, with no hint of Judge Gregory's point about evaluating my fear before I'd left for Kenya. They also unanimously agreed not to allow voluntary departure, though Judge Gregory dissented from the reasoning of the two other judges on that issue.[22]

After an essentially accurate statement of facts,[23] Judge Shedd laid out reasoning closely following the lines Judge Wilkinson had expressed during the oral argument. He accepted Phil's argument that under the *Chenery* case, the court could consider only the reasoning that the board had earlier stated and that it could not make up an entirely new rationale to justify my deportation. But Shedd construed Hess's short statement to be a determination that I had nothing to fear by returning to Kenya, as proven by the fact that no further harm had actually befallen me when I returned. The real issue, Shedd said, was not whether my 1997 return to Kenya was willing or compelled. The real issue was only whether, when I applied for asylum in 2000, I no longer had a well-founded fear of persecution.[24] "There is no evidence that Ngarurih suffered any mistreatment . . . in 1997," he wrote. Echoing Judge Wilkinson almost word for word, Shedd added that "there is perhaps no evidence more relevant [to whether I had a well-founded fear of persecution] than what happened (or did not happen)" when I actually returned.[25]

Turning to Phil's fallback argument that the case should be remanded to the board to decide whether my torture had been so severe as to justify humanitarian asylum, Judge Shedd contended that asylum based on severe past persecution was "reserved for the most atrocious abuse [such as that of] German Jews, the victims of the Chinese 'Cultural Revolution,' survivors of the Cambodian genocide, and a few other such extreme cases." He noted that a Romanian asylum applicant named Rusu had recently appealed a denial of humanitarian asylum to the Fourth Circuit. Under the Ceaușescu regime, the secret police had removed Rusu's teeth with pliers and a screwdriver, but the BIA and the Fourth Circuit had found that "although the persecution he suffered was horrible, it wasn't persecution of the scale warranting a grant of asylum." Shedd added that my torture was no worse than what the Romanian secret police had done to Rusu.

Finally, Shedd turned to Phil's request that the court retroactively stop the voluntary departure clock on the day that I filed my appeal, so that I would have a few more days in which I could still leave without suffering the ten-year bar. He concluded that the 1996 legislation had overruled the *Ramsay* case and that the court now lacked the power to allow me to depart without an order of deportation. He acknowledged that several other courts of appeals had concluded that they retained equitable powers to suspend the expiration of voluntary departure; but, speaking for the Fourth Circuit, Shedd disagreed with those courts. Shedd thought that his conclusion was fair as well as required by law. Someone like me, who had voluntary departure and wanted to appeal the loss of an asylum case, should have to choose between going home right away and appealing from abroad or giving up voluntary departure by remaining in the United States for the court appeal. "Having made his election, however, the alien takes all the benefits and all the burdens of the statute together."[26]

Judge Shedd's conclusion that the court could never grant a stay drew Judge Gregory's dissent. Gregory wrote that the 1996 law did not explicitly bar the court from granting stays and added that "we should not force aliens with possibly meritorious asylum appeals to choose between preserving [voluntary departure] and their safety."

When I finished reading the decision, I felt numb. I tried to talk to Melissa, but I couldn't find any words. In the six months that had passed since the argument, I'd begun to hope that the judges were taking extra time with my case because they disagreed about it, and that Judge Gregory might win over Judge Shedd. Now I had to give up that dream and face the fact that the United States of America seemed determined to expel me.

NINE

Exiled

The decision by the court of appeals was a dreadful blow to my recent marriage. Either Melissa and I would have to live separately, or she would have to give up her legal studies and move with me to another country, provided that some country would accept both of us as immigrants. We had few financial resources. We had been trying to start a venture in Madagascar that might allow us to live there, but we couldn't afford two airplane tickets to Madagascar, and we had no savings with which to start a new life there.

Phil explained the few legal options available. "I can ask the full Court of Appeals for the Fourth Circuit to reconsider the decision that its three-judge panel rendered. Unfortunately, that request would have almost no chance of succeeding because the panel that heard your case was representative of the court as a whole, and the court seldom agrees to rehear cases, especially immigration cases. I could also ask the U.S. Supreme Court to review the decision. That is also unlikely to succeed. The Supreme Court gets about seven thousand requests for review annually, but it accepts only eighty cases. In the past twenty-five years, since asylum became part of American law, the Supreme Court has agreed to hear only two or three asylum cases.

"A third option is to ask the Department of Homeland Security to reinstate voluntary departure for a few more weeks. Even though the court denied you this relief, DHS can grant it.[1] But the department gave short shrift to the request for reinstating your student visa. It's equally likely to deny a request for more voluntary departure time."

Phil paused. "I know it's hard for you to think clearly at this time. But even though it's likely none of these procedures can succeed, I can try any or all of them in good faith if you want me to. At the very least, going through the motions would give you several more weeks to get your affairs in order.

"A fourth option isn't inconsistent with the other three options, and you might want to consider it. You can leave the country and petition the department to waive the ten-year bar against your return to the United States.[2] I can't predict whether DHS will agree to let you return, but I do think the chances of getting a waiver are much greater than the chance of winning asylum or voluntary departure."

Phil added, "Don't make a decision now. But think about these options, and let me know how you intend to proceed."

It was no longer a matter of whether the immigration agents would come for me—rather, it was a matter of when. Melissa warped into overdrive. She packed an emergency backpack that I could easily grab if immigration agents arrived at night and whisked me away to Kenya. She included a first aid kit with bandages, stitching needles and thread, ointments, antiseptics, a reflecting blanket, rehydration salts, a first aid booklet, and a pharmacy of painkillers and prescription antibiotics from her earlier overseas travels. She also added several utility knives, waterproof matches, a reel of thin wire, twine, duct tape, compasses, and safety pins. Then she measured and ground up a full bottle of my prescription sleeping pills, cooked up a sugar solution, dissolved the powder into the syrup, and stirred it into melted chocolate. Several hours later, a pile of small individually wrapped chocolates sat on the counter.

"They aren't for you, so don't eat them!" she instructed. "If you are ever kidnapped, try to get your captors to eat them. It should take only one chocolate to knock a person out. That could give you a chance to escape."

For a week, Melissa and I analyzed our legal options. We divorced ourselves from the painful predicament by debating the legal options abstractly. We enjoyed these discussions so much that we forgot we were talking about our lives.

Finally, we decided that I would not appeal further or ask for more time. Remaining for a few weeks longer would completely drain our funds without significantly improving the chance of success. Even if the Supreme Court miraculously reversed the deportation order, my case would be sent back to Judge Churchill, who likely would create some new reason to deport me. I couldn't endure that again or put Melissa through that ordeal.

In a last attempt to prevent me from being barred from the United States for ten years, Phil asked a contact in the senior ranks of DHS to try to persuade the department to join him in an application to the Board of Immigration Appeals for a few extra days of voluntary departure time. Phil reasoned that if the department joined such a petition, the board would probably grant it. "You would still have to leave, but then you wouldn't need a waiver to return as the husband of an American citizen," Phil advised.

But his contact reported that DHS refused to join in such a request and that, if Phil asked the board for more time, the department would vigorously oppose the extension. Its lawyers reasoned that as a result of the Fourth Circuit's decision, I had overstayed my permitted voluntary departure. That overstay rendered me ineligible to receive any further immigration "benefits," such as additional voluntary departure time. Therefore, even the board couldn't give me more time.

According to Phil, the department's legal theory could have been challenged. But I couldn't afford to wait while more legal maneuvers failed. I also didn't want to risk being arrested and flown to Kenya.

Melissa and I decided that I would leave. "But I will bring you home," she swore. "If I have to pester every government official in sight, I will, but I will get you back."

I couldn't return to Kenya, given the threats to my safety and the culture of corruption there. I settled on two other potential destinations: Madagascar and Tanzania.

While waiting for the Fourth Circuit decision, Melissa had flown to Africa. On behalf of our fledgling company, she had negotiated and signed memorandums of understanding with government agencies in Madagascar to set up and operate waste management system projects. While she was gone, I began negotiating an agreement with officials at the Tanzanian embassy. Either country would allow me to take up residence if I brought in foreign investment and operated a business. Although we had not yet lined up financial support, our efforts in Madagascar appeared promising. Madagascar's embassy in Washington stood ready to issue me a visa whenever we were ready to begin the project. I therefore decided to go to Madagascar while Melissa pressed the American government to let me return home to finish my legal studies and resume my life with her.

Generous friends and relatives raised thousands of dollars for my fare and temporary housing in Madagascar. Melissa's sister-in-law Kathy offered to have Melissa live with her in Bowie, Maryland. Jay and Kathy Sugnet donated frequent flier miles. Our friends Kyla and Everett P'an appealed to their friends and family and loaned us $500; one of their friends, Joseph Desloge, an MIT graduate, was so moved by our situation that he sent $500 in cash with a message saying, "It's not a loan." Our friends from Tulsa, Oklahoma, Mark and Catherine Graddy, loaned us $3,000. Jeannie Williams, Melissa's brother's mother-in-law, offered to buy me a round-trip ticket to Madagascar.

We organized a yard sale and sold nearly everything we owned. "We can get it all back when you come home," Melissa confidently promised. By the end of that week, we had enough money to allow me to fly out with dignity rather than being arrested and forcibly deported on a government plane.

The night before my departure, Melissa and I spent the evening reminiscing about our lives and exploring our future. As we talked, she cut strips of her hair and used embroidery thread to weave them into a cord.

"While Viking husbands sailed, the women managed the farms and households and raised their children," Melissa said. "Before their husbands' journeys, the women made bracelets from their hair and tied them to their husbands' sword arms. The hair would protect their husbands and bring them home alive."

"Why hair?" I asked.

"Human hair is pretty itchy. The itching likely was a constant reminder that their wives expected them home alive." She pulled out a small black stone with what looked like a fat centipede on it. "My grandma gave me this trilobite. She loved a geologist." She paused. "It represents our past."

She attached the fossil to the hair strand. Next, Melissa dug further in her jewelry box and pulled out a baby ring with a tiny diamond on it. "This baby ring came from my parents. I wore it, and I'm to give it to my baby." She paused again, closed her lips together, and tried not to cry. "I never wanted to have a baby until I met you. This represents our future." She secured the ring on the cord, next to the fossil.

Melissa draped the hair necklace around my neck. Her teardrops fell on my shoulder. "You're going to battle. My hair will protect you and carry the past and our future. Bring it back to me, and you will come back home alive."

That night, I saw our future through her eyes. I tasted her breath, felt her warmth, touched her heart, and lived every moment of her being before and after I met her. Every time Melissa cried, her amazing energy and charisma filled me. I couldn't imagine a life without her. "Being human has never been so beautiful until you came along," I whispered. "I'm hoping not to leave this life until I've shared every moment of it with you." We held each other and listened to the silence and darkness of the moment.

We kissed. "When this is all over, we'll move to the suburbs, live a quiet life, drink wine every day, and make babies. We'll probably be bored out of our minds," Melissa grinned.

The hair necklace scratched my chest. I knew for certain that I would come back. The next morning, we went with our friends to Dulles airport, prepared for a tearful farewell. But a severe late afternoon thunderstorm moved into the Washington area, forcing my flight to be postponed and giving us a week's nervous reprieve.

A week later, Melissa and I set out again. The weather was clear. I walked toward the security line and looked back to face her. She smiled and waved. "I'll stay here in case they cancel the flight, but whatever happens, don't die," she said.

. . .

Even though I left on my own accord, the law considered my departure to be a deportation because I left under Judge Churchill's order of removal. Unless the U.S. government waived the bar, I could not return home for ten years. Obtaining such a waiver required two distinct steps. First Melissa had to prove that our marriage was bona fide. Then we had to persuade the government to grant the waiver.

Phil had never helped anyone apply for immigration on the basis of marriage before. Fortunately, CALS always has two experienced immigration lawyers who serve as teaching fellows on its staff. They help supervise students, and they earn Master of Law degrees at Georgetown. At the end of two years, they usually become professors at other law schools.

In 2004, Diane Uchimiya, who later became a professor at the University of La Verne in Los Angeles, was a CALS fellow. Since she had handled marriage immigration cases before, Phil asked her to help Melissa bring me home. This project was beyond her normal duties at CALS, and, as it turned out, it would take more than a hundred hours of her time. But Diane gladly volunteered.

Diane's first task was to help Melissa file an I-130 petition asking the Department of Homeland Security to recognize our marriage.

The I-130 form itself is only two pages long. But special rules apply when a citizen marries a person who is in deportation proceedings or is appealing a deportation order. Regulations require DHS to deny petitions based on such marriages, because foreign nationals faced with deportation are presumed to be so desperate to remain in the United States that they would pay Americans to enter into sham marriages. However, the department can grant an exemption if the citizen can prove by "clear and convincing evidence" that the marriage is genuine.[3] To seek this exemption, Melissa was required to provide, among other things, evidence showing that we jointly leased property and that we commingled our financial resources. She also needed affidavits from our friends and neighbors attesting to the authenticity of our marriage.

Melissa's request for an exemption was 176 pages long. The application laid out, as if on a surgeon's table, our life and our experiences as a married couple for the department to examine. Her submission included all the addresses where either of us had lived during the last five years, all the jobs we had held, our marriage certificate, our joint apartment leases, our commingled debts, our joint bank account statements, our utility bills, our health and dental care enrollment forms, our joint tax returns, our wedding invitations, photographs of our wedding, pictures of us attending the weddings of other family members, photos of me playing softball with her office team, pictures from the cross-country trip during which we became engaged, a number of our love letters, and twelve affidavits from relatives and friends, including one from Dean William Fox of Catholic University's law school.

The affidavits were both funny and endearing. One friend described how we finished each other's sentences, held each other's hands, and dressed in coordinating colors. Another described how she saw us "sneaking quick kisses in the parking garage" at the law school. A fellow law student revealed how we sought medical advice about the health risks of pregnancy because Melissa was more than thirty-five years old. Melissa's sister-in-law asserted that she had never seen two people more in love. Our landlady described rushing to our apartment at 2:00 A.M. to deal with a burst pipe in our ceiling. "After Niagara Falls flooded their bedroom, they joyfully made me breakfast and African tea, with a smile on each of their faces," she wrote. "How many people are so in love that this is how they treat one another and me at 4:00 in the morning?"

Even if DHS granted the exemption and recognized our marriage as genuine, we would then need a waiver of the ten-year prohibition against reentering the United States. Diane prepared our I-212, an "Application for Permission to Reapply for Admission after Deportation or Removal." She attached several important items to the I-212: a copy of the Fourth Circuit's decision to show that my asylum case, while unsuccessful, had not been fraudulent; my airline ticket to Madagascar to show that I had departed; my Kenyan passport; and Melissa's lengthy application to have our marriage recognized. Before I left, I gave Diane a cover letter with a personal plea to the unknown bureaucrat who would ultimately read this application.

"We feel so lucky to have found each other and to have grown so close so quickly," I wrote. "We want to be together as soon as possible so that we can start a family. We are both in our mid-thirties and feel that we don't have time to waste. Again, we feel very fortunate in some ways, but also feel torn about our current status—married, but separated by continents. We would both appreciate anything that you can do to help expedite this process so that we can be together, start a family, and continue spending the rest of our lives together."

Meanwhile, a question arose about where to file the applications, because DHS has offices all over the country. Diane was kayaking outside cell phone range when the applications were completed. A local immigration lawyer advised Phil to file the forms in Washington, D.C., and, on his advice, Melissa did so. But when Diane returned from her vacation, she pointed out that although the forms could be filed in Washington, they would be processed more quickly if they could be sent to the Vermont office. Diane began trying to locate the application in the bowels of Homeland Security so that she could request its transfer to Vermont. If she had been able to show DHS a receipt for the filing, the Washington office might have found the application quickly by tracing it from the receipt's serial number. But, although DHS had cashed Melissa's check for the $435 filing fee, it had not sent her the receipt.

.   .   .

While Melissa and Diane filed forms in Washington, I was experiencing the frustrations of trying to start a business in Madagascar. My airplane landed at Antananarivo, the capital, on Saturday, August 24, 2004. The air felt warm, and the earth smelled spicy.

Antananarivo, also known as Tana, is built on a geologic basin ringed with rice paddies and surrounded by hillsides and ridges. It is a great city to explore by foot; it reminded me of San Francisco without the bay. The iron balconies of its poorly maintained colonial edifices overlook narrow streets that snake around slopes, bisected by stairways running up the hills. But in my short hikes around the town, I was hounded by beggars and street vendors.

My first appointment was a routine commercial briefing session offered by the U.S. ambassador, Wanda Nesbitt, and her commercial officer. At the end of the briefing, she warned, "This is a great place to be, but a lot of people come to Madagascar with high hopes and are disappointed. As you explore your options, be careful. Don't go around fishing."

"What do you mean by that?" I asked.

"Make sure you have a contract and an agreement signed by the right people," she cautioned. It didn't take me long to realize why she had offered that advice.

I soon found that Madagascar had no functioning capital market. The banks were not meaningfully regulated. I visited one of the biggest banks in Madagascar, a Middle Eastern–owned bank, and asked the manager for an overview of its commercial financial services. He simply told me in perfect English, "People just come and open an account. When they want their money, they come, and we tell them when they can get it."

The minimum balance to open an account in Tana is 5 million Malagasy francs, about $500. The average citizen makes $250 a year. But someone who manages to save $100 a year is literally prevented by the banks from opening an account and earning interest on it. Inflation soon reduces the meager savings to nothing. I found myself trying to start a business in a country with no savings or investment, bad credit, a sharply negative trade balance, limited reserves, no infrastructure, no research facilities, and no functioning banking systems.

Shortly after arriving, I met with two local potential business partners and the local minister of industry. They arranged a meeting with several Tana city officials responsible for the city's industrialization. After I explained the initial stages of our proposed project, the translator responded, "We were told that you are willing to give some money to the city. My colleagues want to know how you intend to distribute it and how much each of us will get."

"What?" I asked, startled. Everyone laughed briskly and whispered to one another. I wondered whether I had clearly explained myself. I re-stated that I wanted to create a public/private partnership to manage and operate Tana's solid and liquid waste projects. My primary objectives were first to initiate the project development process, as spelled out in the agreement, and then to assemble a project development team.

"We don't care about the contract," the translator said, not bothering to translate the details. "We care about the money."

I held up a copy of the memorandum of understanding for everyone to see. "Under this agreement, signed by your minister of industry, the city government is supposed to fund the initial stages of the development process until the proposed partnership is organized. Your government has many ways to raise funds for such a project. All it needs is your commitment to the project. If you want to make money, you have to first commit to the initial development process," I explained.

The translator smiled coldly before translating for the rest of the group. They immediately broke themselves into small groups, whispering among themselves. Everyone seemed disappointed.

"Look," I continued, "anyone who told you that I was just going to give money to you wasn't giving you accurate information."

The translator interjected, "The deputy mayor wants you to understand that the central government does not have authority to enter into contracts on behalf of the city. You must first give us half of what you intend to invest in the partnership. That is how things work here. If you can't do that, then you should tell the minister to do the project with you." Stunned, I ended the meeting and reconsidered the idea of starting a business in Madagascar. I realized that my chance of starting a business venture here was worse than my chance of returning to the United States, so I decided not to bet our future here.

My inability to move my business projects forward was not my only problem in Madagascar. In addition, I couldn't stay in the country indefinitely. Officials in Madagascar's embassy in Washington had given me only a temporary visa. They had advised me to apply for a long-term visa upon arrival. But the immigration officials in Tana told me that they could not issue a long-term visa because my Kenyan passport, which the Kenyan embassy in Washington had refused to renew, was valid for only a few days longer than six months. They couldn't attach a long-term visa to such a short-term passport. I would have to renew my Kenyan passport before Madagascar could issue a visa for an extended stay.

Kenya did not have a consulate in Madagascar. The two nearest Kenyan consulates were in Pretoria, South Africa, and Dar es Salaam, Tanzania. I didn't have a visa permitting me to enter South Africa, nor did I have the funds to fly and live there while awaiting my new passport. Furthermore, there was no certainty that the Kenyan consulate there would renew my passport. If it refused, I would have to return to Madagascar and have only an emptier pocket to show for my trouble.

. . .

After about six weeks in Madagascar, I decided to move to Tanzania. I could afford the plane ticket to travel there, and the government of Tanzania had already given me a business visa. That visa, too, was a short-term three-month visa. If I couldn't return to the United States by the time it expired, in December 2004, I would need a renewed Kenyan passport so that I could get a long-term visa from Tanzania.

To fly from Madagascar to Tanzania, I had to change planes in Nairobi. Once again, I faced the risk of being arrested at the airport. I judged that an airport arrest was unlikely because nobody was expecting me and I was only passing through briefly rather than going to my district.

I landed without incident in Nairobi and called Wash from the airport. He agreed to meet me in a few days in Dar es Salaam, Tanzania's capital.

I checked into an inexpensive hotel in Dar es Salaam and began to look for an apartment I could afford on my dwindling savings. I also started to meet with government officials about the waste management project. But the problems bedeviling foreign investors in Madagascar were equally pervasive in Tanzania. As in Tana, the local officials claimed that the national government with which I had signed a memorandum of understanding had no authority over them. They too expected to be paid off.

I also set out to renew my Kenyan passport. I went to the Kenyan embassy and met with a junior consular officer. He politely received me and had me fill out the passport renewal form, which he thought would be approved routinely. When I returned the next day, he seemed nervous. He said softly that he had made some inquiries and had been surprised by the response. "Nairobi isn't very friendly to you," he confided. "The officials there want you to travel there and apply for this renewal in person." He paused. "But, personally speaking, I advise you not to go. It wouldn't be a good day for you."

Because of my earlier encounter with Chris Murungaru and the warnings from Dr. Kituyi in Washington, I was not completely surprised to find out that I was on some sort of list. The consular official agreed to send my application to Nairobi anyway, although we both expected that the officials there would find some reason to deny it. He told me to return in two weeks. Fortunately, I didn't have to relinquish my expiring passport in order to apply for a new passport, so I wouldn't be accused of residing in Tanzania improperly.

In the meantime, after more than a month's wait, the Department of Homeland Security informed Melissa that it had located her application to certify our marriage. But it couldn't act on the file or transfer it to Vermont until Melissa supplied proof that I had in fact left the United States. As soon as I arrived in Madagascar, I had visited the vice consul at the U.S. embassy. He wrote to Homeland Security to say that I had indeed met with him in Madagascar, but he forgot to specify our meeting date. Therefore I had to send copies of my boarding passes to Diane so that she could prove the date of my departure. Connecting this documentation with Melissa's original application consumed another month. By this time, I had left Madagascar and moved to Tanzania. But Melissa's application said that I was living in Madagascar and that embassy officials could interview me there before issuing a visa. My move to Tanzania had further complicated an already procedurally complex request.

A few days after my visit to the Kenyan consulate, Wash called to let me know when he would arrive at my hotel. I anticipated a cheerful reunion with my best friend. When a knock sounded on my hotel door, I flung it open, grinning. Wash stood there, looking terrified. He pushed his way in and shut the door.

"Just now, in the hotel lobby, a man ran up behind me and grabbed my arm," Wash reported, shaking a little. "He identified himself as a Kenyan security agent who had followed me all the way from Nairobi. He warned me, 'I know where you came from, which bus you took from Kenya, where you crossed the border, what you're doing here, and with whom you're staying.'"

"Don't worry about it," I reassured him, elated to see my best friend after years of separation.

"Well, Rambo, the security forces in Kenya know you're here, and now they know where you live."

"Relax, Wash. Kenyans don't have jurisdiction here," I said, realizing that I sounded like a law student.

"Who do you think you are? Lakwena?" We both laughed over his reference to the Ugandan rebel leader who convinced her now-deceased followers that bullets wouldn't kill them if they covered themselves with her magic paint.

Soon we rented an apartment near the U.S. embassy, in a compound protected by a concrete wall and an iron gate. Roberto, the Italian owner, worked for a Kuwaiti company and spent most of his time in the Middle East. "In Dubai, cars are disassembled and reassembled with certain extras for East African buyers," he told me. It was actually common knowledge in East Africa that guns are safely hidden inside these imported vehicles.

One morning, he came by the apartment to check whether his handymen had repaired the plumbing system. In the shade of the courtyard, we talked about the local business culture. He expressed the frustration he had experienced trying to do business with officials in Tanzania.

"I hope you brought your patience with you. What takes a few minutes to do in America takes a couple years to do here in Africa," he casually commented. "A lot of local people will come to you with all kinds of proposals to develop a partnership. Don't go for them. Africans are their own worst enemy. They expect that one day someone will come by and make them rich overnight, so they sit there, wait, and work very little. And why should they exert themselves, only to have to pay whatever they earn to officials and to gangsters who threaten to burn down their businesses? Their best bet is to prey on foreigners like us."

Two days after Wash and I moved in, we noticed that a car followed us whenever we left our compound. When we returned, the same car parked outside the gate. It had a diplomatic license plate, and we took down the numbers. We started paying more attention and noticed that sometimes, when we walked through crowded areas, two men followed us. If we walked faster, they walked faster to keep up with us.

I suspected they were Kenyan security personnel. I emailed Melissa about it. She emailed the U.S. embassy security officer and sent a copy to a contact we had met at the State Department. In her email, she included my telephone number in Dar es Salaam.

Soon thereafter, I received a call from a security official at the U.S. embassy. He told me that the men following me were probably Kenyan security officers and that I might be in danger. He further advised me to report the agents' presence to the Dar es Salaam police and gave me the number of a Tanzanian police contact who could assist me.

I met the police officer the next day and filed a report. He introduced me to the commanding officer of a police station located only blocks from our compound. The following evening, two police officers introduced themselves and told me that they had been assigned to patrol our neighborhood. They gave me their cell phone numbers and advised me to call them if I saw anything suspicious.

With David Wachira Kiguta ("Wash") in Tanzania

Two days later, the security attaché from the U.S. embassy called me again and informed me that Tanzanian officials had identified the Kenyan agents. I emailed Melissa, who alerted our State Department contact. Three days later, the agents disappeared, and we never saw them again.

Wash and I grew friendly with the local police officers. We joined their gym and worked out with them. Some of our neighbors even mistook us for new police recruits. I felt safer for having befriended the local police, but I had even greater doubt that my Kenyan passport would be renewed. I didn't dare return to Nairobi. After two weeks, accompanied by Wash, I returned to the Kenyan embassy to check on the status of my application.

We left our backpacks at the guard office outside the consulate building and walked through the gates of the fenced embassy compound. At the reception area, the secretary took my receipt for my passport application and, after checking, found that no passport had been forwarded from Nairobi. I asked to see the junior consular official I had met earlier.

"Come on in," a familiar voice said from inside the office. I slowly opened the door and walked in. The official immediately stood up from behind his desk and offered to shake my hand. He seemed surprised to see me. "Please, have a seat," he gestured, pointing to an empty chair facing him. I sat down, and he smiled wryly.

"Look, I'll be honest with you," he said. He sounded apologetic. "I sent your application to Nairobi. Nothing has come back. I don't know whether they will renew your passport or not." He lowered his voice. "I don't know who you are, but certain officials don't like you. I'm very sorry, but I can't be in the middle of this." He stood up and opened the door. "Leave this building quickly," he urged.

"I appreciate your time," I said to him. I knew that in the embassy I was on Kenyan territory, where the Tanzanian police could not protect me. I had to restrain myself from running down the stairs. Wash sat waiting for me in the lobby, looking discouraged. At my request, the receptionist returned my receipt.

"Let's get out of here," I said to Wash as I quickly gathered my papers and stuffed them in my pockets.

"What's the matter?" Wash asked.

"Ask me after we get out."

As we walked toward the guard station, I noticed that the vehicle that had been following us was now parked outside. I knew the license plate numbers. I strode to the guard station and retrieved my bag. As I was signing the visitor exit register, the guard's phone rang. He picked up the phone as I turned to leave his small office. A few seconds later, the guard suddenly yelled, "Drop everything you're carrying, and come back here!"

His icy command cut through me like a razor. Suddenly it was 1992, and I was back in detention. In my mind, I recalled the immigration officer who had helped me get my first Kenyan passport in 1995. I had heard that he had disappeared, and I imagined security officers beating him and throwing him from a ten-story building. I faced the guard, who was about twenty feet away from me.

"No, I'm leaving," I said.

The guard quickly stepped in front of me and tried to block my path.

"Don't you dare touch me," I warned the guard. The hairs on the back of my neck rose, my gut seethed with anger, and I tasted sweat. I looked around and saw Wash a few feet away in the courtyard. Behind him was the large steel gate through which vehicles entered. It closed.

Next to the gate was a smaller door, the one through which Wash and I had earlier entered the embassy. It was probably locked against outside visitors, but I hoped that it was not locked from the inside.

Suddenly the guard leapt at me, his hands outstretched. Terror drove me. He was about five feet six inches tall and must have weighed around 150 pounds. Wielding my seven-foot, 240-pound frame, I reached down and grabbed both his shoulders, twisted him toward me as hard as I could, and swiftly moved to my right side. He lost balance and fell forward. I placed my left arm across his right shoulder, stepped behind him with my left foot, and pulled his left shoulder blade as I shoved him forward. Both his weight and my force threw him across the courtyard, where he landed face first in the dirt. I ran toward the gate, opened the small door, and darted out of the embassy. In a flash, I crossed the street and stood safely on Tanzanian soil. I sat down on the curb and started laughing with relief.

Then I realized that Wash, who I thought was running behind me, was still inside the embassy courtyard. Before I could decide whether to go back for him, I heard voices from behind the gate. The guard was interrogating Wash and asking him for the passport receipt. Wash played dumb, claiming that he didn't know me. They couldn't do anything to him—or so I hoped.

Then I heard Wash tell them to open the gate so that he could find me and get the receipt for them. The Kenyans may have realized that holding Wash wasn't worth their trouble. Sure enough, about five minutes later, Wash walked through the gate toward me, with the guard following him. As Wash crossed the street, leaving Kenyan territory, he called out in a loud voice, "Jeff, come back here! Bring those papers back to the consulate." He was literally laughing. The minute he crossed to the Tanzanian side of the street, I joined him. We walked away from the guard, laughing together as we had when we were children.

"If I were the ambassador, I would fire that guard," Wash gasped from laughing. "He was an embarrassment."

The following weekend, Wash and I traveled to Bagamoyo, a small town about thirty-five miles north of Dar es Salaam. The name Bagamoyo comes from the slaves of years past; it is a word that meant "surrendering your soul." This town was the starting point from which Westerners began exploring the East African interior. We visited a cemetery where some of the earliest Christian missionaries in East Africa were buried and saw a four-hundred-year-old mango tree where runaway slaves had been hanged by Arabs and later by German colonialists.

During our weekend trip, the Tanzanian police discovered that after the Kenyan security police who had followed us in their car were withdrawn, other Kenyan plainclothes operatives continued to observe our compound. The police arrested a man who had been hiding with a camera in a market near our apartment after the market's 11:00 closing time.

. . .

Being chased out of the embassy, tracked by Kenyan agents, and denied a new Kenyan passport only added to the urgency of Melissa and Diane's efforts to seek a waiver. In early November 2004, Diane learned that Homeland Security had finally approved Melissa's request to have our marriage recognized. However, it had not acted on our accompanying request for a waiver of the ten-year bar.

By this time, four months had passed since I left Melissa. I was persona non grata in Kenya, I had no prospects in Madagascar, I couldn't start projects in Tanzania without resorting to bribery, and I had neither the inclination nor the funds to fill the pockets of all those who were in line. Both my Kenyan passport and my Tanzanian visa were running out, and when they expired, the only place on earth to which I could go was

Kenya, where I might again be jailed. I was truly a man without a country. My last hope was to be allowed to return to America.

As soon as I arrived in Tanzania, I had tried to make an appointment with a consular officer at the U.S. embassy. My phone calls were never put through to the appropriate people. At this point, I decided to go to the embassy to try to see a consular officer. On each of several occasions, the Tanzanians at the security post in front of the consulate demanded that I pay them to enter the building. When I refused, they laughed. I finally asked to use their phone to speak with someone at the consular desk. One of them picked up the phone, spoke quietly into the receiver, and gave me the instrument.

I spoke with a Tanzanian staff assistant named Olivia. I explained that I was the husband of a U.S. citizen and that I needed to meet with a consular officer to expedite my visa.

"Work with the guards. Otherwise, there isn't anything I can do to help you," she replied curtly.

"But they asked me for a bribe in order to allow me to get through the gate. I don't think that is appropriate," I responded.

"That is why you need to work with the guards. Otherwise, if you want an appointment, bring your American wife with you," she said before hanging up on me.

Africans often use roundabout, inexact expressions or metaphors (such as "salt the water to encourage the cows to drink") in order to get their meaning across without explicitly soliciting bribes. I was certain that she was endorsing the guards' request for a bribe.

The guards laughed at me as I left the security building. I was out of options and had hit bottom.

TEN

The Witch Arrives

That evening, I emailed Melissa and told her what had transpired. "This is a nightmare," she replied. "I'm coming."

A week later, when Melissa's law school classes ended, she postponed her fall exams and bought her ticket to Tanzania. I did not tell Wash that she was coming.

On the morning of the day she was scheduled to arrive, Wash sat in the courtyard of the compound, watching people walk past, while I ate breakfast inside. I saw a middle-aged lady approach Wash. "Where is the tall man?" she asked.

"Who needs him?" Wash responded.

"I do," the woman said. Wash saw my curious expression through the open gate.

"What do you need from him?"

"My daughter is thirteen." The woman offered various prices at which I could buy her daughter.

"He's a married man," Wash said.

"I don't care."

The local raven flew to its usual morning perch on the top of the gate.

"If I were you, I would get out of here as fast as I could," Wash advised the woman.

"I am not leaving until I talk to him. My daughter is beautiful, she's half white, and she can make a beautiful baby to sell. I'll let him have my daughter for free," she insisted.

"His wife is a witch," Wash said, trying to keep a serious face. "She's watching you right now. You should run! You see that raven? She watches him through that bird."

The woman scoffed, and Wash continued, "I'm telling you, she can see you. And she'll call her husband any second now to ask why you are here, so please run."

Just at that moment, my cell phone rang loudly. Startled from its perch, the raven flew toward the woman, who screamed in horror, ran from the compound, and just missed being run over by a passing motorist.

Choking back my laughter, I answered the phone. "What's all the laughing about?" Melissa asked.

"We're laughing because you are a witch. You almost caused the death of a crazy woman who wanted to sell me her daughter."

"Cool," she replied, unfazed. "Are you guys stoned?"

Wash was still laughing loudly.

"Sounds like you're having fun. Keep up the party," she told me. "I'll be arriving in twelve hours. I love you," she said as she hung up.

I simply told Wash that we had to go to the airport that evening to meet one of my friends. At the airport, Melissa emerged from behind a glass door, dragging two large backpacks behind her. She had never looked more beautiful. Her eyes reflected the sunset's tropical orange glow, and her wavy hair blew in the wind across her face. She scanned the baggage claim area, clearly hoping to see a familiar face.

"That woman's beautiful," Wash observed.

I smiled to myself. "Maybe it's our lucky day. Let's go help her," I suggested.

"No way. You see those ravens over there?" With a laugh, Wash pointed at the birds in the nearby palms. "I don't want to be chased away."

Then I blurted out, "Actually, that is my wife."

As soon as she saw me, she yelled, "Jeff, over here!"

"She is a real witch," Wash blurted out, shocked. Melissa jumped into my arms and dangled several feet above the ground.

As an American citizen and a white woman, Melissa was able to do things in Dar es Salaam that I could not accomplish. She also took umbrage at the corruption that had begun to seem more normal to me with each day I spent back in Africa.

Melissa arranged a personal interview with a U.S. consular officer, Elizabeth Jordan, and took me with her to the meeting. But at the consulate's security station, the guards, who were by now familiar with me, stepped past her and stopped me from entering the security screening area.

"What are you doing? That is my husband, and he is coming with me," Melissa said authoritatively as she presented her U.S. passport to the supervising guard. The guard glanced at me, with disdain, "*Hata kama wewe una mzungu, hupitii hapa bila ela,*" he said in Swahili.

"What did he just say to you?" Melissa asked.

"Even though I am with a white woman, I can't get through without paying them a bribe," I translated.

"Son of a bitch," Melissa said loudly. "Does the security attaché know this is happening?"

"I am sure he doesn't. No one would dare tell him. But this practice is common knowledge among the Tanzanians I've talked to who have come here."

"You mean any local person who pays these guys can walk through these gates?" Melissa asked.

"That's right, honey. I haven't seen it myself, but the locals say that they will even let your possessions go through without screening if you pay them a bribe, unless a white person is watching."

"Do any of you understand how dangerous this is to all of you?" Melissa asked the supervising guard, who did not respond. "He's coming with me. Ms. Jordan is expecting us, and, if necessary, I will call her now on my cell phone and inform her that we are here. You will check his possessions," she barked, "and you will not demand money from him now or later." The guard looked me with a grim expression and let both of us through the metal detector. As we walked toward the consular section of the embassy, Melissa grumbled, "We should meet with the security attaché about this. What a security threat! I'm surprised that no one has blown up the embassy again. I wouldn't want to be in this building for more than an hour." We entered the consular section through a second metal detector. We sat on a long bench near heavy Plexiglas windows that separated the consular officials from the public waiting room.

"Honey," Melissa said to me, "you have to tell Elizabeth Jordan about your experience with the guards."

I just wanted to go back to the United States. "I said too much to the consular officer in Nairobi, and I got punished for it. This time, I can't afford the punishment."

"But it's a huge danger. This kind of corruption is really dangerous. I just saw it too, so you have an American citizen as a witness. She needs to be told of the danger they're in," she demanded.

"Okay, I promise I'll tell her." Melissa smiled.

As soon as we met Elizabeth Jordan, she told us that the State Department had already informed her about the Kenyan agents who had been following me in Tanzania. Obviously, our State Department contact had emailed the consulate to pave the way for our arrival. Jordan and the security attaché had also read the email in which I described the attempt to detain me in the Kenyan consulate. Turning to Melissa, she said, "I also know that Homeland Security has approved your application to recognize your marriage."

I pointed out that I had been under a deportation order, so I needed and had applied for a waiver of the ten-year bar on reentry.

"As of now, there is no record in the system showing that a deportation order was entered against you," Jordan asserted. "Therefore, it would be best for us to issue a visa now, instead of waiting for Homeland Security to do the I-212 waiver paperwork."

Melissa and I looked at each other, shocked. We did not expect a consular officer to be so helpful, and Diane hadn't said anything about an exception to the ten-year bar.

"Can you do that without having the waiver?" Melissa asked her. "Our lawyers in Washington are still working on getting it approved."

"Yes. Since you are here and he has documented all the attacks against him, I can issue an emergency visa based on hardship, just like that." She snapped her fingers for emphasis. "You just have to work with me. Please don't involve any lawyers in this. I've been in this place long enough to know how to make things happen." Melissa and I glanced at each other, puzzled and speechless.

"Is that legally possible, Melissa?" I asked, loudly enough for Jordan to hear.

"Based on hardship, I can process your visa in a few days and have you and your wife safely back in the United States. Your I-212 application can be processed while you are in the United States because you're bona fide married to a U.S. citizen." She turned to Melissa and emphasized, "If you work with me, I can get this done before going on my vacation this Friday. But if you wait for Homeland Security, his passport will expire, and then I can never issue him a visa."

I started to interrupt. Melissa shushed me. "What do we need to do?" she asked.

"You need to contact the National Visa Center and have them email me your approved I-130. I can override the need for a Kenyan police certificate and tax documents because it is way too dangerous for him to try to get those from Kenya right now." She scribbled her email and personal phone number on a piece of paper and handed it to Melissa. "Don't give this out to anyone. In the meantime, he needs a medical exam. When you get the medical exam done, come back and see me. Don't talk to anyone else. Just ask for me, and if I am not here, call me on my direct number," she explained.

"Thank you," we both said at the same time, delighted.

"By the way, why didn't you set up an appointment with me right after you arrived in Tanzania?" she asked.

"I tried on three different occasions," I told her. "But the guards refused to let me in. When I tried to set up an appointment with a member of your staff, she also told me that I must bring my American wife with me." I thought this would be a good opportunity to deliver on Melissa's promise. I glanced at Melissa, who glanced back at me and urged, "Tell her what just happened on our way in here."

I explained our experience with the guards at the gate. Jordan listened, nodding, but she didn't reply. Just then, a siren went off. Melissa and I panicked and looked at each other, but a voice on a public address system announced that it was only a test. Nevertheless, it disrupted our meeting, which ended at that point.

We called Diane in Washington to report our conversation with the consular officer. We asked Diane to request that the National Visa Center email the marriage certification to Jordan.

"I'm sorry," Diane informed us, "but I don't think that what Ms. Jordan told you is correct. If she issues a visa before you receive an I-212 waiver, the visa won't be valid. I'll email her to ask how she's planning to get around the waiver."

A few days later, I was examined by a doctor at a downtown medical center. As he wrote up my clean bill of health, Melissa's cell phone rang.

"I just received an email from your lawyer wanting to know the details of our discussion," Jordan yelled. Melissa held the phone away from her ear. Both the doctor and I could hear the shouting from across the room.

"I gave you specific instructions not to involve lawyers, but you did. Now you and your husband can go and rot in hell!" she screamed. And she hung up.

"What was that?" the doctor asked.

"That was Elizabeth Jordan from the consulate, and she's pissed," Melissa said, shaking, as she put the phone back into her purse. "The woman who referred us to you."

The doctor said, "That was her? I'm very, very sorry."

"We'd better go back to see her," Melissa said.

"I'll hurry this up so you can get back there," he promised.

At the consulate, we walked through the security screening without incident. We came face to face with Jordan, sitting on the other side of

the Plexiglas window that separated her from the hundreds of petition-
ers she saw every year. She was seething.

"Your husband is a liar!" Jordan screamed at Melissa. "How dare you
come here and insult my staff based on what he told you!" She stood up
and repeatedly jabbed her index finger toward the glass, pointing first at
Melissa and then at me. "Do you think we would insist that you come to
Tanzania to help these fucking niggers get through these gates? My staff
would never advise Africans to have Americans come here to assist them,
because having Americans here makes our job harder!"

I couldn't believe that a highly trained American official was gesturing wildly and screaming foul language at Melissa.

"Do you even have an idea what you have with you here?" she asked
Melissa, pointing at me again. Putting her hands on her hips, she mocked
Melissa. "You think that you can come to my office, drop names, and pre-
tend to be educated people who know what they are doing."

Melissa tried to say something, but Jordan shot back at her. "Listen,
you stupid bitch, that thing is not going through these gates as long I am
the consular officer here." She was not pointing to the door, and I took
it to mean that she was shutting the gate to America. "I don't care who
you know; they aren't going to help you here."

Melissa got scared and started crying. I hugged her, and she burrowed
her head into my chest.

"Listen," I said to Jordan. "It's okay if you don't want to help us. I can
understand that, but please don't yell at my wife. I think your staff's conduct creates a security threat that your office should be concerned about,
but you don't have to take our word for it. In any event, my wife doesn't
deserve that kind of treatment. If you think I'm lying, then call me anything you want, but don't hurt my wife for it. Now, all we ask is that you
process my visa within the guidelines provided under the law."

"Is that how you want it?" she asked.

"Yes, ma'am," I responded. I wanted a quick approval, but I was mind-
ful of Diane's warning that if Jordan didn't follow the required procedures, I might end up with a worthless visa.

"Fine. I'll now do it according to the law, and we'll see how far you'll go," she retorted, "because I am not going to issue you a visa."

"Well, please at least give us some paperwork showing that I came to your office and stating why you will not issue me a visa."

She stared at me for about three seconds. "Don't threaten me," she warned. "I don't have to write anything down or explain myself to you." But she pulled out a form and checked the section stating that I was ineligible to obtain a visa under section 221(g) of the Immigration and Nationality Act because I was missing a police certificate from Kenya, two full-face photos, and Melissa's original tax documents.

"Is my husband going to have any problems bringing these documents to your office if I return to the United States before he gets them?" Melissa asked.

The consular officer glanced at Melissa and smiled coldly. "There should be no problem with him entering here if he brings those documents. But I will not issue him a visa."

. . .

We didn't believe that Elizabeth Jordan would be able to refuse the visa if we followed every procedure and collected every document that the immigration law specified. Therefore, in the following days, we worked hard, making many calls to Diane and Phil and to Melissa's relatives, who searched through her file cabinets and sent her tax records to Diane. Melissa introduced Wash and me to the U.S. Information Service, an amazing resource that was located in the embassy. The guards on the embassy side of the building never attempted to ask for money, and the Tanzanian staff of the Information Service was always helpful. We could send and receive emails there, and we could search for information on visa requirements.

While we waited for the tax documents to arrive, Melissa insisted that we explore parts of Tanzania. One weekend, we traveled to the isolated, privately owned Kibiji beach, about forty miles south of Dar es Salaam. We camped on the beach and built sand castles. We watched local fishermen catch giant leopard lobsters and chased spider crabs across the beach. One morning, we woke up and found that the tide was so low that the water seemed miles from the beach. We didn't know what to make of it.

Melissa slept in, so Wash and I spent that morning collecting sea shells and watching fish trapped in small ponds of water across the beach. As we were walking back to the campsite later that morning, Melissa sat in front of the tent, gazing blankly at the ocean, which was still far away. "Jeff, we're not staying another night," she declared. "We need to leave this beach now." She stood up quickly and hurriedly started packing. Wash and I sat confused, wondering why she seemed panicked.

"Why do we have to leave?" I asked her.

"I don't know," she said. "But I know that we have to leave this beach before three o'clock this afternoon. Let's go, now!"

I started packing, as Wash and I shrugged our shoulders at each other. We caught the first dalladalla, a small van crammed with passengers, back to Dar.

A few hours after we arrived in Dar, we learned that an earthquake had struck deep under the Indian Ocean and that a huge tsunami had hit Tanzania. The tsunami killed tens of thousands of people in a dozen countries along the ocean's coast lines. Ten people were reported to have died near Kibiji beach.

"How did you know?" Wash and I asked Melissa that evening as we devoured pizza and beer at a local café.

"I didn't. I've never seen a tsunami before. I just felt this urge to leave the beach," she explained. Her instincts might have saved our lives.

"She's a Good Witch," Wash said in English. We laughed.

Melissa asked Wash about his past experiences with white people, especially those from the United States.

"Are white Americans different from other white people?" Wash asked.

"White people are as diverse as Africans," Melissa replied. "Europe is inhabited by different tribes who speak different languages. Until recently, they fought each other and were never able to understand each other." Wash laughed at her description of whites as members of tribes.

"White people all seem the same to me," Wash said, "and we Africans have our own ideas about how white people perceive us. We think they believe everything we tell them." To illustrate, he shared the story of his first encounter with whites. As teens, Wash and his friend bumped into white hikers who were looking for lions. The boys pretended that they knew where to find lions, even though they had never seen the animals either. After several hours, Wash climbed a tree and spotted a lion farther ahead. Astounded, his friend ran ahead to look at the lion.

"Well, that day we learned that lions come in groups," Wash related. When his friend ran too close to the unseen cubs, several lionesses appeared from nowhere and charged him. The boy sprinted to the nearest tree and climbed onto an overhanging branch. Several cats surrounded the tree. Wash watched helplessly as the branch cracked and dropped his friend smack onto the back of a lion. The boy grabbed the lion's back and ears. The lion freaked and ran, and the boy rode the lion past a shocked Wash and the cheering hikers.

"How wonderful to see someone actually ride a lion!" one of the hikers exclaimed. "Do you ride them often?"

"Yes, of course," Wash recovered enough to reply to the hiker. "That's why we call ourselves the Lionriders."

We laughed together. "To the Lionrider!" We toasted to Wash's ingenuity, clinking our beers.

.   .   .

The year 2005 approached quickly. Melissa would soon have to leave to take her law school exams. I still didn't have a U.S. visa, and my passport would expire soon.

At the end of December, I asked the Tanzanian authorities to renew my expiring visa. They agreed to a one-month renewal but informed me that I had to notify them by January 28 that I was departing the country; if I didn't leave by that date, I would be deported to Kenya. They also emphasized that I could not renew the visa again in Tanzania: if I wanted to remain after January 28, I would first have to leave the country and apply for another short-term Tanzanian visa. The official then made a notation on my passport specifying that if I left the country and applied for another short-term visa, it would be good for two months rather than only one.

To deal with the issue of my Kenyan passport, Melissa dressed up and took a taxi to the Kenyan consulate. She introduced herself as an executive of Ngarurih Investment Group and presented our official incorporation papers from the State of Virginia and packets from the Corporate Council on Africa with our company listed as a member. She was then permitted to meet with a senior consular officer, someone much higher up than the junior consular officer who had helped me.

Melissa explained to him that our multinational company was interested in doing business in Kenya and that its Kenyan president needed his passport renewed so that he could continue the work of the company and hire more Kenyans to manage the business. Dealing with a white businesswoman, the consular officer said that he would have the passport expedited. He also had Nairobi wire a police certificate for me. In early January, Wash collected my new Kenyan passport.

Melissa had to go back to Washington on January 2 to take her law school exams and to return to her day job. On the day of her return flight, we both refused to cry. We felt hopeful, because it appeared that I would soon have all the documents Elizabeth Jordan required for the visa. Just before she left, Melissa had managed to schedule an interview for me on January 3 with Maria Ijames, Jordan's assistant consular officer, who also had the power to issue visas.

On the morning of January 3, I went to the U.S. consulate. The guards claimed that Ijames wasn't in the office, so they couldn't admit me. Using my cell phone, I called Jordan's number, which she had given to Melissa. At first Jordan refused to speak to me, but when I blurted out that I was bringing her the police certificate she had requested, she spoke to the guards, and they let me in. Ijames was there. She looked at the certificate and rejected it because it didn't include a copy of my fingerprints.

Wash returned to the Kenyan embassy. The senior consular officer who had obtained the certificate had a copy of my fingerprints wired from the police in Kenya. But when I returned to the U.S. consulate, Jordan informed me that she still could not issue the visa. She said that she would have to get an approving cable from Washington before I could be given a visa.

That day, Wash received an emergency call from his family and had to go back to Kenya. I took him to the bus station. As we waited for the bus to take him back to Nairobi, we talked about all the painful experiences that Jordan had put me through. But we thought that the process was finally at an end.

"This is not a hard experience for you," Wash commented, "because you had Melissa with you. What would be hard is to go through this with someone who doesn't understand what it means to love another person. You have a super woman who loves you, a woman who understands the value of persevering. You should be proud because she will always love you. You are just one lucky dog."

The bus pulled up. "You and Melissa are too good to be real," Wash said. "People get frustrated with themselves when they meet people like you." We hugged, and he continued, "Bad things happen to good people, but good people don't get lost in bad things. Bad people don't recover from good things. You are a good person."[1]

Nonetheless, I went back to the compound feeling completely empty and hating my life.

I started worrying about the questions on the visa application that had caused so many problems with Margaret Hartley at the U.S. embassy in Nairobi back in 2002. When asked whether I had been charged with or arrested for a crime, I would again have to check a box simply marked "yes" or "no." If I told Jordan about my imprisonment by Moi's security forces, she might accuse me of lying, for I had a clean police certificate. If I said I had never been arrested, I would actually be lying. Diane advised me to check "yes" and to attach an explanation, which she wrote for me. But I was terrified, and so I decided to leave both boxes blank and attach the statement.

A few days later, the consulate called me and told me to come for a visa interview on January 10. Once again, the guards insisted that I didn't have an appointment. Again I called Jordan from my cell phone. She directed me, "Mr. Kenney, I'm going to ask you one question, and I want you to answer it correctly. If you don't answer it correctly, I'm not going to help you. This is a yes or no question."

I expected her to ask about my arrest in Kenya, but she had a different yes or no question. "I just received a message from the State Department saying that you were deported by DHS. Were you deported by DHS?"

Standing on a busy street corner near the consulate, I felt confused about how to answer her. Despite her view of things, this was not a yes or no question. DHS had ordered my deportation, but I had not been deported by DHS—I had deported myself. DHS never even mailed a notice telling me to show up for deportation. "I would like you to refer to the email that my attorney wrote to you about that question," I replied, ready to explain the whole situation to her.

She interrupted, asking again, "Were you deported by DHS?"

"I really don't know," I said.

"You claim to be a law student, and you don't know whether you were deported by DHS or not!" she exclaimed. "You're wasting my time. Don't ever call here again." And she hung up on me.

In just a few seconds, the visa that I could almost touch had flown away.

Obviously, DHS had finally told her that I'd been ordered deported, just as Melissa and I had admitted in our first meeting with her, when she told us not to seek a waiver because she had no record of any deportation order.

The only chance of getting a visa now was to get DHS to waive the ten-year bar. I emailed Diane and told her to go ahead and try to expedite the I-212 application.

I thought that Melissa and I might never hear from Elizabeth Jordan again. But Melissa received an email from her a few days later. Melissa's tax documents had arrived from the IRS and were in order, Jordan reported. But because I had been deported, she apparently couldn't issue a visa to me unless I received a waiver. She had asked DHS to specify what I should do.

By this time, my Tanzanian visa was only a few days away from expiration. Once again, I prepared to leave a country, hoping that I would be able to return. But because I couldn't work in Tanzania and had been unable to start a business there, my funds were nearly exhausted. I couldn't afford to fly to any country with a Tanzanian consulate. The bus from Dar es Salaam to Kampala, the capital of Uganda, went through Kenya. A train ran westward from Dar es Salaam to Kigoma, and then south to Zambia, but I could only afford a ticket as far as Kigoma. From there I could either take a boat south on Lake Tanganyika to the Zambian border or head north by bus to the Ugandan border. Once I was in Zambia or Uganda, I could apply for a new Tanzanian visa.

But both routes were extremely dangerous. In 2003, an overloaded ferry had capsized on Lake Tanganyika, killing more than a hundred people. In the desolate region of Tanzania south of the Ugandan border, Congolese bandits and rebels operated with impunity, raiding buses and trucks to supply their fight against the Congolese government. The choice was made, however, when I learned that I would have to wait a week in Tanzania for the boat across the lake to Zambia.

On January 24, 2005, four days before my planned departure to Uganda, I learned from Diane that she had succeeded in having my I-212 application considered on an expedited basis. Even more wonderful, DHS had approved it. Jordan had told me never to call her again, but as soon as I heard this critical news, I left her a message and asked for a final visa interview. Unfortunately, the only possible date for this interview was February 28, the very day that my visa would expire, after which the Tanzanian authorities could arrest me and deport me to Kenya.

That afternoon, while I was waiting to hear back from Jordan, I learned from Melissa that her trip to visit me in December had been a greater success in more ways than we already knew. She was pregnant.

Map 2.   My route from Dar es Salaam to Uganda

This news raised the stakes considerably. Even if I was able to return to Tanzania, unless I could persuade Jordan to issue the visa, I couldn't see my wife through her pregnancy. I might even miss the birth of my child in September.

The next morning, my cell phone rang. Jordan was on the other end of the line. DHS had not sent her any official notice of the approval of my waiver application. "They must have sent the notice by mail," she said, and added, "Unfortunately, mail service to Dar es Salaam can be very slow." I had no choice but to leave Tanzania.

. . .

I packed my bags and headed toward the train station. The ticket office was closed for lunch break. I had tried to buy a ticket a day earlier, and the clerk had refused to sell it to me because I couldn't part with a bribe. This time, as I stood in line behind a middle-aged couple and waited for the ticket office to reopen, I grew determined to buy a ticket.

The ticket office finally opened after several hours. Behind the counter sat a heavy Tanzanian woman in the usual depressed state of slow motion. She looked at the couple in front of me with disdain and said to the man, "It does not matter whether she is your wife. You two aren't traveling in the same cabin." The man looked at his wife sadly and pleaded, "Please, we've been married for a year now. This is our first train ride. I plead and beg you, please sell us a first-class ticket to Tabora."

"All tickets to Tabora are booked," the clerk responded dismissively. Disappointed, the two hugged each other and slowly walked away. I realized the clerk was not going to sell me a ticket without a bribe. I leaned forward and asked her, "Please provide me with the train schedule."

"Where are you going?" she asked, nonchalantly.

"Through Tabora to Kigoma." I abruptly added, "And if you're thinking about denying me a ticket like you did to that couple, I will not hesitate to talk to your supervisor or the managing director. You should have helped that couple. Can I get my ticket now?" I demanded. My voice must have been louder than I expected. One of the women standing in line behind me said angrily, "I know there are tickets, but they don't want to sell. This is pathetic; we shouldn't have to pay bribes to buy a ticket." Other people in line started mumbling.

"Oh, shit, I'm about to start a revolution again," I thought.

The ticket clerk eyed me and handed me a small piece of paper with a reference number written on it.

"Go see the supervisor at the back door," she ordered. I took the paper and walked through the back door into an office. A voluptuous, smiling woman was seated behind a desk. I started to explain that the clerk wasn't selling tickets for my route. "Have a seat," she said, gesturing me to an empty seat next to her desk. "We aren't refusing to sell you the ticket. Where are you going?"

"Kigoma," I responded. She immediately handed me a ticket

"I have two other friends who just got married. They are returning to Tabora from their honeymoon. I would also like two other tickets for them in first class, and it would be nice if you didn't put them in separate cabins."

"Are you paying for their tickets?" she asked.

"Yes, this is my wedding present to them."

"Here you are," she said, as she handed me two first-class tickets.

I quickly rushed out into the street, hoping that the couple had not left. I later found them at a kiosk down the street, drinking a Coke from a single bottle that they were holding together. I stopped and stared at the moment, thinking of Melissa. I handed them the two tickets, smiled, and walked away.

That evening, I sent farewell emails to Melissa and Diane because I would be out of contact for as long as this trip would take. I took a train to Tabora in central Tanzania and then to Kigoma, on the eastern shore of Lake Tanganyika. I didn't know it at the time, but just after I left Dar es Salaam, DHS sent an email to Jordan to notify her that it had waived the bar to my return.

Kigoma is a small fishing town located on the Tanzanian bank of Lake Tanganyika. It is inhabited by Congolese, Rwandan, and Burundian refugees. Kigoma's main attraction is the Jane Goodall resort, where the renowned conservationist spent several years studying gorillas in a nearby forest south of the town. It was the only decent hotel in the town and therefore the only place I wanted to spend the night before embarking on what I knew would be the most dangerous leg of my trip.

The bus trip to Bukoba, just south of the border with Uganda, was advertised as taking nine hours. Most people in the region, however, knew that it usually took twelve to fifteen hours because of breakdowns and other problems that often occurred en route. The region is one of game reserves, Tanzanian police and military bases, and U.N. refugee camps. The route, largely through forest, was a poorly maintained rut so damaged by heavy rains that the bus could rarely travel at more than twenty-five miles an hour, and it sometimes hit potholes so deep that elderly riders broke bones.

At 5:00 A.M., I put my large backpack in the luggage compartment under the dilapidated bus and climbed aboard, taking with me only a small camera bag and my daypack. I had selected clothing that identified me, as much as possible, as an American: Columbia shorts, Nike shoes, a t-shirt, and a baseball cap with a Georgetown logo. I was quite worried about how safe this trip would be. I figured that if trouble arose, I would be less likely to be harmed or kidnapped if people thought I was an American rather than a Kenyan, because Kenyans are not well regarded in Tanzania. A woman sat next to me, and after the bus departed, we began to chat. We couldn't talk much, though, because the road soon became so bumpy that all we could do was try to hold on. Chatter could easily result in a lacerated tongue.

We passed a Tanzanian military base and stopped to take on a police officer as an escort. This escort was necessary, the driver told us, because we were about to enter a stretch of territory in which criminal gangs and small bands of rebels from neighboring countries operated.

We traveled for a few more hours. At about 11:00 in the morning, I realized that something strange was happening. The bus was still moving, but people were starting to crouch behind the seats. There were gasps of "Oh, my God." The woman next to me warned, "Put your head down."

"Why?" I asked.

I couldn't hear her response because the bus was still bumping along slowly.

"What did you say?"

"Rebels!" she exclaimed. "You don't want to look at them."

I wanted to hide behind the seats, as everyone else was doing, but it wasn't possible. The average Tanzanian is about five feet three inches. There was no room for me to crouch behind a seat.

The bus stopped. I felt strangely curious about the rebels and who they were. The police escort in the seat in front seemed to be asleep, his AK-47 rifle dangling loosely on his arm. Other passengers tried to wake him, without success. I knew he was pretending to be asleep; either he was too frightened to act, or he was working with the rebels.

The bus door opened, and about nine men entered the bus, all of them carrying AK-47s. They didn't storm the bus; they just got on as though they were regular passengers whom we'd picked up at a regular stop or police officers who were checking to make sure everything was secure. But we were smack in the middle of the forest. I thought they might be Tanzanian military police out of uniform.

The men walked through the bus. One of them came up to me and smiled. He looked at my Georgetown hat and said to me, in Swahili, "You're American, aren't you?" This man had no way of knowing what languages I spoke, so I had to make a quick decision about whether to reveal that I understood him. I decided to stick to the plan of pretending to be American.

I responded, in Swahili, "Yes, I'm an American. I'm with the Peace Corps." I figured that on the hatred spectrum of Americans that ranged from CIA operatives to nuns, Peace Corps volunteers were somewhere close to the nun end.

His face stiffened, and he bit his lower lip.

"Get up and come with me," he ordered. "Off the bus." He turned around to lead me off the bus.

"Who are you, and why do you want me to leave the bus?" I asked. He looked at me with a fierce expression.

The woman seated next to me slowly raised her head and grabbed my hand while looking at the man with the gun. "You can't take him!" she said defiantly in Swahili. "He's my husband."

The man with the gun seemed confused. "He can't be your husband."

"Yes, he's my husband," she insisted. "If you take him, you have to take me too."

The man hesitated for a moment, unsure what to do with her. He ordered both of us off the bus. When we got to the ground, I saw several others dressed in ragtag military uniforms. The luggage compartment was open, and some of the men were removing bags. A few remained on the bus, watching the passengers. "Maybe they are rebels," I thought.

As I watched, I realized the tenuousness of the situation. I had put myself in great danger. To these people, an American Peace Corps worker was not a friend. A member of the Peace Corps was an American, and Americans could be the enemy.

"Why did you say that I'm your husband?" I whispered to the woman.

"Be quiet now," she told me. "Rebels take a man off a bus for only one reason—to shoot him." For the moment, she had saved my life by claiming me as her husband. But as soon as they learned she had tricked them, or perhaps even if they never found out, they would probably shoot me anyway. I thought back to the night when the Kenyan security forces were about to shoot me in another forest, in another country, but not so far away. I was afraid, back then, but ready to die. I had led a movement that would go on without me. This time, I was not ready to die. I had a wonderful wife at our home in the United States. My child was growing within her, a child who would never know me if these men killed me now.

Meanwhile, the men had unloaded most of the luggage on the ground. They were emptying and searching nearly every compartment and arguing with each other. Apparently something was wrong: they were looking for something that they couldn't find.

They didn't have what they wanted, but now they had a different prize. The man who had taken us off the bus and who seemed to command the rest said to the others, "It's okay anyway. At least we got ourselves an American."

"Well, it depends on how much money his family has," one of the men responded.

My heart sank. I didn't have family with money. I pictured how happy my older brothers would be when they got the news of my execution. "Someone finally did it for us," they would gloat. I thought of my little sister and how sad she would be. "We've never spent enough time together," I reflected. I imagined my little brother asking questions: "What was he doing in western Tanzania?" he would wonder, probably for the rest of his life. I visualized Melissa, pregnant, making unsuccessful efforts to get the American government to negotiate for my release. "The American government never pays ransom for its own citizens," I realized. "It certainly won't pay ransom for a Kenyan it has banished."

"If these people hate Americans, perhaps my safety might lie in showing them that I am not an American," I mused. Meanwhile, the rebels closed up the luggage compartment, and the other gunmen left the bus. They ordered the driver to take off, and the bus left. The rebels, the woman, and I stood in the middle of the forest, surrounded by luggage, though I didn't see my own backpack on the ground.

The senior rebel approached me. "What part of America are you from?" It took me a second to realize that he had addressed me in perfect American English.

"You speak English so well! How did you learn English?" I asked him in the same language.

He stared at me with an angry expression. "You niggers think that we Africans are so dumb," he said, slowly shaking his head.

His remark reminded me of the racism I'd experienced, particularly the black-on-black racism. I thought of the man in Chicago who was prepared to shoot me because I rode in a car with a white person, and the restaurant in Nairobi where the Africans seated white tourists ahead of native Kenyans. This man with the gun was an African, and I could tell from his speech that he had lived in America. White Americans might have treated him badly, but, if my own experience in Virginia was any guide, African Americans probably had never let him forget that he was a newcomer and a foreigner. I had often met African Americans who acted deferentially to whites but aggressively toward African immigrants.

African Americans might have treated him with more contempt and disrespect than the whites had.

To him, I was a typically insensitive African American.

"I lived in America," he confirmed. "I was at Georgia Tech for four years. I worked harder than any of you niggers can ever work, and I got nothing but shit from black people like you," he emphasized. "And then you kicked me out."

I could see how angry he got as he spoke to me. He could have shot me at any moment. Surprisingly, his mistaken assumption seemed funny, and I tried not to laugh. "Look, man," I said in English. "I'm Kenyan, and they kicked me out, too." His attitude changed immediately, disbelieving.

"My passport is in my back pocket," I said. "I'm going to take it out very slowly." I showed him the Kenyan passport. "They kicked me out last summer. I was in law school, but they didn't care. I had to give it up and get on a plane back to Africa."

The other rebels hustled us off the road, aware that when the bus reached the next police post, Tanzanian troops would come looking for us. They quickly scavenged through the luggage and packed their loot into small loads, which they distributed among themselves. They didn't seem to be paying much attention to my conversation with their leader; they didn't appear to understand English. The more he and I talked, however, the more comfortable they seemed to become with me.

We kept going further into the forest so the troops couldn't find us. As we walked, I explained my situation to the man from Georgia Tech. "You think you're angry? I can't even go back to my own country because they'd kill me there. There isn't anything you can get by shooting me or kidnapping me. The Americans won't care what happens to me. Neither will the Kenyans," I explained.

After walking for about an hour, we took a break under a huge tree. I sat down, my back against the tree, and thought about what I had told him. Finally he adjusted his gun, and, for a moment, I thought he was about to shoot me. But he shouldered the gun and told me to get up.

Then he hugged me. "I'm Jesse," he said. "That's my American nickname. Don't consider yourself a hostage . . . you're not my hostage. I thought you were one of those American niggers. I was going to shoot you. I wasn't even going to try to exchange you for anything, no matter how much your parents would have paid for you. Even if they paid, I was going to shoot you."

"I have a nickname, too, but I acquired it in Africa," I said to him. It was difficult to conceal that my whole body was shaking. "I'm Jeff. It's short for giraffe." He laughed. We made more small talk to keep the conversation going.

We soon got up and started walking. I got more worried. Even if we got out of this mess alive, the woman and I would never find the road or catch up with the bus. I was also worried about my backpack, still in the luggage compartment of the bus, which contained my camera, my clothing, and my return bus ticket. All I had with me in the day pack was a map, a snack, the kit with the doctored candy that Melissa had given me, and a little cash. I couldn't even remember the name of the bus company. I'd taken a picture of the bus, but that picture was still in the camera.

We kept walking. Jesse and I walked ahead of most of the rebels and the woman who had claimed to be my wife. I thought of trying to knock him out with the doctored candy. But I realized that I couldn't escape and leave the woman with them—she was the reason I was alive. The rest of the men were moving more slowly; one of them had suffered a leg injury, and others were carrying the stolen luggage. The woman was engaging them in a conversation as they walked.

I started asking Jesse questions about their life in the forest. "Me and my boys are barely surviving," he said. "When I came back from the United States, I spent two months in Kinshasa trying to get a job. There was nothing for me to do. One way or the other, I had to earn something. I am from this region, so I came back home, and we put this squad together. I trained these boys, and we've been fighting ever since. I've lost so many of my men—not to combat injuries but to regular injuries and diseases that can be easily cured. But we have no medical supplies. We need medicine badly, and that is why we came out here. We paid the local police to send a shipment through for us, but I think we stopped the wrong bus. We were expecting a bus with weapons and medicine."

Jesse demanded my day pack and confiscated my map, stuffing it in his pocket. "We badly need that map, so I have to keep it," he said, almost apologetically.

After walking for about two more hours, we sat down at a spring. The woman and the other men caught up with us. Even though we were only a few miles off the road, the rebels seemed to feel very comfortable and familiar with the area. Apparently, they weren't worried about being followed.

The men found food in the luggage and passed it around. I learned that one of the rebels was a geologist who had studied in Paris. He'd returned to his native Congo because he wanted to do something useful for his region, but the area had been so destroyed by war that nothing was left for him to do. "The government in Kinshasa didn't care about the people in the east," he asserted. "They only wanted the uranium and the oil under the ground so they could enrich themselves." He believed that only by taking over the country could he and others like him begin to rebuild it.

I told these rebels that I really wanted to get back to the road and go on to Uganda. I asked Jesse if he would be willing to point me and the woman toward the road.

"I will do better than that," he offered. "I will escort you back. In fact, you'll need me to escort you, because there are other groups in this forest who might harm you if you're not with me."

We walked back with Jesse. Eventually, we sighted the road, and Jesse faded back into the forest. We anticipated a long walk up the road to find a telephone or a police post, but within less than a mile, we saw the bus conductor with several police officers. The driver had taken the bus to a nearby U.N. refugee camp and from there had called the nearest police post. On instructions from the police, he'd driven the bus to the police post, about sixty miles farther north, and deposited the passengers. Now he had returned to the place where the bus had been stopped, along with several officers, to look for me and the woman. We walked to the refugee camp, and from there the police took us in one of their Land Rovers to rejoin the other passengers at the police post. My backpack was still in the bus, so covered with the dust and dirt blown in during the trip that the rebels never spotted it in a back corner of the luggage compartment.

The other passengers were so overjoyed to see us again that they didn't seem to mind that their trip had been delayed by many hours. I was so exhausted that I could barely relate what had happened to us, but the woman told them the whole story. We all returned to our seats and drove on to Bukoba. The woman sat once again in the seat next to mine. All the way, I kept wondering how I could thank a stranger who had risked her own life to save mine. She had left the bus and walked toward an unknown fate in the forest to help a man she had just met.

"I was planning to connect with the bus to Kampala tonight," she told me. "But now we can't possibly arrive in time. I will have to stay overnight in Bukoba and take the morning bus."

I offered to pay for her hotel stay in Bukoba that night. It was the least I could do, and since I too was going to Uganda, I would ride the morning bus with her to Kampala. Later, I learned during our brief conversation that her brother taught at Makerere University Law School in Kampala. As a law student, I thought that spending a day or two with him would be interesting—and I also hoped that it would afford me a rest break after the frustrations of Dar es Salaam and the ordeal of the bus trip. As it turned out, when we got to Kampala, he arranged housing for me for two nights in a university apartment.

I couldn't face the prospect of risking my life again by taking a bus back through northern Tanzania. I decided to spend the last of my savings on a flight to Dar es Salaam, but I couldn't fly directly from Kampala. The immigration commissioner in Tanzania had specified that in order to get a two-month visa, I must apply at a border crossing, not at a Tanzanian embassy or consulate. So I took my leave and boarded a bus for Bukoba. When I crossed the border back into Tanzania, the immigration inspector looked at the commissioner's notation and gave me a two-month visa.

. . .

From Bukoba, I flew to Dar es Salaam. As soon as I returned to my apartment, I checked my email. The first message I read revealed that the National Visa Center had sent Elizabeth Jordan the approved I-212 waiver completion form. In my mind, I started getting ready to return to Melissa.

Then I read the next message. Two days after receiving the approved form, Jordan had written to Melissa that the DHS office in Nairobi "insists that your husband was indeed deported and requires an I-601 waiver in addition to the approved I-212. They have asked us to send your husband's entire file to them."

Jordan had mentioned the I-601 form once before, in passing, during her first meeting with us. But then, after she advised us not to try to expedite the I-212 application, she had dropped the subject. With this message, I knew that I had become the prince in the fairy tale who can wed the king's daughter only by succeeding in a quest ordered by the king. Each time the prince completes a quest, however, the father demands a new one. I had applied for asylum, won and then lost voluntary departure, won the diversity visa lottery, had my marriage recognized by the American government, and received a waiver of the ten-year bar. Now the Department of Homeland Security had concocted a new obstacle to prevent me from being with my princess.

Ironically, Jordan had been trying to reach me because she needed my signature on a form so that she could send my file to Nairobi. I hadn't answered my cell phone, of course, because her delays had forced me to go on a dangerous week-long trip to Uganda.

My email box had other messages. Phil had insisted that Jordan explain why DHS thought it needed an I-601 waiver. The department used this waiver form, he noted, when a would-be immigrant had committed any of several different kinds of transgressions: crimes, frauds, or employment in the United States without permission. Which, if any, of these things was I accused of doing?

Jordan apparently didn't know; she just wanted to send the file to Nairobi and let someone else deal with it, however long that would take. Since I couldn't safely go to Nairobi, I would have no ability to deal with U.S. officials there. Also, having flown from Bukoba, I was very low on money. If Jordan ever decided to let me have a visa, I would have to borrow money just to pay the application fee.

Once again, what mattered was who my lawyers knew. Phil had a contact at a senior level in DHS, who called the Nairobi office to find out why officials in Nairobi thought they needed an I-601 application. Rather than answer this inquiry from officials of their own department back home, the people in the Nairobi office backed down. They notified Jordan that I didn't need to go through the I-601 process after all.

When the U.S. consulate got that news, Maria Ijames called me and invited me for a visa interview, scheduled for Monday, February 21. I emailed Diane to tell her the good news and the date. Diane checked the consulate's web site and discovered that the interview was scheduled for President's Day, a federal holiday on which the building would be closed.

I persuaded the consulate to reschedule for February 22. Jordan didn't even come to the interview; Ijames conducted it. I answered the questions about Kenyan arrests and U.S. deportation exactly as Diane had instructed me. That very day, at last, American officials granted me an immigrant visa.

The documentation they presented to me consisted of a fat sealed envelope to give to the airport immigration officer and some other papers. When I looked at the other papers, I realized that the consulate had listed my citizenship as Tanzanian, not Kenyan. So I had to return to the consulate and have them cancel the visa and reissue it correctly.

Even after I had what seemed the correct documents and had bought a plane ticket to Washington, I wasn't sure that I would actually be allowed into the United States. When I looked at the papers again, it appeared that the consulate had stamped the visa correctly. However, the signature line above Elizabeth Jordan's name was blank.

I didn't know whether the blank line would cause me a problem at Dulles airport. But Melissa had another contact at DHS, who told her that, after getting off the plane, I should find the oldest immigration inspector and get in that line. The older inspectors, he said, were more experienced and didn't feel a need to demonstrate their power by giving arriving immigrants a hard time.

Flying to the United States for the fourth time since 1995, I focused on this advice, and on Melissa, who would be waiting for me. They just couldn't send me back to Africa. I was totally out of money, and if they put me on a flight back to Tanzania, I would be out of hope as well.

My inspector was in his mid-fifties. I gave him the fat envelope, still sealed. He looked at it and said, "Oh, my, we've got one of these."

I wondered what he meant. He opened the envelope and stamped it. The first thing he pulled out was a picture of Melissa. "Is that your wife?"

"Yes, sir, that's my wife," I said, smiling. I knew that she was in the airport, just a few yards away, but she couldn't communicate with me unless I cleared immigration and customs.

"Where did you two meet?" the inspector asked.

"At a Halloween party," I responded.

"She's beautiful," he observed.

"Thank you." My heart kept pounding. There was only one door between me and safety in America.

He carefully examined my passport. "You know," he commented, "we get an immigrant visa only one out of a thousand times these days. Not so many are being issued in Africa now, so it's a surprise to see one."

He sifted through the other papers and kept flipping through the stack of documents, apparently looking for something he couldn't find. I got worried. Finally, he found what he was looking for at the bottom of the envelope, a single piece of paper not stapled to the others. It was the I-212 approval.

"I got it. It's supposed to be on top of the stack, but I guess they wanted us to work for it." He pointed to a long hallway to the left of his glass-caged office, with a door at the end. "Now, go through that door on that side. There will be another immigration inspector, a very calm gentleman with a mustache. Just go in and see him. I'm going to put this I-212 form on top, because that's the first thing he'll want to see," he explained as he put the papers back into the envelope and handed them back to me together with my passport. Relieved, I took the papers, smiled, and walked toward the hallway.

The man on the other side of the door was indeed very calm and reassuring. He went through the thick packet of documents in the envelope, one by one, reading my whole long immigration history, including the entire opinion from the Fourth Circuit. He collected my biographical information and took my fingerprints, matching them with the prints that had been sent from the consulate in Tanzania.

After about two hours, he looked up from his work, put all the papers back into the envelope, made a notation on my passport, and handed it to me with a smile. "Welcome to America," he said. "Now you can get your bags and go through customs."

I walked through customs in a daze. At the end of the counter, I walked through a door. Melissa stood on the other side of the door, holding a bouquet of roses and a big balloon. The printing on the balloon didn't read "Welcome to America"—instead, it read "Welcome Home."

I walked to her, and we slowly wrapped our arms around each other, and for a long time we just held each other, unable to speak.

The Lawyer's Epilogue

I have practiced law for forty years. For more than thirty of those years, I have directed a law school clinic, first at Columbia University and then, since 1981, at Georgetown.[1] My students and I have won and lost many cases. Several decisions that went against my clients seemed unjust, but I don't think that any unsuccessful case has ever made me as angry, or as ashamed of my country's legal system, as the case that became known as *Ngarurih v. Ashcroft.*

What distressed me so much about how our immigration system treated Jeff was that he had a stronger claim for asylum than many of the dozens of clinic clients who easily won their cases. He was a classic political dissident, thrust into an opposition role by an oppressive political and economic regime in which he had no voice. He was tortured and put into solitary confinement for his temerity in speaking up for his fellow farmers. He left his country for the United States, abandoning the twins he had brought up since infancy, only when it became clear that there was no hope and no future for him in Kenya. Despite very little schooling, he learned English as a third language. He came to the United States legally, with a student visa. Upon arrival, he not only began the studies that eventually earned him a college degree but also was instrumental in helping to create the first four-year Catholic college in Oklahoma. He

had hoped to return home eventually and applied for asylum only because President Moi remained in power. At that point, asylum was his
only way to avoid the risk of being imprisoned again in Kenya.

Jeff was, in short, an exemplary refugee and future citizen of the
United States. His one "failing" was that he loved his brother Njoka so
much that he risked his own life to try to save Njoka from torture. Yet at
every turn, federal agencies and courts responded to his pleas for help
with denial and rejection.

Jeff is amazingly resilient. He bounced back from each legal rebuff;
from imprisonment, torture, and isolation; and from his three near-death
experiences: at the hands of his older brothers, the Kenyan security
forces, and the rebels in the forests of western Tanzania. He came up
smiling each time, full of wry observations about his treatment.

I am neither as resilient nor as cheerful as Jeff. When I get angry about
an injustice, I want to appeal and expose and denounce it. In this instance,
my feelings were intensified by how much I liked Jeff from the moment
I met him and by how our friendship grew after Dave and Bernie left the
clinic and my personal and professional contacts with Jeff—now *my*
client—began to proliferate.

In my first meeting with Jeff, on the eve of his scheduling hearing, I
was amazed by his height. But what I really loved about him was his
British-influenced African accent. I later learned that he wrote in English
with difficulty. But he spoke English elegantly, with a rolled "r" that
made my own voice seem pathetically flat. For days, I practiced his name,
trying to say the middle part as he did, Ga—rrrurrr—ee, feeling my
tongue vibrate in the back of my throat.

In late summer 2002, my relationship with Jeff became much closer.
When we decided that his best bet was to risk arrest by returning to
Kenya to try to obtain the diversity lottery visa that awaited him, I felt
comfortable that we'd made the right decision. But I didn't hear from
him for days at a time when he was out of telephone range in Kenya, and
I worried constantly that he was in prison and that I was responsible.
That fear gave way to fist-pounding frustration when Margaret Hartley,

the consular officer, refused not only to issue his visa but also to allow me to explain his situation to her. We lawyers are used to making arguments, even losing arguments; we are not so accustomed to having American officials slam doors in our faces. I wanted to get up from my law school desk, take a taxi to the airport, fly to Nairobi, and confront her in person. But lacking the time, money, or access to do any of those things, I tried, unsuccessfully, to help Jeff through emails to the consulate and the State Department.

As Jeff resumed his law school studies that winter, our personal relationship deepened much further. My wife, Lisa, became his faculty advisor at Catholic University, and I was standing only a few feet away from him when he met her student Melissa. He came to Thanksgiving dinner and a Passover seder at our house. He and Melissa took us to a cheerful Italian restaurant to kick off their westward trip to meet her parents. But the more our friendship grew, the more I felt that I was betraying him personally by giving him one piece of bad news after another about the progress of his case. In early January 2003, as I set off to teach a class, I picked a letter out of my mailbox. On the way to class, I read Hess's brief rejection of Jeff's appeal, and I could hardly teach. A day or two later, I felt like a surgeon delivering news of a fatal illness when I met Jeff in my office and told him that the Board of Immigration Appeals had ruled against him and that his chances in the Fourth Circuit were poor. And more than a year after that, after I'd celebrated at his wedding and struggled in vain with Judge Wilkinson in Richmond, I sat glumly with Melissa at the airport, watching helplessly as the plane took off, carrying Jeff to a continent from which he might never be able to return.

Those simultaneous feelings of deepening friendship and anger at my government's indifference carried me through four years of frustrating litigation and three years of collaboration on this book. Jeff's safe return was certainly welcome, but it did little to end my anger. Although he eventually got lucky, many other deserving asylum applicants may be deported because of restrictive or arbitrary decisions by American officials, particularly in the wake of the September 11 tragedies.

Some American policy-makers, including several members of Congress quoted in the introduction to this book, want to put still more legal obstacles in the path of asylum applicants, claiming that asylum is an immigration loophole through which terrorists can easily pass. Jeff's ten-year quest for safety in America suggests that their fears are overblown. To the contrary, even victims of torture face formidable challenges as they try to prove their claims and persuade the American government to allow them to remain in the United States. They must submit to identity and security checks and document every aspect of their lives to an asylum officer or immigration judge—surely not the route a terrorist would choose.

Of course, not every asylum applicant experiences as many successive disappointments and defeats as Jeff did. But many do, and much of the suffering and anguish that the American government imposes on them is completely unnecessary. Because tens of thousands of people apply for asylum in the United States each year, the government necessarily maintains an elaborate administrative structure for adjudicating their cases. Congress and successive administrations have tried to establish a system that is both efficient and fair. But Jeff's encounters with this system suggest that further improvement is necessary. He and I wrote this book to expose some of the flaws in how America treats would-be immigrants, particularly asylum applicants, and to make some recommendations for improving the adjudication system, as outlined in the following sections.

· *Reduce the Role of Luck*   My most important recommendation is to reduce the role of pure chance in the asylum adjudication process.[2] Chance played a major role in Jeff's legal case—and not just in his winning the diversity visa lottery, which is the one and only aspect of the U.S. immigration system in which luck is deliberately part of the process. The most critical event in his case was the random assignment of his file, by the clerk of the Arlington, Virginia, immigration court, to Judge Joan Churchill (who has since retired). The reason this assignment was so critical is that the more than two hundred immigration judges in the United States grant asylum at widely differing rates, even to applicants from the same country and in the same time frame. Within the immigration court within a single city, such as Arlington, enormous and persistent variations make the outcome of cases highly dependent on the identity of the judge.

Of course, I can't prove that a different judge would have granted Jeff asylum, but the odds of prevailing would have been much better. From January 2000 through August 2004, five judges in Arlington (one of whom was appointed late in that period) heard nineteen asylum cases from Kenyan applicants, and they collectively granted asylum in five of them, a 26 percent rate overall. But Judge M. Christopher Grant, who heard six of the cases, granted asylum in four of them (67 percent); whereas Judge Churchill heard eight cases, including Jeff's, and granted asylum in none of them (0 percent).[3]

This particular disparity may be a fluke, and no firm conclusion can be drawn from the decisions in such a small number of cases. But the disparity in the Arlington judges' decisions in Kenyan cases is all too consistent with the pattern of their decisions in asylum cases from all countries combined (a large database consisting of 869 cases in that five-year period): Judge Churchill's grant rate was 17 percent, whereas every other judge in Arlington had a grant rate of at least 30 percent. For the 463 applicants from Kenya during this period, the combined *national* grant rate for all immigration judges was 42 percent; and for all 140,428 applicants from all countries, the national grant rate was 38 percent. Judge Churchill's 0 percent grant rate for Kenyan applicants and her 17 percent grant rate for all applicants who came before her therefore seem exceptionally low.[4]

A recent article entitled "Refugee Roulette," which I co-authored with two colleagues, shows that the judges of the immigration court in Arlington are actually *more* consistent in their asylum decisions than those in other cities.[5] For example, the San Francisco immigration court has seventeen immigration judges who each decided at least fifty cases involving Indian nationals seeking asylum between January 2000 and August 2004.

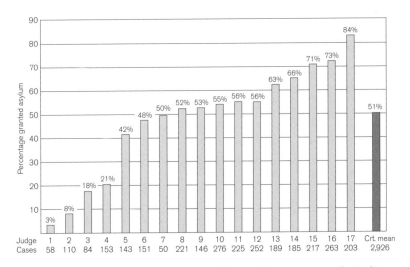

Figure 1. San Francisco immigration judges' asylum grant rates for Indian applicants, January 2000–August 2004. Each judge (identified by a sequential number) decided a minimum of fifty such cases. The court mean and the total number of cases include 272 decisions by judges who decided fewer than fifty such cases. *Source*: "U.S. Immigration Judge Decisions in Asylum Cases, Jan. 2000 to Aug. 2004," www.asylumlaw.org/legal_tools/index.cfm?fuseaction= showJudges2004 (visited Oct. 17, 2007).

In Figure 1, each bar shows the grant rate of an individual judge for asylum applications by Indian nationals. The sequential number under each bar is merely a serial number assigned to a particular judge. The number of cases involving Indians decided by that judge appears under the serial number. As the figure demonstrates, one of these judges granted asylum to 3 percent of the applicants from India, whereas a judge down the hall granted asylum to 84 percent of the applicants from that same country.

Among the twenty-two immigration judges in Miami who each decided at least fifty cases, one granted asylum to 5 percent of Colombian applicants, while another granted asylum in 88 percent of the Colombian cases. And consider the situation of Chinese asylum applicants in the immigration court in Los Angeles. As Figure 2 shows, they may be assigned

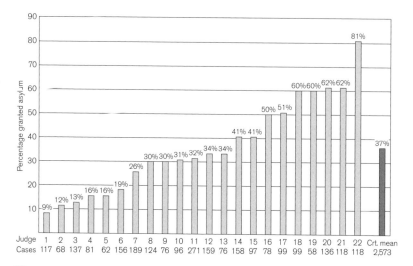

Figure 2.   Los Angeles immigration judges' asylum grant rates for Chinese applicants, January 2000–August 2004. Each judge (identified by a sequential number) decided a minimum of fifty such cases. The court mean and the total number of cases include 172 decisions by judges who decided fewer than fifty such cases. *Source:* "U.S. Immigration Judge Decisions in Asylum Cases, Jan. 2000 to Aug. 2004," www.asylumlaw.org/legal_tools/index.cfm?fuseaction= showJudges2004 (visited Oct. 17, 2007).

to a judge who grants asylum in 9 percent of the cases or a judge in a nearby courtroom who grants asylum in 81 percent. The prospects for refuge depend largely on random assignment by a clerk.

Random chance may also have diminished Jeff's chances of prevailing at his initial Asylum Office interview with Patricia Craddock. I can't be certain of this, because I don't know Craddock's grant rate compared to the grant rate of others in her regional Asylum Office. The Department of Homeland Security has, however, made available both the grant rates of each asylum officer, without identifying names or regional offices, and the grant rates for cases involving eleven countries that generate a high number of applicants. Some of DHS's eight regions show considerable consistency from officer to officer, but others show the same kind of

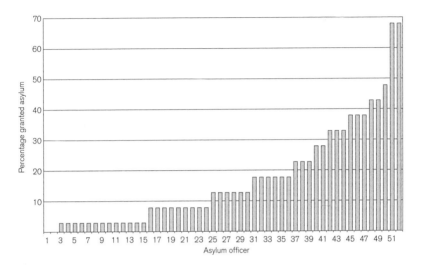

Figure 3.   Asylum officers' grant rates for Chinese applicants, Department
of Homeland Security region "H," fiscal year 1999 through fiscal year 2005.
In the original DHS data, the grant rates were stated in ranges of 5 percent;
this chart shows the midpoint of each range. Thus an officer who granted
asylum 31–35 percent of the time is shown here as having a 33 percent rate.
Source: U.S. Citizenship and Immigration Services, Department of Homeland
Security, "Refugees, Asylum, and Parole System, Grant Rates by Asylum
Officer, FY99 through FY05," www.law.georgetown.edu/humanrightsinstitute/
refugeeroulette.

grant rate spread that is evident in immigration court. Figure 3, for
example, shows decisions made by asylum officers from fiscal year 1999
through fiscal year 2005 in an area DHS identifies only as Region "H."
Each officer decided at least twenty-five applications from Chinese nationals. In these cases involving Chinese, fifteen officers had grant rates
of 3 percent or less, while eight other officers had grant rates exceeding
35 percent.

Because I don't know whether Jeff's asylum interview took place in
a region of high or low consistency, I am therefore uncertain whether
chance assignment strongly affected his chance of prevailing when he

first applied. But I do have reason to believe that bad luck made it almost impossible for him to prevail at the other end of the process, on his appeal to the federal courts. Ultimately, his asylum application was rejected by the U.S. Court of Appeals for the Fourth Circuit. As noted in chapters 7 and 8, this court is generally the most conservative federal court in the nation, and its treatment of asylum cases is no exception.

In calendar years 2004 and 2005 (combined), this court considered 269 appeals in which asylum had been denied by the Board of Immigration Appeals. It sent only 5 cases back to the board for reconsideration, a remand rate of 1.9 percent. Jeff's case came before the Fourth Circuit because, during his year of practical training, just before he applied for asylum, he had left his job with Hertz and moved from California to Virginia to take a job with MCI. He had no way of knowing that by moving from west to east, he was seriously reducing his chances of winning asylum. If he had applied for asylum in the San Francisco Bay Area, he would have had a 71 percent chance of being granted asylum by an immigration judge (the San Francisco immigration court's 2000–2004 grant rate in Kenyan cases). In addition, if the immigration judge had denied his claim, his appeal would have gone to the Court of Appeals for the Ninth Circuit rather than the Fourth Circuit. The Ninth Circuit's remand rate for asylum cases in 2004 and 2005 was 19.5 percent, compared to the Fourth Circuit's 1.9 percent.[6]

Also, just a few months after Jeff lost his case in the Fourth Circuit, the Ninth Circuit unanimously disagreed with the Fourth Circuit on the very issue that his case had raised. Nasser Karouni, a Lebanese national, had been persecuted by Hezbollah because he was gay. He fled to the United States, entering with a tourist visa, which he overstayed. He returned twice to Lebanon before applying for asylum, once for two months to visit his father, who was dying of cancer, and once for one month to visit his dying mother. The immigration judge denied asylum, stating that Karouni had not established a well-founded fear of persecution. This judge specifically found that Karouni's two returns to Lebanon "cut against" his claim of fear of future persecution in Lebanon because these actions did "not appear to be the actions of an individual who fears persecution because he is gay." The Board of Immigration Appeals summarily affirmed this decision. Deborah Misir wrote the brief for the Department of Homeland Security, as she had done in Jeff's case. But the Ninth Circuit rejected the board's decision. It reasoned, just as I had tried to argue in Jeff's case, that Karouni's return was justifiable:

> Faced with the difficult choice of returning to Lebanon to see his dying parents or remaining in the safe haven of the United States, we do not fault Karouni for his choice to return to Lebanon to see his parents one last time. Accordingly, we do not believe that Karouni's two return visits to Lebanon constitute substantial evidence that his fear of persecution was not well-founded. Rather, the [judge's] conclusion to the contrary was "personal conjecture" about what choice someone in Karouni's unfortunate position would have made. An immigration judge's personal conjecture cannot be substituted for objective and substantial evidence.[7]

I do not mean to suggest that every asylum officer or immigration judge should have the same grant rate for asylum applicants of a given nationality, or that every U.S. court of appeals should have exactly the same remand rate for cases of this type. Some variation is to be expected. But the statistical variations that exist seem excessive. They call to mind a report by the attorney general more than half a century ago, commenting on disparities in criminal sentences meted out by federal judges:

> It is obviously repugnant to one's sense of justice that the judgment meted out to an offender should be dependent in large part on a purely fortuitous circumstance; namely, the personality of the particular judge before whom the case happens to come for disposition. While absolute equality is neither desirable nor attainable, a greater approach to similarity of treatment than now prevails appears to be desirable, if not essential.[8]

Rather than imposing a target grant rate that each immigration judge should strive to meet, it might be sufficient for the Department of Justice to require all the judges in each immigration court, or in each region of the country, to sit in on each other's cases from time to time, meet periodically, compare grant rates, and discuss why any substantial disparities exist. Those in the middle might persuade those with exceptionally high or low grant rates that they are too gullible or too suspicious of applicants' tales, that they misunderstand the human rights conditions in certain countries, or that they are misinterpreting the law.

The Department of Justice seems to be aware that inconsistency from judge to judge in the adjudication of asylum cases is a problem. In January 2007, the attorney general's office advised the U.S. Commission on International Religious Freedom that it was exploring unstated "mechanisms" to address the commission's 2005 recommendation that it adopt procedures to address the significant variations in approval rates among immigration judges. However, it conceded that the process remained "under internal review within the Department."[9]

The court of appeals judges in each circuit do have annual regional conferences at which they talk among themselves and are informed about new developments in the law. But these conferences do not provide an opportunity for judges from different circuits to discuss why remand rates in asylum cases are more than ten times higher in some circuits than in others, even when the cases under consideration are limited to the same set of fifteen countries with particularly bad human rights records. Similarly, the chief judges of each circuit hold an annual conference, but since only chief judges participate, a discussion of the remand rate differences at that conference is unlikely to effect a significant change in the cultures of the circuits with particularly high or low remand rates.

The Federal Judicial Center should convene a national conference of court of appeals judges to help the judges understand the causes of the remand rate disparity and to decide whether measures should be taken to reduce it. For example, it might be desirable for judges from courts with low rates of remand to participate in some asylum appeals, as visiting judges, in courts that have high rates of remand.

· *Train the Immigration Judges and the Federal Judges*   Another approach would be for the government to provide regular training for immigration judges and for the judges of the U.S. courts of appeals. The Department of Homeland Security does offer frequent periodic training for its more than nine hundred asylum officers, which could account for the fact that the disparity among the grant rates of asylum officers within several of the regional offices is much less pronounced than the spread among the grant rates of immigration judges who work in the same regional courts. The training for asylum officers includes sessions on the relevant law, current human rights conditions around the globe, and intercultural sensitivity when dealing with asylum applicants. Periodic continuing education of the other adjudicators in this system, particularly the immigration judges, could only improve the quality of justice. In Jeff's case, it might have acquainted Judge Churchill with the Justice Department's *Basic Law Manual*, of which she claimed ignorance.

In the past, immigration judges had annual training conferences. In 2006, however, the president of the National Association of Immigration Judges complained that no training conference had been held in three years because of funding cuts.[10] The Department of Justice did provide national training conferences in 2006 and 2007 but made no assurances of annual training, much less more frequent training at the local level.[11]

· *Provide Legal Representation for Asylum Applicants*   Although Jeff did not win asylum, he had a reasonable chance of prevailing only because he stumbled by accident into Georgetown University's asylum clinic while trying to seek admission to the school as a law student. If he had been represented by a lawyer before he applied for asylum, he would have prepared much more effectively for the interview with Patricia Craddock, the asylum officer. A lawyer probably would have referred him to a psychologist, as Dave and Bernie eventually did, and he would have been able to straighten out the dates of the protest and his arrest. He might have been able to talk about rather than suppress his ordeal in the water cell.

When he applied for asylum in 2000, he could not have paid for a lawyer out of his meager earnings as an MCI trainee. He might have requested more financial help from the industrialist who had supported him through college, but he was too proud to ask. Most people in his shoes do not have the assistance of either law school clinics or wealthy financial backers. The American government does provide free legal help to indigent persons who are accused of crimes, even misdemeanors and juvenile offenses, but it does not provide lawyers for indigent asylum applicants who face possible deportation. To the contrary, Congress has prohibited the federally supported neighborhood offices sponsored by the Legal Services Corporation from representing asylum applicants.[12]

The government should end this policy, which effectively forces indigent asylum applicants to navigate the complex asylum process without representation. As a nation, we deem it imperative to offer legal representation to indigent individuals accused of crimes. It is equally imperative to provide indigent asylum seekers with legal assistance. An erroneous denial of asylum can result in imprisonment, torture, or death; these are consequences equivalent to or worse than incarceration in the United States. Lawyers make a huge difference in the likelihood of success for an asylum applicant. Among nondetained asylum seekers such as Jeff, those who have representation in their immigration court proceedings are nearly three times as likely to win asylum as those who are unrepresented (39 percent versus 14 percent); and detained asylum seekers are six times more likely to win if they are represented.[13]

Donald Kerwin, executive director of the Catholic Legal Immigration Network, Inc., has suggested that the United States create a system of public defenders for indigent respondents in immigration court. Alternatively, at less cost, the U.S. government could provide funds for an organization to screen cases and match those that seem most meritorious with charitable organizations that would arrange for free representation. Adoption of either of these plans would significantly improve the fairness of the present system, which in essence deprives most poor refugees of a fair chance to prove their cases. Another plan, relying more on private attorneys than on those paid by public or nonprofit organizations, would have the government pay the attorneys' fees, up to a reasonable amount, at least for asylum applicants who actually win asylum.[14]

· *Restore the Appeals Process*   At the Board of Immigration Appeals, Jeff's case got short shrift because Attorney General John Ashcroft had essentially destroyed the board as an effective appellate body. He and his appointees politicized the board by firing only certain members appointed during the Clinton administration, reduced the quality of review by directing a single member rather than a panel of three to review nearly all asylum decisions, and ensured that many decisions would be incoherent by allowing cases to be affirmed without opinion or with a sentence or two, as in Jeff's case. He also ordered such a swift reduction of the large backlog of cases that cursory review was inevitable during the period in which Jeff's case was decided.

Asylum cases often determine whether a person will live in freedom in the United States or be returned to risk imprisonment or death in a country with a dreadful human rights record. These cases are too important to be decided summarily by a single board member who merely signs his or her name or writes a line or two of text. In addition, the cases are too important to be decided by a board that is subservient to the attorney general and is therefore subject to political influence.

At least for cases involving requests for asylum or protection under the Convention Against Torture, the board should return to its former practice under which a team of three members evaluated each appeal and wrote an opinion of at least two or three pages explaining their disposition of the case. The opinions should, at a minimum, address the arguments that were made by the losing party. If, as in Jeff's case, the board leans toward deciding against an immigrant on a ground other than one raised by the immigration judge, it should ask the parties to brief the new issue rather than denying the appeal on a ground that the immigrant had no reason to address. The mutual accountability of three-member panel decisions would improve the quality of decision-making. So would requiring the panels to address the parties' contentions in their opinions, because board members would not then be able to gloss over troubling issues by signing unreasoned affirmances.

In 2006, Attorney General Alberto Gonzales announced twenty-two "measures" to improve the immigration courts and the Board of Immigration Appeals. One such measure stated that new rules, not yet written, would allow the use of three-member opinions "in a small class of particularly complex cases."[15] So minuscule an expansion of the use of panel opinions in no way meets the need of asylum applicants for thoughtful, debated, and reasoned responses to their arguments on appeal.

To depoliticize the board's decisions, the board should be moved out of the Department of Justice, where the attorney general can influence decisions by threatening to fire any members who do not share his or her philosophy. The board should become an independent executive branch agency, whose members are appointed by the president with the advice and consent of the Senate.[16]

Restoration of the board as a genuine appellate body would not only improve justice for asylum applicants but also relieve the terrible burden that the Ashcroft "reforms" put on the U.S. courts of appeals, where the load of immigration cases rose precipitously (from two hundred cases per month to about nine hundred cases per month) because immigrants and their lawyers no longer trusted the Board of Immigration Appeals to take their cases seriously. In addition to dealing with the increased case load, the courts have also been stressed by having to review poorly reasoned immigration judge opinions that the board has approved. Some of the language used by the courts of appeals in relation to these opinions reflects their frustration. These are but a few samples (not, of course, from the Fourth Circuit):

> The immigration court was "not aware of the most basic facts of [the immigrant's] case."
>
> The immigration judge's unexplained conclusion is "hard to take seriously."
>
> "The elementary principles of administrative law, the rules of logic, and common sense seem to have eluded the Board in this as in other cases."
>
> "It is the [immigration judge's] conclusion, not [the immigrant's] testimony, that 'strains credulity.'"[17]

If immigrants and their representatives had confidence in the Board of Immigration Appeals, both they and the taxpayers would save substantial amounts of money that are now being wasted because appeals must be taken to a U.S. court of appeals before the parties can trust that their arguments have been examined with care. One of the major advantages of an administrative rather than a judicial appellate body is that the administrative appeals process is less formal and less costly.[18]

· *Fix the Diversity Visa Lottery System*   Probably through an oversight, since fewer than one hundred individuals are affected each year, the diversity visa lottery system utterly fails to take into account the problems of lottery winners who are also asylum applicants. The State Department requires them to be interviewed in their home countries, where their lives are in danger. Few if any of the people in this small group have a valid immigration status at the time of the scheduled interview. If they ever held valid visas, as Jeff did, the validity of their visas would have expired during the months in which an asylum case is adjudicated in immigration court. Current law bars these winners from receiving their visas in the United States. Assuming that Congress doesn't end the diversity visa lottery altogether,[19] the law should be changed so that the immigration court itself, rather than a consular officer abroad, can determine whether the lottery winners meet the other qualifications, such as medical and financial fitness, and, if they do, allow them to become permanent residents.

In addition, some provision should be made for lottery winners like Jeff who are told to appear for interviews during the final month of the fiscal year and are then asked to produce additional documentation. They should not lose their chance to emigrate to America simply because their interviews were scheduled so late that they could not compile the required papers within a few days. In many countries, it takes many days of contacts with numerous bureaucracies to produce the documentation. These winners should be given at least a month's grace period before their lottery success is canceled.

Federal courts have concluded that they lack power to order the State Department to issue diversity lottery visas, even when the applicant has applied in a timely manner and the State Department has dragged its feet until after the fiscal year has ended. But the courts are not happy about having their hands so tied. One such court recently noted that the law is being implemented "in such a fashion as to make the United States appear unfeeling, arbitrary, and capricious, and to render an act of Congress an object of derision," perhaps because of "bureaucratic indifference or mismanagement at a lower level."[20]

· *Provide a Review Process When Consular Officers Deny Visas*   American consular officers have enormous power over people who want to go to the United States temporarily or permanently. In principle, they enforce a statutory standard; they are supposed to deny a visa only if they have "reason to believe" that the applicant is not eligible for the visa.[21] However, that standard is extremely vague and malleable, making arbitrary decision-making all too possible. The risk of unjust and unguided decisions is compounded by Congress's decision to make consular officers' denials of visas nonreviewable.[22] The denial of an immigrant visa is supposed to be reviewed by a more senior consular officer,[23] but the review does not always take place because of the high volume of applications.[24]

Even if review occurs, the applicant is not told of a right to this internal review and is not entitled to participate in it, either personally or through counsel.[25] Also, if the more senior officer agrees with the denying consular officer, no one, not a federal judge or even the secretary of state, for whom all State Department employees work, can overrule the decision to deny the visa.

Jeff encountered three different consular officers in the course of his ten-year effort to flee Kenya for the United States. The State Department's model for respectful, helpful assistance to a person in distress should be Marsha Von Duerckheim, the consular officer in Kenya who expedited his student visa and even provided her home phone number in case he had any problem leaving the country. Margaret Hartley, the consular officer who denied Jeff's visa when he won the lottery, seemed to represent the other extreme. Even though the State Department had severely criticized Kenyan human rights practices throughout the years of Daniel arap Moi's presidency, she apparently could not understand that Kenyan security forces held dissidents in secret prisons without giving the captives receipts to prove their arrests and detentions. She therefore sent Jeff on a wild goose chase for proof of his imprisonment. Although I tried to explain the situation to her and attempted to provide proof of Jeff's bona fides, including Judge Churchill's immigration court finding that Jeff had been truthful, Hartley refused to even pick up the telephone to talk with me and would not return my many calls and faxes. In my decades of practicing law, I have rarely felt so helpless as during those days of fruitless attempts to speak with her while Jeff's lottery ticket was expiring in 2002.

Elizabeth Jordan, in the consulate in Tanzania, was at first extraordinarily helpful, offering to expedite Jeff's visa when her security officer confirmed that he was in danger from Kenyan agents in Tanzania. However, she later became extremely suspicious of Jeff after he informed her of the Tanzanian guards' requests for bribes to enter the consulate and when he violated her instructions not to complicate her efforts by involving lawyers. She then imposed one documentary requirement after another and later directed him to obtain not just one but two waivers from the Department of Homeland Security before she would issue the visa. Eventually, she was advised that Jeff did not need the second waiver, and, to her great credit, she did allow her assistant to issue his visa. But meanwhile, Jeff was separated from his family for months, and he nearly lost his life at the hands of Congolese rebels during his scavenger hunt to be in simultaneous possession of all the necessary valid travel documents.

More than twenty-five years ago, the State Department reported "unevenness" in the performance of consular officers, and the U.S. Civil Rights Commission expressed its concern about these officials' unbridled discretion. The commission found that the process for review of consular visa denials "does not adequately protect aggrieved parties from improper exercises of consular discretionary authority." It recommended that Congress establish a Board of Visa Appeals to consider appeals from denials of visas, particularly when an applicant is attempting to return to a family that includes an American citizen, as Jeff was.[26]

Congress never acted on the commission's recommendation. It should do so now, in the post-9/11 world, when consular officers have a greater incentive than ever to deny visas based on vague suspicions, given that granting a visa to a terrorist could well be a career-ending decision. Even if Congress does not act, the secretary of state should establish a more formal review process for visa denials, in which the unsuccessful applicant is informed of the review procedure and allowed to participate in it, personally or through a legal representative.

Meanwhile, the Department of State should train its consular officers to cooperate with applicants and never to lose their tempers. The department's training should instill in consular officers the realization that many visa applicants who come before them have a desperate need to go to the United States, whether to visit a dying relative or to remove themselves from mortal danger. These officers are the face of the United States to thousands of foreign nationals, including many individuals who will never receive the requested visas. These officials should receive human rights training, and they should be particularly attentive when an applicant claims to have been a victim of persecution. In addition, when communication issues arise, they should welcome, not spurn, the efforts of American lawyers to explain the situations of their clients.

· *Clarify That Federal Courts Can Suspend the Expiration of Voluntary Departure While They Review Asylum Cases* In Jeff's case, the Fourth Circuit held that it lacked the power to stop the voluntary departure clock while an asylum applicant appealed a deportation order to a court of appeals. This is a bad decision because people who are at risk of being killed in their home countries should not have to return and somehow hide from their governments while federal appeals courts consider their cases. Furthermore, the Fourth Circuit is at odds with the other circuits in holding to such a limited view of its power. Six circuits have considered this question since the Ninth Circuit first addressed it in 2003. All five others have concluded that at least in asylum cases, they could suspend the expiration of a period of voluntary departure until after they decide whether the Board of Immigration Appeals made an erroneous judgment.[27] Only the Fourth Circuit believes that it lacks this power. It should reconsider its view.

· *Recognize That Genuine Refugees May Risk Persecution in Family Emergencies* I close with a recommendation for a change in policy that will affect only a few individuals each year but can make the difference between doom and safety for those persons. Training materials for asylum officers still state that a person can be considered to have a well-founded fear of persecution in his or her home country even if the person chooses to return to that country for a family emergency. This principle has not yet been codified in a more formal pronouncement, however, such as an official regulation of the Department of Homeland Security or a precedent of the Board of Immigration Appeals.

The policy should be transmuted from a training manual to a regulation or precedent, making it binding on immigration judges. Asylum should never again be denied to individuals because they temporarily overcome their fear in order to care for an ailing sibling, say good-bye to a dying parent, or attempt peacefully to obtain the release from prison of a family member who is being tortured. American asylum law should not enforce the cynical bumper stickers that proclaim, "No good deed goes unpunished." Instead, it should reflect the humanitarian spirit in which Congress sought to create a safe haven for those who come to the United States needing protection from persecution.

. . .

Jeff's life changed dramatically when the immigration inspector at Dulles airport cleared him to go through customs and meet Melissa at the exit. Thirteen years after he was imprisoned in Kenya, his struggle for a safe refuge was over. He had lost his plea for asylum, but he had gained something better: status as a lawful permanent resident of the United States.[28] For the first two years after he arrived from Tanzania, that status was provisional. To prevent marriage fraud, the government approves the permanent resident status of an immigrant spouse only conditionally; if the marriage does not last for two years, it revokes the visa. If the couple is still married after two years of residence in the United States, however, an immigration officer interviews them to make certain that the marriage is genuine. If the marriage is judged to be genuine, the officer removes the condition attached to the visa.[29]

After some brief family celebrations, Jeff resumed his legal studies. He and Melissa bought a house in the suburbs of Washington. Melissa graduated from Catholic University Law School and began working at a law firm, where she represents parents of students in need of special education. Jeff remains a student at Catholic, completing a legal education that was twice interrupted by having to leave the country as a result of his immigration travails.

Four freedoms

As of summer 2007, Jeff and Melissa had been married and had lived together in the United States for more than two years after receiving his conditional visa. The government has now granted their application to have the condition on his visa removed. The next and last step for Jeff will be to apply for naturalization as a citizen of the United States.

And there is one more event to relate. . . .

The Client's Epilogue

Back in Kenya, I knew many women who died. Some were close relatives; others were friends with whom I grew up or even dated. Each year, two or three never came home from the hospital. They died alone, tended by impersonal doctors, without husbands or family members at their sides.

. . .

On a sunny September afternoon, Lisa Lerman and I sat with Melissa in a darkened hospital room in Washington, D.C. I was frightened. The idea of driving back home without Melissa was so vivid to me that I had called Lisa, Phil's wife, the night before and asked her to meet us at the hospital. Lisa sat in a chair next to me preparing for her next contracts class, while I daydreamed about writing a book that would convey my struggle for safety in America.

After a while, I got hungry and went to the hospital cafeteria. I was besieged by gawkers. "How tall are you?" one asked. "Do you play basketball?" another inquired. As soon as I could, I beat a retreat back to Melissa's room.

The only light in the room spotlighted Melissa, leaving everything else in shadows. She breathed through a clear oxygen mask, holding my hands. Assisting her was a staff of doctors and nurses.

Soon Lisa stood on one side, holding Melissa's leg. A nurse held the other leg. I held her hand. A doctor stood at the foot of her bed. "Here it comes again . . . one . . . two . . . three!" the doctor exclaimed. At each count, Melissa held her breath, crunched forward, and pushed like a weightlifter on her final rep.

"That's good, stop now," the nurse said, encouraging her.

Melissa inhaled and looked deeply into my eyes. "You look scared," she said and pulled off the mask. "It's okay . . . it doesn't hurt. I love you," she whispered. "Thank you for making this moment happen."

I leaned over and kissed her.

"Ouch," she exclaimed, "my hand."

"Oops." I loosened my grip on Melissa's hand as she prepared for another push.

Suddenly, a gush and a flurry of movement . . . Melissa immediately saw him from her curled position. "Oh, it's a boy!" she blurted out, laughing. We all started to laugh.

As the nurse moved him onto the drying table, he grabbed the stethoscope from around her neck. The nurse quickly removed his tiny hand, but he grabbed the tubes that were attached to Melissa. I could feel his panic; I watched him try to hold onto something, to prevent himself from falling.

"Whuaaaaahh! Whuaaaahhh!" he cried. The nurse placed him down and quickly wiped his tiny body clean. "Would you like to cut the cord?" she asked, pushing the scissors into my hands.

"No," I responded impulsively. The nurse quickly cut him free and began to examine him. Then she bundled the infant into a blanket and handed him to me. As soon as I held him in my hands, Mackenzie stopped crying.

I recognized him. I could feel the spirit of my father around him. We gazed at each other for a moment that seemed to last forever.

I turned to look at Melissa. "It's him," I said, "it's my dad." I placed him gently into her cradling arms. "Meet your mother," I told him. Macken-

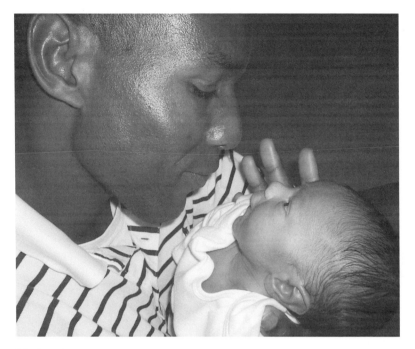

Mackenzie

zie nuzzled at her breast, learning her scent. I wondered what he would say when he woke up. I wondered what I would tell him. I was certain he would want to know where he was and how he got here. I lay down on the bed next to Melissa and held them close.

"Welcome home," I whispered.

ACKNOWLEDGMENTS

This book would not have been written without the support of T. Alexander Aleinikoff, dean of the Georgetown University Law Center and an authority on immigration law, who personally encouraged us to write it. We are grateful to him and to the faculty of the Law Center for creating the Center for Applied Legal Studies (CALS), which has successfully represented more than one hundred asylum applicants since 1995. We also want to thank Geri Thoma and Naomi Schneider (our editor at University of California Press), each of whom provided valuable editorial advice; Zachary Schrag, who gave this book its title; and Professor David A. Koplow, co-director of CALS, who urged us on and introduced us to the University of California Press. We appreciate the willingness of Getaneh M. Getaneh to allow us to tell the story of his asylum case in chapter 5. We also acknowledge with gratitude the research on asylum adjudication statistics conducted by Professors Andrew I. Schoenholtz and Jaya Ramji-Nogales, summarized here in the first epilogue.

This struggle for safety in America could not have succeeded without the help of many people, including some who are named in the text and others whose names are unknown or cannot be revealed. They include Joyce Aschenbrenner, Father Nicholas Ast, OSB, Fredrick Ballard Jr.,

Everett Bellamy, Karen Bouton, Marc Cassidy, Phil Chinnici, Danielle from Chicago, Samantha Daniels, Hartmut Fischer, Robert and Nancy Foster, William Fox, Mark and Catherine Graddy, Tauna Hanson, Charles Henck, David Herzog, Bernardine Huang, Arthur and Karen Ingram, Grant Ingram, Peter Kano, Mike and Katherine Kenney, Rob and Amanda Kenney, David Wachira ("Wash") Kiguta, Lucy Ngaruri, Peter Njoka Ngaruri, Georgia Niedzielko, Judy Okawa, Pitman Orr, Everett and Kyla P'an, Ricardo Patton, Frank Pfaff, Mike and Linda Ramelot, Meg Riley-Jamison, Debi Sanders, David Scalise, Jay and Kathy Sugnet, Diane Uchimiya, Marsha Von Duerckheim, Tracy Walbert, Carl and Vicki Warden, Gary Williams, Richard and Jannie Williams, and Donald Yamamoto.

We owe more than we can put into words to two people who supported us in uncountable ways during both the search for refuge and the writing of the book: Melissa Kenney and Lisa Lerman.

NOTES

INTRODUCTION

1. The story of the *St. Louis* is told in Gordon Thomas and Max Morgan Witts, *Voyage of the Damned*, 2d ed. (Stillwater, Minn.: Motorbooks International, 1994), and in an extensive exhibit in the U.S. Holocaust Memorial Museum in Washington, D.C. Much of it is also available at the museum's web site, at www .ushmm.org/museum/exhibit/online/stlouis/ (visited Feb. 14, 2007). See also Nicholas Day, "No Turning Back," *Washington Post*, Aug. 26, 1998. Some details of the "*St. Louis* Affair" as well as the larger story of America's rejection of Jewish refugees before and during World War II are presented and analyzed in Richard Breitman and Alan M. Kraut, *American Refugee Policy and European Jewry, 1933–45* (Bloomington: Indiana University Press, 1987), and in the outstanding Public Broadcasting Service documentary *America and the Holocaust*, WGBH-TV (1994). Recent evidence has revealed that the United States turned away the family of Anne Frank, among many others who were trying to escape (Patricia Cohen, "In Old Files, Fading Hopes of Anne Frank's Family," *New York Times*, Feb. 15, 2007).

2. 8 USC secs. 1101(a)(42) and 1158.

3. See Philip G. Schrag, *A Well-Founded Fear: The Congressional Battle to Save Political Asylum in America* (New York: Routledge, 2000), 27–34, 55–56.

4. Ibid., 57–190.

5. 151 Cong. Rec. H561 (remarks of Representative Barbara Cubin, Feb. 10, 2005). The 9/11 hijackers entered the United States with temporary visas, not as asylum applicants.

6. 151 Cong. Rec. H563 (remarks of Representative Bob Goodlatte, Feb. 10, 2005); 151 Cong. Rec. H471 (remarks of Representative Mary Bono, Feb. 9, 2005). See also 151 Cong. Rec. H471 (remarks of Representative Randy Neugebauer, Dec. 9, 2005) to the effect that the asylum system "has been abused by terrorists with deadly consequences, by allowing judges to determine whether asylum seekers are truthful."

7. 151 Cong. Rec. H454 (remarks of Chairman F. James Sensenbrenner, Feb. 9, 2005).

8. Pub L 109–113 (2005).

9. HR 1645 (the "STRIVE Act"), 110th Cong., 1st Sess., secs. 221 and 222(c). Like all other versions of comprehensive immigration reform thus far, this bill went nowhere.

10. As a *Wall Street Journal* editorial put it, "The last thing a terrorist would want to do is apply for asylum. Not only would he be bringing himself to the attention of the U.S. government—the first step is being fingerprinted—but the screening process for applicants is more rigorous than for just about anyone else trying to enter the country" ("National ID Party," Feb. 17, 2005).

11. Joel D. Barkan, "Kenya after Moi," *Foreign Affairs* 83, no. 1 (2004): 88.

12. See Korwa G. Adar and Isaac M. Munyae, "Human Rights Abuse in Kenya under Daniel arap Moi, 1978–2001," *African Studies Quarterly* 5, no. 1 (2001), http://web.africa.ufl.edu/asq/v5/v5i1a1.htm (visited May 11, 2007).

13. Barkan, "Kenya after Moi," 89.

14. U.S. Department of State, *Country Reports on Human Rights Practices, 2000*, Kenya, sec. 1(a), www.state.gov/g/drl/rls/hrrpt/2000/af/841.htm (visited Oct. 9, 2007).

15. Pub L 101–513 (1991), 593. Moi did not meet all the conditions imposed by the law, but his Parliament did repeal the statute that had made Kenya a one-party state, and the aid was restored. Opposition parties formed, but Moi continued to win presidential elections, partly because the opposition was divided and partly because elections were "often rigged" and "characterized by unprecedented levels of communal violence and foul play" (Barkan, "Kenya after Moi," 89–90).

16. Jaya Ramji-Nogales, Andrew I. Schoenholtz, and Philip G. Schrag, "Refugee Roulette: Disparities in Asylum Adjudication," *Stanford Law Review* 60 (2007): 295–411.

1. THE FARMERS' BOYCOTT

1. According to our oral history, Kikuyus (my father's tribe) were originally governed by kings, but the people overthrew the kingdom centuries ago in a popular revolution. They created a federation of village councils made up of elders. Judicial committees elected by the councils settled local disputes. Each village also elected a judge, called a *muchiri*, to settle disputes involving land or trading with other tribes. My grandfather's brother was such a judge. Because he raised my father, the word *muchiri* became part of my father's name.

2. BASKETBALL

1. Form I-20, issued by a school approved by the U.S. government, must be filed to obtain a student visa; see 8 CFR sec. 214.2(f)(1)(A).

2. See 8 CFR sec. 214.1(a)(3).

3. See Shelly Wilson, "Becoming Scholarship Savvy," www.tukwila-reign .com/Becoming%20Scholarship%20Savv1.htm (visited Sept. 18, 2007).

3. TEMPORARY SAFETY

1. See U.S. Department of Homeland Security (in 2000, the U.S. Immigration and Naturalization Service), Form I-589 and Instructions; available online at www.uscis.gov/files/form/I<->589.pdf (form) and www.uscis.gov/files/form/I< ->589_Inst.pdf (instructions) (visited March 30, 2007).

4. BERNIE AND DAVE

1. Convention Relating to the Status of Refugees, 189 UNTS 150, entered into force April 22, 1954. Originally, this convention applied only to European refugees, but in 1967 an added Protocol extended it worldwide; see Protocol Relating to the Status of Refugees, 606 UNTS 267 (1967).

2. In rare cases in which an affirmative asylum applicant has another valid status (such as a student visa that is still valid at the time of an asylum officer's decision), an officer can deny the asylum application without referring the applicant for a deportation proceeding. Starting in 1997, asylum officers also became involved in a limited category of cases in which foreign nationals were apprehended

at airports with false documents or no documents and expressed fear of being re-turned home. Under a law passed by Congress in 1996, these persons are inter-viewed in jail by asylum officers to determine whether they had a "credible fear" of persecution. This is a lower screening standard than the "well-founded fear" standard for granting asylum. Those found not to have a credible fear are de-ported forthwith; those found to have a credible fear appear before an immigra-tion judge who determines whether to grant them asylum or deport them.

3. Andrew I. Schoenholtz and Jonathan Jacobs, "The State of Asylum Repre-sentation: Ideas for Change," *Georgetown Immigration Law Journal* 16 (Summer 2002): 739, 766, table 1. For persons of some nationalities, the differences were even more dramatic: unrepresented natives of India won only 1 percent of their cases, while represented Indians won 31 percent of their cases; unrepresented Liberians won 8 percent of the time, while represented Liberians won 60 percent of the time (ibid., 743).

4. Frederic Tulsky, "Uncertain Refuge: Asylum Seekers Face Capricious Legal System," *San Jose Mercury News*, Oct. 18, 2000, A20. The judge-by-judge statistics that Tulsky obtained were posted online by asylumlaw.org at www .asylumlaw.org/legal_tools/index.cfm?fuseaction=showJudges (downloaded July 28, 2005). In August 2005, asylumlaw.org posted more recent figures; see "U.S. Immigration Judge Decisions in Asylum Cases, Jan. 2000 to Aug. 2004," www .asylumlaw.org/legal_tools/index.cfm?fuseaction=showJudges2004 (visited Sept. 19, 2007). During those years, Judge Churchill's grant rate rose from 14 percent to 17 percent but fell further below the grant rates of her colleagues on the im-migration court in Arlington, Virginia. "The Lawyer's Epilogue" in this book dis-cusses the disparities in grant rates among immigration judges at greater length.

5. *Matter of Ngarurih,* transcript of master calendar hearing, Nov. 21, 2000, at 5.

6. *INS v. Cardoza-Fonseca,* 480 U.S. 421 (1987).

7. Voluntary departure at the end of a hearing is not available to many un-successful asylum applicants. To win voluntary departure at that time, respon-dents must prove that they are of good moral character (a fairly easy test for any-one who has not been convicted of a crime), that they have enough money to leave and passports that will allow them to go elsewhere, and that they have been present in the United States for at least a year before receiving the summons that began the deportation proceeding. Since asylum seekers must apply within a year of entering the United States (or qualify for an exception), and an asylum offi-cer's referral of a case to an immigration judge generates a summons to a depor-tation proceeding, many asylum applicants will not have been in the United

States long enough to be eligible for voluntary departure. My case was different because I had been in the United States for several years before the case began.

8. Convention Against Torture and Other Cruel, Inhuman or Degrading Treatment or Punishment, adopted Dec. 10, 1984, 1465 UNTS 85, entered into force June 26, 1987.

9. After 2003, the government stopped providing asylum officers' notes to immigration court respondents.

10. For a full explanation of the educational goals and teaching methods of CALS, see its web site, www.law.georgetown.edu/clinics/cals/. A former CALS student has written an article describing the frustrations and satisfactions of being given so much responsibility in a case that, if lost, could result in the imprisonment or even death of a client; see Agata Szypszak, "Where in the World Is Dr. Detchakandi? A Story of Fact Investigation," *Clinical Law Review* 6 (Spring 2000): 517–530.

11. See U.S. Department of State, *Country Reports on Human Rights Practices*. These reports are updated for each specific country each year and are available online at www.state.gov/g/drl/hr/c1470.htm.

12. See, e.g., *M. A. v. Immigration and Naturalization Service*, 899 F. 2d 304, 307 (4th Cir. 1990) (en banc).

13. U.S. Department of State, *Country Reports on Human Rights Practices for 1992* (Washington, D.C.: U.S. Government Printing Office, 1993), 118, 120, 124.

14. U.N. Commission on Human Rights, *Civil and Political Rights, including Questions of Torture and Detention: Report of the Special Rapporteur, Sir Nigel Rodley, Submitted Pursuant to Commission on Human Rights Res. 1999/32; Addendum: Visit of the Special Rapporteur to Kenya*, E/CN.4/2000/9/Add. 4, March 9, 2000, 3. The report is available online at www.unhchr.ch/Huridocda/Huridoca.nsf/TestFrame/e45663899d2802c3802568b9004ba1bf?Opendocument (visited Aug. 20, 2007).

5. MY DAY IN COURT

1. See *In re Y– B–*, 21 I&N Dec. 1136 (BIA 1998); *In re M– D–*, 21 I&N Dec. 1180 (1998). For an analysis of three Board of Immigration Appeals (BIA) cases requiring that asylum applicants' testimony be corroborated with documentation (when the judge thinks that documentation should be available), see Virgil Wiebe and Serena Parker, with Erin Corcoran and Anna Marie Gallagher, "Asking for a Note from Your Torturer: Corroboration and Authentication Requirements in Asylum, Withholding, and Torture Convention Claims," in *American Immigration Lawyers Association Immigration and Nationality Law*

Handbook, 2001–2002 (Washington, D.C.: AILA, 2001), 1:414. Until 2005, the U.S. Court of Appeals for the Ninth Circuit refused to insist on corroboration in cases arising from the several western states the Ninth Circuit comprises, and the BIA could have changed its own precedent. But in 2005, in the "REAL ID" Act, Congress codified the corroboration rule, thereby making it permanent and applicable throughout the United States; see Pub L 109–113 (2005).

2. "Tea Farmers Stage Big Demo," *Daily Nation* (Kenya), July 18, 1992.

3. "Tea: Moi Warns Inciters," *Daily Nation* (Kenya), July 31, 1992.

4. *In re S– P–*, Int. Dec. 3287 (BIA 1996).

5. U.S. Department of Justice, Immigration and Naturalization Service, *Basic Law Manual: U.S. Law and INS Refugee/Asylum Adjudications* (1994), 24; reprinted in Charles Gordon, Stanley Mailman, and Stephen Yale-Loehr, *Immigration Law and Procedure*, special supp. (New York: Matthew Bender, 1995), 14.

6. Ibid.

7. Convention Relating to the Status of Refugees, 189 UNTS 150, entered into force April 22, 1954, art. 1(C)(1).

8. *In re Getaneh M. Getaneh* (BIA, July 27, 1998) (unpublished). Getaneh later received a diploma in pastoral ministry and founded Watch and Pray International Ministries, calling attention to the plight of persecuted Christians; see www.reachafricanow.org/Ethiopia.htm (visited May 25, 2005).

9. In 2001, lottery winners were required to have either a high school education or two years of work experience at a job that required two years of training.

10. All quotations from the hearing are drawn from the transcript. Capitalization has occasionally been standardized; any other alterations made for clarity appear enclosed in square brackets.

11. Board of Immigration Appeals, *Practice Manual*, sec. 4.6(d)(ii); www.usdoj .gov/eoir/vll/qapracmanual/pracmanual/chap4.pdf (visited Aug. 4, 2005).

12. U.N. High Commissioner for Refugees, *Handbook on Procedures and Criteria for Determining Refugee Status under the 1951 Convention and the 1967 Protocol relating to the Status of Refugees*, para. 118, www1.umn.edu/humanrts/instree/ refugeehandbook.pdf (visited Oct. 9, 2007). The Supreme Court had ruled that this handbook was not legally binding on U.S. officials but that it did offer significant guidance in interpreting the Protocol; see *INS v. Cardoza-Fonseca*, 480 U.S. 421, 439n22 (1987).

13. U.N. High Commissioner for Refugees, *Handbook on Procedures and Criteria*, para. 134.

14. U.N. High Commissioner for Refugees, Response to Request for Advisory Opinion/Ngarurih/Kenya/ROW #71946 (attached to the brief in *Matter of Ngarurih*) (Jan. 15, 2002), at 4 (emphasis added).

15. See Peter J. Levinson, "The Façade of Quasi-Judicial Independence in Immigration Appellate Adjudications," *Bender's Immigration Bulletin* 9 (2004): 1154.

6. WINNING THE LOTTERY

1. 8 CFR sec. 1245.1(b)(5) (restricting adjustment of status, from nonimmigrant to immigrant, for an alien who is no longer in lawful immigration status). "Adjustment of status" is the term used for obtaining lawful permanent residence by order of an immigration court, rather than by the State Department's issuance of an immigrant visa to a person who is physically abroad.

2. 8 CFR sec. 1003.4

3. U.S. Immigration and Nationality Act sec. 208(a)(2)(C); 8 USC sec. 1158(a)(2)(C).

4. U.S. Immigration and Nationality Act sec. 212(a)(9)(A)(ii)(II); 8 USC sec. 1182(a)(9)(A)(ii)(II).

5. See U.S. Department of Homeland Security (formerly the U.S. Immigration and Naturalization Service), Form I-131 and Instructions, www.uscis.gov/files/form/I-131.pdf (visited March 30, 2007).

7. THE FOURTH CIRCUIT

1. *In re Ngarurih* (BIA, Jan. 7, 2003) (unpublished memorandum decision).

2. See the listing for Office of the President at www.kenyaweb.com/government/president-office.html (visited Dec. 9, 2007).

3. Jim McGee, "Federal Wiretaps Rise under Clinton," *Chicago Sun-Times,* July 7, 1996.

4. Board of Immigration Appeals, www.usdoj.gov/eoir/fs/biabios.pdf (visited Dec. 9, 2007).

5. Lisa Getter and Jonathan Peterson, "Speedier Rate of Deportation Rulings Assailed; Ashcroft's Goal to Clear a Backlog of Immigration Appeals Has Board Members Deciding Cases in Minutes," *Los Angeles Times,* Jan. 5, 2003. Hess would not speak to the *Times* reporter, but the Justice Department replied that it was unfair to count the number of cases signed in a day because that date "reflects the date the case was mailed to the parties, not necessarily the date it was

decided." But "board members privately do not dispute the *Times*'s findings that some members are deciding as many as 50 cases a day."

6. 8 USC sec. 1252(b)(2).

7. Laura Sullivan, "Fourth Circuit's Reputation Is Polite, Conservative; Bush Administration Steers Sensitive Cases to Friendly Panel of Judges," *Baltimore Sun*, Nov. 18, 2003; Brooke Masters, "Fourth Circuit Pushing to the Right; Federal Court Tests Supreme Intentions," *Washington Post*, Dec. 19, 1999; Tony Mauro, "Fourth Circuit Seen to Be the 'Right' Place," *USA Today*, March 9, 1999.

8. *Dickerson v. U.S.*, 530 U.S. 428 (2000).

9. Masters, "Fourth Circuit Pushing to the Right."

10. E.g., *Estrella v. INS*, http://vlex.com/via/18217/60 (4th Cir. 2003) (unpublished) (visited Dec. 9, 2007).

11. *Ramsay v. INS*, 14 F. 3d 206, 213 (4th Cir. 1994).

12. *Ayalew v. INS*, no. 99–1673, http://pacer.ca4.uscourts.gov/opinion.pdf/ 991673.U.pdf, 1999 U.S. LEXIS 32852 (4th Cir., Dec. 20, 1999) (unpublished) (visited Dec. 7, 2007).

13. 8 CFR 214.2(F)(16), as of January 2003. The rules subsequently became more restrictive.

14. Nita Bhalla, "Kenya Opens Up Torture Chamber," *The Scotsman*, http:// thescotsman.scotsman.com/international.cfm?id=172052003 (visited Feb. 26, 2007); Zachary Ochieng, "Stunning Revelations," www.newsfromafrica.org/ newsfromafrica/articles/art_1282.html (visited Feb. 26, 2007).

15. World in Brief, *Washington Post*, Oct. 27, 2005, A23.

16. Federal Rule of Appellate Procedure 32(a)(5).

17. Dorsey and Whitney LLP, "Board of Immigration Appeals: Procedural Reforms to Improve Case Management," www.dorsey.com/files/upload/ DorseyStudyABA_8mgPDF.pdf (2003) (visited Feb. 28, 2007).

18. William Shakespeare, *The Tragedy of King Richard the Second*, ed. Stanley Wells and Gary Taylor (Oxford: Oxford University Press, 1987), act 1, scene 3.

19. *SEC v. Chenery Corp.*, 332 U.S. 194, 196 (1947).

20. *Sanon v. INS*, 52 F. 3d 648, 651–652 (7th Cir. 1995); *Osuchukwu v. INS*, 744 F. 2d 1136, 1142 (5th Cir. 1984); *Turri v. INS*, 997 F. 2d 1306, 1309 (10th Cir. 1993).

21. *Turri v. INS* at 1309.

22. 8 USC sec. 1255(e)(1). There is an exception to this rule, but it seemed that I would have to apply to Judge Churchill for this exception. Even then, it was not clear whether the exception would apply to someone who had been ordered deported but had not yet left the United States.

23. The degree of deference federal courts grant to federal agencies depends on several factors. Traditionally, these factors include the nature of the case: whether the question being reviewed is a purely legal issue; whether it involves an application of settled law to the established but unique facts of a case; or whether it is a determination of what the facts really were. Appellate courts give some deference to agency decisions even on pure questions of law, particularly when the agency is thought to have "expertise" in interpreting the authority Congress has given it. But the appellate judges themselves have the greatest expertise when it comes to the interpretation of statutes, so they defer to agencies less often in that realm than in the two other types of cases.

Reviewing courts defer the most to an agency's fact-finding, because the agency's adjudicator (in this instance, Judge Churchill), who sits through the actual hearing, is in a much better position than the appellate court to decide how probative the evidence was. The amount of deference appellate courts give to an agency's application of settled law to the facts is somewhere in the middle, between that shown in the other types of cases.

In deportation cases, Congress has imposed what seem to be particularly severe limits on court review. Findings of fact by the Board of Immigration Appeals cannot be altered "unless any reasonable adjudicator would be compelled to conclude to the contrary"; 8 USC sec. 1252(b)(4)(B) (2007). Fortunately, I wasn't disputing any facts in either Judge Churchill's decision or Hess's short order. Rather, my appeal concerned the legal consequences of those facts. Congress has also decided that the "Attorney General's discretionary judgment whether to grant [asylum] shall be conclusive unless manifestly contrary to the law and an abuse of discretion"; 8 USC sec. 1252(b)(4)(D) (2007). This additional restriction on judicial review is not quite as strict as it appears, however, because asylum determinations theoretically include two separate questions: first, whether the applicant is legally eligible for asylum; and, second, once eligibility is established, whether the attorney general will exercise his or her discretion to grant asylum. (Technically speaking, the first question is whether the applicant meets the statutory definition of a "refugee," and the second question is whether the immigration judge, employing power delegated by the attorney general, exercises his or her discretion to grant asylum.) The congressional restriction on judicial review limits review only over the second, discretionary aspect of this determination. By contrast, the denial in my case, like most denials of asylum, was a decision stating that I was not eligible to be considered for asylum.

24. There are twelve regional federal circuits, but the court of appeals in one of them, the District of Columbia Circuit, hears no asylum appeals because no immigration court is located within the district.

25. Brief for Respondent (Attorney General Ashcroft), 15 (July 8, 2003).

26. *Zazueta-Carillo v. Ashcroft*, 322 F. 3d 1166, 1170 (9th Cir. 2003).

27. The policy argument in favor of reinstating voluntary departure was stronger for unsuccessful asylum seekers than it was for other immigrants, because if the denial was erroneous, unsuccessful asylum applicants would be deported to countries where they would be persecuted, rather than having a month to try to find an alternative destination. They would arrive home identified as targets, on a government-funded flight, accompanied by a federal officer, and perhaps in shackles, instead of being able to return on their own terms.

28. In addition, two of the three judges in *Zazueta-Carillo* said that although it could no longer reinstate voluntary departure, the court might retain the power to stay (postpone) the expiration of the board's thirty-day period of voluntary departure. Zazueta-Carillo had asked the court to issue a stay, and the court had denied it because it did not think that his case was strong enough to merit the stay. The third judge had definitively said that the court did have the power to stay the expiration of that period, and she even noted that the equities in favor of granting a stay were greatest when the applicant was an asylum applicant. If this decision had been issued and published before February 7, 2003, when my thirty-day period expired, Phil would have applied for such a stay on my behalf. But *Zazueta-Carillo* was not decided until March 13.

29. U.S. Department of State, *Country Reports on Human Rights Practices, 2001*, Kenya, www.state.gov/g/drl/rls/hrrpt/2001/af/8386.htm (visited Oct. 7, 2007).

30. U.N. Commission on Human Rights, *Civil and Political Rights, including Questions of Torture and Detention: Report of the Special Rapporteur, Sir Nigel Rodley, Submitted Pursuant to Commission on Human Rights Res. 1999/32; Addendum: Visit of the Special Rapporteur to Kenya*, E/CN.4/2000/9/Add. 4, March 9, 2000, para. 86. The report is available online at www.unhchr.ch/Huridocda/Huridoca.nsf/TestFrame/e45663899d2802c3802568b9004ba1bf?Opendocument (visited Aug. 20, 2007).

31. Ibid., para. 73.

32. U.S. Department of State, *Country Reports on Human Rights Practices, 2001*, Kenya.

33. Misir also argued that the reason for my return was not as compelling as that of the Canadian refugee who won asylum despite returning home to care for a "dying" parent. But in fact that refugee's parent was only ailing, not dying. See *Shanmugarajah v. Canada*, 34 A.C.W.S. (3d 828) (Fed. Ct. of App. of Canada), 1992 A.C.W.S.J. LEXIS 33598 (1992).

34. *Ayalew v. INS.*

35. Like the Board of Immigration Appeals, the Fourth Circuit had a specific rule allowing lawyers to call a particularly relevant unpublished case to the attention of the court.

8. A COLD DAY IN RICHMOND

1. U.S. Court of Appeals for the Fourth Circuit, www.ca4.uscourts.gov/ (navigate to Argument Calendar, then to Oral Argument Schedule, and then to a particular week and location) (visited Sept. 18, 2007).

2. *Velazquez v. Ashcroft*, 340 F. 3d 573 (1st Cir. 2003), withdrawn but then reaffirmed in 342 F. 3d 55, 59 (1st Cir. 2003); *Loulou v. Ashcroft*, 354 F. 3d 706 (8th Cir., Dec. 30, 2003). Several months after the argument in *Ngarurih*, the Eighth Circuit, without explanation, amended its decision in the *Loulou* case to delete its reinstatement of voluntary departure; see *Loulou v. Ashcroft*, 2004 U.S. App. LEXIS 8347 (2004).

3. *Nwakanma v. Ashcroft*, 352 F. 3d 325 (2003); *Villanueva v. Ashcroft*, 80 Fed. Appx. 590 (9th Cir. 2003).

4. *Villanueva v. Ashcroft.*

5. General Services Administration, "Historic Federal Buildings," http://w3.gsa.gov/web/p/interaia_save.nsf/0/e247b96d59ed24c8852565d90053a0b3?OpenDocument (visited Dec. 10, 2005).

6. Seth Stern, "A Court of Civility and Controversial Conservatism," *Christian Science Monitor*, May 29, 2003.

7. Deborah Sontag, "The Power of the Fourth," *New York Times Magazine*, March 9, 2003.

8. Ibid.; Timothy M. Phelps and Tom Brune, "Supreme Court Seat Shuffle? Judges' Retirements Would Spark First Shift in Decade," *Newsday*, May 18, 2003.

9. Kenneth L. Manning, Bruce A. Carroll, and Robert A. Carp, "George W. Bush's Potential Supreme Court Nominees: What Impact Might They Have?" *Judicature* 85 (2002): 278.

10. DeWayne Wickham, editorial, "With Judicial Pick, Thurmond May Gain Biggest Win," *USA Today*, July 4, 2002.

11. Online NewsHour, "Judging Judges," www.pbs.org/newshour/bb/congress/july-dec02/judges_11–18.html (visited Dec. 9, 2005).

12. National Organization for Women, "Take Action Now! Oppose the Judicial Nominee Dennis Shedd," Nov. 18, 2002, www.now.org/lists/now-action-list/msg00074.html (visited Dec. 9, 2007).

13. Sen Orrin Hatch, speaking on Online NewsHour, "Judging Judges."

14. Sontag, "Power of the Fourth."

15. *Loving v. Virginia*, 388 U.S. 1 (1967).

16. E.g., *Albathani v. INS*, 318 F. 3d 365 (1st Cir. 2003).

17. Two months later, the Fourth Circuit unanimously upheld the summary affirmance procedure. Judge Wilkinson wrote the opinion. See *Blanco De Belbruno v. Ashcroft*, 362 F. 3d 272 (4th Cir. 2004).

18. In the Fourth Circuit, oral arguments are not transcribed, but recordings are preserved and indexed under the court's docket number. The quotations in this summary are taken from the court's recording of the oral argument in *Ngarurih v. Ashcroft*, case number 03–1144.

19. *Tarvand v. INS*, 937 F. 2d 973 (4th Cir. 1991).

20. The practice of trial by drowning is described in "The Witches: Myth and Reality," available in Internet archives at http://web.archive.org/web/20050308224810/www.parascope.com/en/articles/witches01.htm (visited Aug. 20, 2007), though no eyewitness account of such a trial in Europe has been found. In medieval England, however, poor people were tried by "ordeal" in which "the accused crouched, placed his arms beneath his knees, was bound around his knees and body by a rope, and let down into a pool. If the water received him and he sank he was innocent and was, it is to be hoped, immediately pulled out of the water" (Frederick G. Kempin Jr., *Historical Introduction to Anglo-American Law in a Nutshell* [St. Paul, Minn.: West Publishing, 1990], 59). Curiously, there is a report that a witch was tried in Virginia by being thrown into a river. In the late 1600s, neighbors envious of the farming success of Grace Sherwood accused her of witchcraft. In 1706, county authorities tied her up and threw her into the Lynnhaven River. Because she did not drown immediately (she untied her ropes underwater and was later pulled out), she was convicted of witchcraft and served seven years in prison. Three hundred years later, Virginia governor Timothy M. Kaine pardoned her. See Princess Anne County/Virginia Beach Historical Society, "Grace Sherwood and the Witch of Pungo," www.virginiabeachhistory.org/kyle.html (visited July 25, 2006); and Ian Shapira, "After Toil and Trouble, 'Witch' Is Cleared," *Washington Post*, July 12, 2006.

21. 8 CFR sec. 208.13(b)(1)(B)(iii).

22. *Ngarurih v. Ashcroft*, 371 F. 3d 182 (4th Cir. 2004).

23. Judge Shedd's recitation of the facts did not mention Dr. Okawa's findings that the period of sensory deprivation in the water cell amounted to a particularly severe form of torture, a point that should have been relevant to whether asylum was warranted even in the absence of a well-founded fear. Also, Judge

Shedd stated incorrectly that Judge Churchill had denied asylum because the 1997 trip showed that I was willing to return to Kenya. In fact, she had denied it because of her interpretation of one of the cessation clauses in the international refugee convention. It was the board that had substituted the theory that my trip proved that I was not "unwilling to return."

24. In his separate opinion, Judge Gregory concluded that "the BIA incorrectly determined that Ngarurih 'willingly' returned to Kenya. . . . Having been tortured in a Kenyan prison himself, Ngarurih understandably felt compelled to assist his brother . . . even if doing so required him to place his life in danger."

25. Judge Gregory agreed with the other judges on this point, rendering immaterial his view that the board was wrong in viewing my return as voluntary.

26. Judge Gregory dissented from the view that the court could not suspend the running of the voluntary departure period in a proper case, but he thought that this case was not a suitable case for suspension. Gregory didn't explain why, but in a footnote, Shedd added that this case would not be suitable, even if the court had the power to stay suspension, because the stay had been requested after the thirty-day period had run out. Shedd cited cases from two other circuits that had granted stays. He noted that in one of those cases the applicant had sought the stay on the last day voluntary departure was allowed and that the other case had expressly not decided whether a court could stay a departure period that had already expired. Phil had cited the *Villanueva v. Ashcroft* decision, in which the Ninth Circuit did grant a nunc pro tunc application for a stay, but Judge Shedd simply ignored that decision.

9. EXILED

1. 8 CFR sec. 240.25.

2. See Immigration and Nationality Act sec. 212(a)(9)(A)(iii), 8 USC sec. 1182(a)(9)(A)(iii). The statute specifies no standards for granting this waiver.

3. 8 CFR sec. 245.1(c)(v).

10. THE WITCH ARRIVES

1. As I understood Wash, he's saying that the reason bad things happen to good people is to remind them that they are good. They make the right decision even when it goes against their personal interests and actually thrive when bad things happen to them because their experience makes them stronger. In the process, we learn something about the true nature of humanity. As for bad people, think about how

we can only tell how dark it is by lighting a candle. We can tell how bad people are by exposing them to good things and watching how they act. If they fail to reflect the goodness around them and make decisions contrary to that goodness, they ultimately destroy themselves. In other words, "bad people don't recover from good things."

THE LAWYER'S EPILOGUE

1. See Philip G. Schrag and Michael Meltsner, *Reflections on Clinical Legal Education* (Boston: Northeastern University Press, 1998). The final essay in the book (Philip G. Schrag, "Constructing a Clinic," 244–311) describes the creation of the asylum clinic at Georgetown.

2. Jeff's personal life, of course, has been full of very lucky and very unlucky episodes. Luck in life seems inevitable, but the idea that the outcome of legal cases should depend on chance seems inherently inconsistent with the rule of law. The role of luck in the outcome of legal cases, particularly those where life itself may be in the balance, should therefore be minimized where possible.

3. All the statistics on immigration judges' grant rates are from data supplied by the Department of Justice in response to a Freedom of Information Act request and are available online from www.asylumlaw.org, an organization that supports asylum applicants throughout the world; see www.asylumlaw.org/legal_tools/index.cfm?fuseaction=showJudges2004 (visited Oct. 17, 2007).

4. Asylum cases are confidential, so while the judges' grant rates are public information, it is impossible to study the rulings of Judge Churchill in any depth. However, the *Washington Post* reported in 2007 on another ruling Judge Churchill made in 2001, the same year she denied asylum to Jeff. In that case, she rejected the claim of Hussain Hayal al Zaidi, a Shiite Iraqi national who had been arrested in Iraq for shouting slogans denouncing Saddam Hussein. Al Zaidi was blindfolded, strung up with ropes, and beaten. He suffered a detached retina from the beatings, and his genitals were burned with electricity. During his asylum hearing, Judge Churchill received an anonymous letter accusing him of "working as secret service" for Saddam Hussein and intending to kill U.S. officials. The author of the letter turned out to be Khalid Houmadi, al Zaidi's roommate, who was planning to attack a third man. Al Zaidi had threatened to report Houmadi if he went through with the attack, and Houmadi was retaliating against al Zaidi for this threat. Churchill said that Houmadi "cast considerable doubt on the credibility of crucial aspects" of al Zaidi's claim, and she denied asylum. Later, Houmadi did attack the man, al Zaidi testified against him, and Houmadi was sentenced to ten

months in jail. A single member of the Board of Immigration Appeals summarily affirmed Churchill's order deporting al Zaidi to Iraq, and he was detained by the U.S. government. Despondent and evidently depressed, he dropped his appeal to the Fourth Circuit while in jail (Brigid Schulte, "Escaping a Painful Past to Find a Shaky Future," *Washington Post*, March 7, 2007, B1).

5. Jaya Ramji-Nogales, Andrew Schoenholtz, and Philip G. Schrag, "Refugee Roulette: Disparities in Asylum Adjudication," *Stanford Law Review* 60 (2007), 295–411.

6. These statistics have been developed in greater detail in Ramji-Nogales, Schoenholtz, and Schrag, "Refugee Roulette." The court of appeals statistics stated in the chapter text pertain to all asylum appeals to the federal courts, but similar discrepancies from court to court are evident if the cases under consideration are limited to those from fifteen countries with large numbers of asylum applicants and high grant rates from the Asylum Office or the immigration courts (ibid.).

7. *Karouni v. Gonzales,* 399 F. 3d 1163 (9th Cir. 2005).

8. *Annual Report of the Attorney General to the Senate and the House of Representatives,* Jan. 3, 1941, 5–6.

9. U.S. Commission on International Religious Freedom, "Expedited Removal Study Report Card: Two Years Later," www.uscirf.gov/reports/scorecard_FINAL.pdf (visited April 27, 2007).

10. Jennifer Ludden, "Complaints Prompt Government Review of Immigration Courts," *Morning Edition,* National Public Radio, Feb. 9, 2006, www.npr.org/templates/story/story.php?storyId=5198044 (visited Oct. 7, 2007).

11. U.S. Commission on International Religious Freedom, "Expedited Removal Study Report Card."

12. Pub L 104–134 sec. 504 (1996).

13. Donald Kerwin, "Revisiting the Need for Appointed Counsel," *Insight* (Migration Policy Institute), April 2005.

14. Ibid.

15. U.S. Department of Justice, "Measures to Improve the Immigration Courts and the Board of Immigration Appeals," http://trac.syr.edu/tracatwork/detail/P104.pdf (visited April 27, 2007).

16. For a thoughtful discussion of the advantages of moving both the board and the immigration judges out of the Department of Justice, see Stephen H. Legomsky, "Deportation and the War on Independence," *Cornell Law Review* 91, no. 2 (2006): 369–410.

17. These quotations are from cases cited in *Benslimane v. Gonzales,* 421 F. 3d 595 (7th Cir. 2005).

18. For example, for an administrative appeal, briefs do not have to be reprinted if the footnotes use a font that is slightly smaller than the text.

19. In recent years, Congress has considered several different versions of a "comprehensive immigration reform" bill. Some versions have included provisions that would end the annual diversity visa lottery.

20. *Gebre v. Rice*, 462 F. Supp. 2d 186 (D. Mass. 2006).

21. 22 CFR sec. 40.6.

22. The authority of consular officers to grant or deny visas, at their discretion, derives from a provision of the Immigration and Nationality Act stipulating that if a visa applicant "fails to establish to the satisfaction of the consular officer that he is eligible to receive a visa . . . no visa . . . shall be issued to such person" (Immigration and Nationality Act sec. 291; 8 USC sec. 1361). The U.S. courts have held that consular decisions to deny visas are not subject to judicial review; see *Ulrich v. Kellogg*, 30 F. 2d 984 (D.C. Cir. 1929), cert. denied 279 U.S. 868 (1929).

23. The more senior officer is not necessarily the consul; it is "the principal consular officer at a post, or a specifically designated alternate"; see 22 CFR sec. 42.81(c).

24. Administrative Conference of the United States, Recommendation 89–9: "Processing and Review of Visa Denials," 54 Fed. Reg. 53496 (Dec. 29, 1989).

25. Until recently, all "nonimmigrant" visa refusals (for example, for tourist or student visas) were also supposed to be reviewed by senior consular officials. But in 2006, the State Department reduced the level of administrative review of these refusals so that it could devote more resources to reviewing visa issuances, stating that "it will no longer be possible to review all visa refusals" (U.S. Department of State, "Visas: Documentation of Nonimmigrants under the Immigration and Nationality Act, as Amended," 71 Fed. Reg. 37494 [June 30, 2006] and correcting amendments, 71 Fed. Reg. 50338 [Aug. 25, 2006]).

26. U.S. Commission on Civil Rights, *The Tarnished Golden Door: Civil Rights Issues in Immigration* (Washington, D.C.: Government Printing Office, 1980), 49, 53–54.

27. American Immigration Law Foundation, "Protecting the Voluntary Departure Period during Court of Appeals Review," www.ailf.org/lac/lac_pa_ 102505.pdf (as amended Oct. 25, 2005) (visited March 6, 2007).

28. Persons who win asylum may apply for lawful permanent resident status after one year, and then they must wait for another year or so while their applications are processed. But persons who marry American citizens receive lawful permanent resident status relatively quickly, unless, like Jeff, they are subject to legal bars that complicate their eligibility.

29. Immigration and Nationality Act sec. 216; 8 USC sec. 1186.

INDEX

Text: 10/15 Janson
Display: Janson
Compositor: Binghamton Valley Composition
Printer and binder: Maple-Vail Book Manufacturing Group